THE NON-PHILOSOPHY OF GILLES DELEUZE

THE NON-PHILOSOPHY OF GILLES DELEUZE

GREGG LAMBERT

Continuum
The Tower Building, 11 York Road, London SE1 7NX
370 Lexington Avenue, New York, NY 10017-6503

www.continuumbooks.com

First published 2002

British Library Cataloguing-in-Publication Data
A catalogue record for this book is available from the British Library

ISBN 0-8264-5955-2 (hardback)
ISBN 0-8264-5956-0 (paperback)

Library of Congress Cataloging-in-Publication Data
Lambert, Gregg, 1961-
The non-philosophy of Gilles Deleuze / Gregg Lambert.
p. cm.
Includes bibliographical references and index.
ISBN 0-8264-5955-2 – ISBN 0-8264-5956-0 (pbk.)
1. Deleuze, Gilles. I. Title.

B2430.D454 L35 2002
194–dc21

2001047582

Typeset by Aarontype Limited, Easton, Bristol
Printed and bound in Great Britain by
Bookcraft (Bath) Ltd

CONTENTS

LIST OF FIGURES

ACKNOWLEDGEMENTS

I would like to thank the following editors of the journals and collections in which previous versions of some of the chapters first appeared: Lisa Brawley, Ian Buchanan, James English, Gregory Flaxman, Sydney Levy and John Marks. I am particularly indebted to Gregory Flaxman for his support and comments throughout the process of editing this volume, and to Jenny Overton. I would also like to thank my editor, Tristan Palmer, for his support and his patience with the occasional chain of queries. Finally, I would like to express my gratitude to the following individuals whose long-standing support of my writings on Deleuze has been a valued source of inspiration and encouragement: Réda Bensmaïa, Constantin Boundas, Peter Canning, Tricia Daily, Jacques Derrida, Alexander Gelley, Dorothea Olkowski, Gabriele Schwab, Daniel W. Smith and Charles E. Winquist.

Every effort has been made to locate holders of copyright material; however, the author and publishers would be interested to hear from any copyright holders not here acknowledged so that full acknowledgement may be made in future editions.

ABBREVIATIONS

WORKS BY GILLES DELEUZE

B *Bergsonism* (1988)
CC *Essays Critical and Clinical* (1997)
DR *Difference and Repetition* (1994)
F *Foucault* (1988)
Fold *The Fold: Leibniz and the Baroque* (1993)
K *Kant's Critical Philosophy* (1984)
LS *The Logic of Sense* (1990)
MI *Cinema 1: The Movement-Image* (1986)
N *Negotiations* (1990)
Pli *Le Pli: Leibniz et le baroque* (1988)
P *Proust and Signs* (1972 [USA]; 2000 [UK])
S *Spinoza: A Practical Philosophy* (1988)
TI *Cinema 2: The Time-Image* (1989)

WORKS BY GILLES DELEUZE AND FÉLIX GUATTARI

AO *Anti-Oedipus* (1977)
ML *Kafka: Toward a Minor Literature* (1986)
QP *Qu'est-ce que la philosophie?* (1991)
TP *A Thousand Plateaus* (1987)
WP *What is Philosophy?* (1996)

OTHER WORKS

BR *Borges: A Reader* (1981)
C Proust, *In Search of Lost Time*, Vol. 5, *The Captive and the Fugitive* (1993)
FF Eisenstein, *Film Form* (1949)
H Duras/Resnais, *Hiroshima mon amour* (1963)
L Borges, *Labyrinths* (1962)
M Leibniz, *Monadology* (1965)
PS Paul Klee, *Pedagogical Sketchbook* (1968[1953])
T Leibniz, *Theodicy* (1985)
TR Proust, *In Search of Lost Time*, Vol. 6, *Time Regained* (1993)
W Frantz Fanon, *The Wretched of the Earth* (1963)

PREFACE
ON THE ART OF COMMENTARY

Most books of philosophy these days, particularly those written on other philosophers, which claim to explain, to clarify, and even in some cases to rectify the mistakes of the philosopher, all share in something deceitful and malicious. Indeed, they are often written from a certain spirit of 'bad faith,' although, certainly, not many commentators would admit that this is the source of their inspiration. On the contrary, many commentators spend their time before the reader's short-lived attention trying to persuade anybody who happens onto their little tome (in the library or bookstore, or even today on the internet) that it is absolutely worth the time it will take to read. They might argue that it will impart some new knowledge, or a new twist on something already known; perhaps it will serve other uses for the author.

Nevertheless, even while they claim to be providing a useful service to both the author and the reader, in practice they are doing the opposite. The very existence of a book that claims to clarify and explain another writer already makes the first (so-called 'primary') writer redundant to his or her own efforts to say something. We could say that all commentaries introduce a certain amount of 'stupidity' into the relationship between the writer and the reader: the reader actually becomes more stupid and dependent on another (the so-called 'secondary writer') who will explain things; the writer becomes more stupid for the very reason that he or she needs to be explained. Thus, every commentary performs this dual relationship of stupidity and understanding, even if the commentator makes every reasonable effort to avoid it. This is because the rules of representation are already laid down in advance, and even in those rare and exceptional cases where the commentator does not choose to adhere to these rules, there will be plenty of readers who will demand that they be enforced.

The function of commentary can be organized according to two distinct moments: in the first moment, the commentary produces a 'forgetting' of what is known in order that, in the second moment, it performs a recollection of what was forgotten, which often takes the distinct form of revelation (or the simulacrum of truth). It is not by accident that Deleuze locates this backward and forward movement as a logic that governs Platonic reminiscence, that is, the logic of representation itself. In *Difference and Repetition*, he writes:

> For reminiscence only appears to break with the recognition model when in fact it is content to complicate the schema: whereas recognition bears upon

> a perceptible or perceived object, reminiscence bears upon another object, supposed to be associated with or rather enveloped within the first, which demands to be recognized for itself independently of any distinct perception. This other thing, enveloped within the sign, must be at once never-seen and yet already-recognized, a disturbing unfamiliarity. (DR 141–142)

Underlying this act of 'representation,' which continues to be dominant these days despite everything that has been said in the last four decades concerning the evils of representation, are two distinct transformations on the level of sense. First, sense is separated from its material expression, making these two things appear easily distinguishable, as if their relationship is contingent or purely accidental. (In other words, the singular marks that occur when *a life* makes its passage through language are often reduced to the different vagaries that surround the question of 'style.') Second, the primary writer is often turned into a stammerer, a child, or a 'genius,' who thereafter requires the mediation of another in order to be understood. Every 'secondary writer' is first in line to accept this role and will denounce all the others who have gone before him or her as impostures, opportunists, or mere block-heads.

At the same time, everyone knows that Deleuze himself has written a great deal on other philosophers. Some might even go so far as to say that these are his best works, the works of a true philosopher, and not to be mistaken for those somewhat bizarre manifestos he wrote with that other guy.[1] However, even when he wrote on other philosophers, Deleuze's books differed from the usual commentaries, since he claimed immediately and outright that he was not necessarily performing a benevolent service for the author or the reader. His objective was not to clarify or to explain the work of the particular philosopher they examined. Deleuze himself described his approach to the genre of commentary by stating that it was a kind of 'buggery' (*enculage*) and his intention in every case was to take each philosopher from behind, 'giving him a child that would be his own, yet monstrous' (N 6). Many of Deleuze's best commentators have tried to ignore this statement, or have reveled in its iconoclastic energy (which amounts to the same thing). Few have taken the statement seriously, preferring to understand it to apply only to his 'enemies,' Kant, for example, and not also to his philosophical 'friends' such as Nietzsche and Spinoza. Perhaps this is because, particularly in the case of Nietzsche, it is hard to imagine making him more monstrous than he already was for many.

What Deleuze is addressing here must be understood in the context of Platonic *anamnesis*, the proper function of memory, which is sometimes likened to a 'proper birth' where the child resembles its parent. Derrida has also addressed the issue of 'bad or weak' memory within the concept of *writing* (*l'écriture*), which is 'exterior' to the internalizing function of the former. 'Plato said of writing that it was an orphan or bastard, as opposed to speech, the legitimate and high-born son of the "father of logos."'[2] Consequently, the Derridean strategy of commentary ('deconstruction') is premised on the exaggeration of this difference to a hyperbolic degree; the function of commentary itself produces a repressed or marginalized representative by means of the powers accorded to a 'weak and externalized' memory. In a certain sense, the Derridean method can be understood to be the fullest deployment of the logic of representation itself, to the point where representation exhausts itself thereby undergoing a strange reversal around the principle of identity that underwrites this logic: the production of the maximum of difference between the model and the copy.

By contrast, Deleuze does not follow this strategy of representation, even though he seeks to liberate the copy from its adherence to a model by replacing the weak notion of the copy with the power of the simulacrum, or the double. 'In the history of philosophy, a commentary should act as a veritable double and bear the maximal modification appropriate to a double' (DR xxi). Something else happens when the commentator functions as a 'double,' in the sense that Deleuze has defined this role, and perhaps this definition restores to the art of commentary a more upright and direct presentation. As I suggested in the beginning, there is already something essentially 'under-handed' in the portrait of the commentator as a dedicated disciple or pure 'sub-ject' of the author. Rather, we might consider this conceptual persona according to the portrait that has been provided by Henry James in his story 'The figure in the carpet,' where the character of the commentator (or critic) will resort to any form of treachery in order to wrest the author's hidden design as his own source of joy, including designs on the author's daughter, only to end up a miserable wretch and loner.[3] One has to admit, at least according to the portrait of the critic that James provides us, including all the subjacent goals and the motives involved, that it is not much of *a* life. After all, what could drive someone to devote a portion of their life to deciphering the stirrings that take place in the soul of another? Certainly not the truth, which is offered like hollow rationalization, an alibi placed before the reality of desire.

And yet, it is not simply a matter of according the commentator a more 'realistic' or 'passionate' portrait of a rival claimant, a pretender, or a lover. A question would have to be posed concerning the object under contention: 'What is being claimed?', 'Who is posing, who is pretending?', 'A lover of whom, or what?' Unlike the fable by James, the object in question cannot be imputed to the author, as the secret source of his joy, but rather concerns something else, something 'impersonal' that is bound up with the movement of writing itself as a kind of 'passage.' In his or her passage through the work of another, the commentator performs a series of operations (textual, rhetorical, conceptual) that amounts to 'working on the material' and causing a series of modifications to occur, which Deleuze calls 'falsifications.' This can be easily demonstrated in those passages where the commentator writes 'the author says,' 'the author means,' or even more, 'the author believes.' We should understand these moments precisely as falsifying in the sense that the commentator creates a simulacrum of the author's speech, causing the author to appear to be 'saying something' when, in fact, it is the commentator who has been speaking all along. Thus, we might conclude from this that all commentaries lie – and some more than others – and perhaps this is the essential characteristic that belongs to the genre of commentary. And yet, Deleuze does not understand this process of falsification morally, as a defect of representation, but rather vitally, as a supremely creative act; it is by falsification that the commentary functions as a 'veritable double' and 'bears a maximal difference appropriate to a double.'[4]

I prefer to think of the relationship enacted between the original work and its commentary according to the logic of the fold that Deleuze has outlined in his commentaries on both Leibniz and Foucault, where the act of unfolding, which is often given as the metaphor of interpretation, cannot be opposed as contrary to the gesture of folding. The fold and the unfold are not contraries, but rather, are continuous. Deleuze demonstrates this in his concept of the baroque interior where the fold of the inside is at the same time, on another surface, the unfold of the outside and vice versa. In passing through the work the objective of unfolding some aspect, notion, or passage is not to reach a point where the work becomes a flat or empty space – the point of the complete unfold is impossible – but rather to discern the writer's manner of folding (and unfolding) in order to maintain what Leibniz called the *vis activa* (the living potential) that defines the force of creation. As Deleuze writes, 'Reading does not consist in concluding from the idea of a preceding condition the idea of the following condition, but in grasping the effort or tendency by which the following condition itself ensues from the preceding "by means of a natural force" ' (Fold 72). Undoubtedly, this approach to the task of commentary involves a notion of repetition that is distinctly different from representation, which is premised on a too simplistic idea of the fold (and of the unfold). The act of unfolding, of tracing the fold of another mind, is a precarious exercise, one that is more of an art than a straightforward representation of knowledge (in part, because the mind of another person is infinitely folded). Today we have numerous examples where the commentary fails, either by following too closely and failing to maintain the writer's manner of folding somehow independently of the commentator's unfold (in which case the commentary becomes a bad copy), or by losing the sense of the fold entirely and thereby displaying the work on a flat and empty space as something inert or no longer actual, as a frozen or rigidified profile of an object of the understanding.

It is ironic that every commentary already owes its existence to a more original repetition in which it takes part, even without being fully conscious of it, drawing both the work of the writer and the work of a commentary into a wave that lifts them and carries them along helplessly. The cause of this original repetition is difficult (if not impossible) to discern. In their last book, *What is Philosophy?*, Deleuze and Guattari approach the question of the original forms of repetition that have creased through the Western tradition of philosophy. For each epoch they demonstrate the presence of distinct 'conceptual personae' each of which introduces a new image of thought. Thus, we can point to a Platonic wave, a Cartesian, a Hegelian, and even today a Derridean or Deleuzian wave, all of which can be distinguished by the manner in which they remain enigmatic and folded even while the incessant number of commentaries break around their peak. In this sense, the image of thought and the conceptual personae that give rise to it can be likened to a signature of Warhol or Duchamp. What distinguishes one thought from another is a special kind of sign, which is often associated with the 'author-function,' as when we say 'Hegelianism' rather than 'Kantianism' or 'Platonism'; however, what this sign refers to is a multiplicity and also a manner of organizing a multiplicity. As Deleuze and Guattari state:

> There are no simple concepts ... There are no concepts with one component. Even the first concept, the one with which philosophy 'begins,' has several components, because it is not obvious that philosophy must have a beginning, and if it does determine one, it must combine it with a point-of-view or a ground [*une raison*]. (WP 15)

Although repetition gives rise to a form that can be distinguished from other moments, it is primarily to be understood by its force, by the manner in which it maintains its fold even in the process of unfolding.

As I stated above, every commentary already presupposes a certain force of repetition to which it belongs, even though this repetition is often understood as a 'problem' for which there must be a response (e.g. 'God is dead,' 'Being is One,' etc.), or a command that must be obeyed in the sense that 'one must' (as the French say *il faut*) read this or that philosopher or work of philosophy at a given moment. Yet, all commentaries differ from one another precisely around the specific 'problematic' that they try to take up, to articulate, even to pose as a solution in their passage through the work of another philosopher. Finally, it is for this reason that I wonder if there are, in fact, any commentaries; is there rather the repetition of various problems that have been grasped under either too general a concept of the representation, or too particular and individual a concept of the author? In my own passage through the philosophy of Gilles Deleuze, the problem I have constantly engaged in the various essays that are assembled here is the problem of 'non-philosophy' – a problem that encompasses the domains of art, literature, cinema (as well as science, which is not treated here to the same extent). It is around this point that today philosophy seems to enjoy no more sovereignty than these other domains but rather, according to Deleuze's own understanding, constitutes the 'relation of the non-relation' with other planes of expression around the problem of a general co-creation. Another way of putting this is that the relation between philosophy and 'non-philosophy' takes the form of a general co-dependence and distribution among these other planes all of which are attempting to gather a little bit of the chaos that surrounds us and carries us along and to shape it into a *sensible form.*

A final aspect I would like to take up concerning the art of commentary is the degree of clarity that is often accorded to the work under the logic of representation. Under this logic, a complete and clear understanding is already posed in advance. Recalling the allusion to 'the figure in the carpet' in the story by James, all that is needed is a certain angle of vision, or a moment of personal revelation, to make it appear. On the contrary, it is because I do not believe that Deleuze has already 'figured everything out in advance' that I do not consider that the task of the commentator is *to understand everything*, to become a 'know-it-all,' or a specialist of 'Deleuze' (whatever that means!). Nothing could be further from the truth and I take Deleuze very seriously around this point when he says that a thinker does not proceed methodically, but more like a dog chasing a bone, in leaps and starts. As an illustration of this, we might take many of Deleuze's concepts where he resorts to a kind of poetic refrain: 'the Other Person as the expression of a possible world,' 'Time off its hinges,' or 'real without being actual, ideal without being abstract.' If Deleuze must resort to poetic expression or refrain at these moments, in my view, it is because these concepts are not concepts of the understanding (in the Kantian sense), but rather indicate problems of expression. It is precisely at these moments that the problem of expression in Deleuze's philosophy intersects with the art of concept creation, and we must suppose that there are still concepts that Deleuze could not resolve or express adequately and this might explain the repetition of various poetic refrains throughout his writings, refrains that he called '*ritournelles*.'

A *ritornello* is a 'short repeated instrumental passage in a vocal work, or of the full orchestra after a solo' (*Oxford English Dictionary*), and both definitions can be employed to characterize the moments designated by the above refrains.[5] In part, these refrains indicate moments where the problem of expression is most acutely reached and Deleuze must resort to these refrains in order to mark an incomplete passage, a potential interruption, or an ellipsis; to repeat a melodic line in order to keep from getting lost, or from falling silent. In other words, these refrains can also be understood as the points where Deleuze himself can be heard 'to stutter,' and it is important to remark that these refrains are present throughout his entire philosophical project, particularly from the period of *Différence et Répétition* (1968) to the final period of *Qu'est-ce que la philosophie?* (with Guattari 1991). Thus, if these refrains continue to remain obscure for us as well, it is not because they hide some profound meaning, the secret source of the author's joy, but rather because they express a more pragmatic problem of unfolding a plane that Deleuze says constitutes the ground of concepts. This is a ground that Deleuze remarked many times by the term 'immanence,' and he cautioned that any concept that installs itself on this ground can only be partial, or relative, to 'the base of all planes,' although 'immanent to every thinkable plane that does not succeed in thinking it' (WP 59). Thus, 'incapacity' (defined as the inability 'to unfold,' 'to become immanent to . . . ,' or 'to create a concept' as a solution, even partial, to a problem of philosophy) is not an occasion for criticism, which would assume that the problem is already in the state of being solved (on some ideal plane) and it is only a question of correcting or perfecting its expression. Rather, it is the case of a problem in which there have already been multiple solutions in the history of philosophy, 'and each time we can say that the solution was as good as it could have been, given the way the problem was stated, and the means that the living being had at its disposal to solve it' (B 103). In each case, therefore, it falls equally to the writer as well as to the commentator to choose the best solution possible, assuming here that one of the possible choices also includes those solutions that have yet to be invented, or created.

PART ONE

ON THE IMAGE OF THOUGHT FROM LEIBNIZ TO BORGES ('TIME OFF ITS HINGES')

1

PHILOSOPHY AND 'NON-PHILOSOPHY'

If, as Heidegger said, every great philosopher is motivated by only one fundamental problem that remains 'unthought,' then we could say that everything Deleuze has written (*with* himself, *with* Félix Guattari, *with* Claire Parnet, but also *with* Kant, Hume, Spinoza, Nietzsche and Bergson) concerns the Idea of difference that remains 'unthought' under the requirements of representation. As Deleuze writes in the conclusion of *Difference and Repetition*,

> Difference is not and cannot be thought in itself, so long as it is subject to the requirements of representation. The question whether it was 'always' subject to these requirements, and for what reasons, must be closely examined ... From this, it is concluded that difference in itself remains condemned and must atone or be redeemed under the auspices of a reason which renders it liveable and thinkable, and makes it the object of organic representation. (262)

This statement is not reductive, since it is precisely the nature of a 'problem' to create a field of questions that are coordinated and bear a certain univocal or singular trait of organization. That difference remains an 'Idea' is what accounts for its absence under the conditions of what Deleuze calls 'organic representation' since, as Deleuze writes, 'ideas are not given in experience, they appear as problems, and unfold as objects of a problematic form' (LS 103). What are the objects of a problematic form but the concepts by means of which philosophy proceeds in the sense of making a little headway through the chaos of sensation?

Concepts comprise a properly philosophical means of understanding the chaos that surrounds experience, and runs underneath it, in the sense that concepts attempt to grasp the diversity that makes up the conditions of experience. Therefore, philosophy progresses by means of its concepts, and there is no philosophical understanding *per se* that does not also represent an advance in the art of creating concepts. However, this constitutes only one-half of the equation, since Deleuze immediately stipulates that philosophy does not only need a philosophical understanding, but a non-philosophical one as well. Philosophy needs both wings to fly (N 139). As Deleuze argues, 'philosophy has an essential and positive relation to non-philosophy: it speaks directly to non-philosophers' (N 139–140). As an example of this duality, let us take up the question 'What is called thinking?' Even in its effort to propose a new concept in response to this question, or even a new manner of understanding the question, philosophy must continue to presuppose an 'image' that defines thought, even though this image is only the expression of a non-philosophical understanding of what it means to think. Nevertheless, if it is to remain immanent, that is, to share a plane of immanence that is occupied or populated by others, philosophy must presuppose an image of thought that becomes the 'ground' of its concepts. This is because only a non-philosophical understanding provides the absolute ground for philosophy, and philosophy can differentiate itself from this ground only by passing through it (or over it) in such a manner that its own image of thought becomes modified.

'It is true,' Deleuze and Guattari write, 'that we cannot imagine a great philosopher of whom it could not be said that he has changed what it means to think,' that is, 'to have changed planes and once more found a new image' (WP 51). However, in *What is Philosophy?*, the plane of immanence is not defined as being a concept, nor is it to be confused with the concepts that populate it at any given time (such as the Cartesian *cogito*, Kantian 'pure reason,' Hegelian 'spirit'). Rather, the 'plane of immanence' is given as the internal condition of thought; it is thought's 'non-philosophical' image, which does not exist outside of philosophy although philosophy must always presuppose it. 'It is presupposed not in a way that one concept may refer to others but in a way that concepts themselves refer to a non-conceptual understanding' (WP 40). On an immediate level, this is the simplest thing to understand and subscribes to a simple notion of pragmatism. In order for its signs and concepts to be 'recognized,' philosophy must occupy a plane that is open and populous. However, according to Deleuze, pragmatism begins to go astray when it confuses this immanent plane with the representation of a common sense (*cogitatio natura universalis*), under the false presupposition that the more simple and direct understanding is for that reason more open, more gregarious, more 'democratic' and, consequently, is considered to be more immanent thanks to the qualities that define it. However, it is precisely this model of 'recognition' that Deleuze most vehemently rejects from *Difference and Repetition* onward.[1] Throughout his interviews and his writings, he maintains that philosophy is not 'communication', that philosophy gains nothing from either argument or discussion with the 'common man.' Does this mean, however, that philosophy, according to Deleuze's understanding, simply abandons the idea of communication entirely and leaves the field to information specialists and '*ideas men*' (WP 10)? Were this the case, then it certainly would raise a problem for readers of Deleuze: if philosophy no longer develops or refers its concepts to a plane occupied by 'common sense,' how should we understand this position? How will it communicate? Would a philosophy that rejects a certain notion of common sense not risk becoming solipsistic, at least a little schizophrenic, or assuming the lofty attitude of 'the beautiful soul'?

While classical philosophy (from Plato to Descartes) has traditionally grounded its operation and its 'image of thought' on the ground of non-philosophy, the ground was often determined as common sense (*cogitatio natura*). In this sense, the philosopher's image was always extracted from an idiot's point-of-view, the bastard child of natural consciousness. By positing a vulgar and common image of thinking, more often defined by 'error' or 'falsehood' than by stupidity, philosophy was able to differentiate its own image of thought, often by means of a special faculty that only philosophers possessed. 'In this sense,' Deleuze writes, 'conceptual philosophical thought has as its implicit presupposition a pre-philosophical and natural image of thought, borrowed from the pure element of common sense' (DR 131). However, what is distinctly modern about the style of philosophy that appears after the Second World War (even though we can find certain forerunners of this style in certain exceptional or untimely thinkers such as Kierkegaard, Leibniz, Nietzsche and Spinoza) is that common sense no longer offers a sufficient ground for the philosopher's conceptual activity; the statement *everyone knows* no longer marks the commencement or recommencement of the dialectical movement between truth and its negatives (DR 130).

Consequently, the modern idiot is no longer the child of 'natural man,' but is the one who is deceived or the one who deceives (that is, the one who feigns idiocy while all the time pursuing his own ends in the world of action under the mask of a more sovereign ignorance). Deleuze himself suggests this in his seminal essay 'Plato and the simulacrum,' where he shows that the classical figure of evil, shaped by 'finitude' or 'natural error,' has been supplanted by the appearance of this new idiot. His character is less likely to be found in the figures of the common soul in either Plato's dialogues or Aristotle's *De Anima*, than in the dramas of Shakespeare.[2] In place of the childish ignorance of the natural idiot, instead we awaken to a world that is populated by figures of an overpowering 'will to stupidity' in such characters as Hamlet or Lear, or the 'malicious cunning' of Macbeth, Edmund, Iago and Richard III, who would prefer to blot out the eye of the world and steal away through the hubbub of the chaos that rises up in their wake. Of course, there are other idiots that can be found to populate Deleuze's philosophy, such as the figures of Artaud or the enigmatic 'Bartelby' from Deleuze's last work *Critique et Clinique* (1993).[3] However, Deleuze will differentiate the latter from 'the terrifying models of *pseudos* in which the powers of the false unfold' (DR 128).

Deleuze asks: 'Can we, flailing in confusion, still claim to be seeking the truth?' (N 148). In other words, it is not from 'common sense' that the greatest problems can be posed, but rather from a more radical stupidity, or from a recalcitrant being that refuses to be rectified by the concept of reason, even to the point of willing the impossible and the unthinkable. We have an example of this in what Deleuze calls a 'primary nature,' illustrated by Kleist's Penthesilea or Melville's Ahab, as '*innately deprived beings*' who make nothingness an object of their will' (CC 79–80). Behind the dumb-show of idiocy, for the situation confronted by contemporary philosophy there is another power that must be accounted for, a power that has the appearance of a strange and malevolent desire, the 'cunning of reason' itself, or as Deleuze suggests later on in his description of 'a society of control,' the effects of a powerful automaton, or a nearly impenetrable and concerted organization that is discovered to be operating deep within the order of things.[4] Perhaps this is why common sense or the error caused by finitude does not comprise the plane of immanence for philosophy today, because there are new and more imposing problems that have emerged, as well as a different species of illusions that must be addressed.

If philosophy 'institutes' a plane, as Deleuze said, by 'presupposing' this plane in a certain sense as a position it *already* occupies, then the image of thought will be quite varied depending on the plane that philosophy presupposes as its condition. For instance, although classical philosophy grasped this plane of immanence as the representation of the idea within natural consciousness, we cannot help but notice that today philosophy constructs its concepts upon other planes, most notably the planes expressed by science, art, literature and, most recently, modern cinema. We say that common sense is no longer posed as the beginning of a philosophical construction, in the sense that it no longer provides the ground of philosophy itself. Rather, as Deleuze writes, contemporary philosophy has taken on other measures – even those measures that 'belong to the order of dreams, of pathological processes, esoteric experiences, drunkenness and excess' (WP 41). For example, it is a characteristic unique to modern commentaries on Descartes to highlight the passages in *The Meditations* on madness, or even to refer to the philosopher's dreams, including the dream that mysteriously ends with the inexplicable and strange gift of a water-melon.[5] How can we explain this except to point out the fact that there is something in this surreal, enigmatic water-melon that seems closer to determining the ground of our existence than the propositions concerning the *cogito* as a foundational certainty. In fact, it is precisely the *cogito* itself that appears to us now as a fantastic and illusory premise. Deleuze responds to this illusion when he argues that the possibility of thinking can no longer be understood as something innate or predestined for the *cogito* – that the mere possibility of thinking in no way guarantees the presence of a subject who is yet 'capable' of it.

What does the above observation concerning the image of thought imply for us today? On one level, it implies that to an even greater degree contemporary philosophy erects itself on the ground of 'something that does not think' – for example, although it could be said that the unconscious thinks, it is certainly not an image of thought that we could say is rational. Thus, this something that does not think in us returns as a question concerning the possibility of thought itself, the possibility that 'I am not yet thinking' (a Heideggerian statement that Deleuze frequently employs to indicate the horizon of the greatest problem that philosophy must confront, but which it is incapable of confronting if it remains within the boundaries of the logic of representation). And to a greater and greater degree, contemporary philosophy poses its own *ground* in what is 'other than consciousness,' or what stubbornly remains outside the powers of representation, whether this is defined as the subject of the Unconscious (Freud), as the subject of a virtual linguistic structure (Saussure and Hjemslev) or of the 'Being of Language' as such (Heidegger), as a determinate moment within the economic sphere of production (Marx), the series or Markov chain in modern biology, or, more recently, in terms of the brain that is just beginning to be discovered by neuro-physiology. These can be described as the different 'spiritual automatons' (Deleuze) that have assumed the position of the ground for contemporary philosophy, or could be variously described as the avatars of one great spiritual automaton which modern philosophers have sought to determine as the form of an immanence that is immanent to itself alone – as either pure consciousness or as a transcendental subject from which nothing, neither internal nor external, escapes (WP 46).

On a second level, if philosophy can no longer extract its image of thought from simple common sense, and can no longer illuminate or correct the simple 'error' of the understanding, then its orientation both to natural consciousness and to higher principles (such as the 'Good') is exposed to a more profound *disorientation*. The creation of the concept of the fold in Deleuze's philosophy after the 1980s is precisely a diagrammatic figure of this extreme disorientation, a state of suffering that Leibniz once described as a dizziness or even a 'swooning' (*l'étourdissement*) which occurs when the external and internal attributes of an object are confused and the soul loses its ability to orient itself to either the external world of perception or the interior domain of psychological representation (memory, dream, fantasy, etc.). The crucial significance of the Baroque is that it provides a more precise understanding of a new image of thought that corresponds to how the mind is folded with the body (or *le corps*), that is, of an absolute 'inside,' which is deeper than any interiority, which is co-implicated with a pure 'outside,' which is further away than any external object of perception. In fact, I will argue that by turning our attention to the state of extreme disorientation that 'the Baroque' often represents, we might be able to *orient* ourselves to the peculiar cause of our own state of suffering.

As Deleuze asks, 'if "turning toward" is the movement of thought toward truth, how could truth not also turn toward thought? And how could truth itself not turn away from thought when thought turns away from it?' (WP 38). Here we note a precarious movement which, first of all, admits the possibility of a more profound disorientation than error or falsehood, which is the disorientation of thinking itself and, as a result, the point where the relation of thought and truth essentially assumes the form of *non-relation*. It is a turning-away from one another 'which launched thought into an infinite wandering rather than error' (WP 51). This sounds uncannily like the Heideggerian interpretation of the profound 'Error' of the metaphysical tradition descending from Plato; at the same time, something striking (and distinctly non-Heideggerian) occurs if we accept from this the possibility that this 'non-relation' becomes the only form of the relation between truth and thought. Therefore, it is only by tracing this paradox that we are able to discover the contours of an event that caused – and continues to cause – their mutual disorientation. Can we not see, in the modern period, that each and every manner by which thought loses its way (including deception and madness) becomes precisely the means of locating the missing relation to truth?

The above observations imply that the false becomes a special 'power' that orients for us today the (non-) relation between thought and truth: *the false is the force that causes us to think the relation to truth as a (non-) relation.* Turning once more to the question of those other regions where contemporary philosophy attempts to ground its concepts and to 'institute a plane of immanence with the world' – since 'Philosophy is at once concept creation and institution of a plane' (WP 41) – Deleuze defines a non-philosophical understanding as rooted in what he calls 'percepts and affects,' which points to the special relationship that philosophy entertains with literature, modern cinema and the arts. As Deleuze writes, 'percepts aren't perceptions, they're packets of sensations that live on independently of whoever experiences them. Affects aren't feelings. They're becomings that spill over beyond whoever lives through them (thereby becoming something else)' (N 137). As the domain proper of *percepts* and *affects*, the question of art can no longer be subordinated to the specialized or minor analytic of aesthetics; therefore, it is not surprising that Deleuze revitalizes this bastard form of philosophy (following Kant) and gives back to it a more vital sense of 'non-philosophy.' In *Difference and Repetition*, Deleuze writes:

> It is strange that aesthetics (as science of the sensible) could be founded on what can be represented in the sensible. ... Empiricism truly becomes transcendental, and aesthetics an apodictic discipline, only when we apprehend directly in the sensible that which can only be sensed, the very being of the sensible: difference, potential difference and difference in intensity as the reason behind qualitative diversity. (57)

'Affects, percepts and concepts are three inseparable forces, running from art into philosophy and from philosophy into art' (N 137). For Deleuze, therefore, art now occupies the position of a pre-philosophical understanding that was formerly reserved for natural consciousness or common sense. It could easily be demonstrated that much of a certain tradition of contemporary philosophy can be remarked by a fundamental encounter between itself and the domain of the modern arts. We have several prominent examples: Heidegger and poetry, Merleau-Ponty and painting, Derrida and literature. The question remains as to why? Why are philosophy and the different domains of modern art inevitably drawn toward an encounter with each other and, at the same time, to a point 'outside' of common perception or intuition? It is as if both are under the spell of another point or dimension of the real which is hidden precisely because it is too open and chaotic, that is, too near for the power of intuition (or imagination) and too far for the power of perception (or concepts of the understanding) to represent?

The first response to this question would be that there is a relation between this outside and time. If time is the form of subjective intuition in Kant, then Deleuze remarks that point where the classical subject is no longer capable of grasping time as the form of its own interiority (the form of an 'inner sense'), and thus is no longer equal to the task of representing 'What happened?' or 'What's going to happen?' (two locutions that I will employ for the past and future, in order to render more vividly as subjective problems of orientation in time). That is to say, there is the excessive character of an 'event' which has caused time to shatter its cardinal frame of representation, and, simultaneously, which has outstripped the subject's power to synthesize a temporal space of the given, exposing the subject of representation to 'something = x' that, on the one hand, is *outside* its powers to render thinkable, livable, or as an object of possible experience (that is, 'organic representation') and, on the other hand, is also the determinate condition of both knowledge and communication: the being of the sensible.

Contrary to the metaphysical tradition, which always grasps thought as an object of representation (in the form of the 'idea' in Plato, 'reason' in Kant, or 'spirit' in Hegel, for example), Deleuze situates this object of non-relation on the plane of expression. The concept of philosophy, as Deleuze and Guattari address it in *What is Philosophy?*, becomes nothing less than a diagram of the brain (*le cerveau*) that is traced from the limits of sensibility to the condition of thought, '*du dehors au dedans*,' attempting to discover in the perceived a resemblance not as much to the object of thought, but rather to the force that causes us to think: the condition of sensibility and no longer the representation of its sense. Here again, we might discern the special power that is accorded to the role of art, literature and cinema in Deleuze's philosophy, since the conditions of thinking this form of immanence can no longer be said to be common or innate to the Ego, but can only be approached by means of a constructivism. Art researches the conditions for rendering this plane of immanence discernible by making the bare possibility of feeling more intensive and raising the minimal powers accorded to perception and intuition into a form of 'vision.' Consequently, the false is trans-valued into a special and positive power that is now charged with the discovery of new *percepts* and *affects*, that is, with researching the conditions for restoring at least the possibility of immanence to the powers of philosophical discernment.

Deleuze argues that if philosophy is to survive it is only through a creative engagement with these forms of non-philosophy – notably modern art, literature and cinema. In other words, philosophy today can only hope to attain the conceptual resources to restore the broken links of perception, language and emotion. This is the only possible future left for philosophy if it is to repair its fragile relationship of immanence to the world *as it is*. In its attempt to think the immanence of this world, which is neither the 'true' world nor a different or 'transformed' world, philosophy has returned to its original sense of 'ultimate orientation' as its highest vocation and goal. However, something new, and distinctly modern, occurs in the philosophy of Deleuze when we recognize that the sense of ultimate orientation is no longer described in terms of verticality – a dimension of transcendence that Deleuze takes great pains to avoid – but rather in terms that are essentially horizontal, or terrestrial.

As Paul Klee once wrote, 'If the vertical is the straight line, the uprightness, or the position of the Animal, then the horizontal designates its height and its horizon – and each one is entirely terrestrial, static.'[6] Consequently, one concept that I will highlight in my commentary of Deleuze is the concept of 'the Other

Person' (*Autrui*), which appears in *Difference and Repetition* and, finally, in *What is Philosophy?* The creation of the concept of the Other Person represents perhaps the most profound and yet most subtle transformations in Deleuze's entire philosophical system, and it is not by accident that the concept of the Other Person is given as the first concept in *What is Philosophy?* – a place usually reserved for the concept of God as 'first principle' in traditional metaphysics (particularly the scholastic philosophy of Duns Scotus who bears a special importance for Deleuze). In other words, Deleuze's philosophy 'begins' with the creation of the concept of the Other Person, and in Deleuze's attempt to orient thinking purely in terms of the horizontal relationship that is introduced by the problem of the Other Person, perhaps we have no better indication of the overturning of transcendence as the highest problem for contemporary philosophy.[7]

2

HOW TIME PLACES TRUTH IN CRISIS

Certainly one of the most enigmatic points of Gilles Deleuze's philosophy is the poetic statement 'time off its hinges.' This statement receives its most succinct formulation in the preface to the English edition of *Cinema 2: The Time-Image* (1989) where Deleuze introduces the reader to what he calls the 'adventure of movement and time' in modern cinema:

> Over several centuries, from the Greeks to Kant, a revolution took place in philosophy: the subordination of time to movement was reversed, time ceases to be the measurement of normal movement, it increasingly appears for itself and creates paradoxical movements. *Time is out of joint*: Hamlet's words signify that time is no longer subordinated to movement, but rather movement to time. (TI xi)

Sometimes it is in the nature of poetic saying to obscure rather than to clarify, and here we find only the announcement that 'something happened' that caused time to fall off its hinges, to increasingly appear for-itself (to engender sensory-motor paradoxes). This event will signal a point of irretrievable crisis for philosophy itself since, as a result of this reversal, 'every model of truth collapses' and its models will ultimately fail in discerning the new relationships between the real and the imaginary, or to differentiate between true and false pasts (TI 131).

If we accept the premise that the role of classical philosophy was to 'fix time,' that is, to save truth at all costs (since time itself is the fundamental problem of philosophy), then we need to ask 'How is it that time can place truth in crisis?' 'What happened?' Taking up these questions, the following discussion will attempt to clarify the relationship between the statement 'time off its hinges' and what Deleuze will call the crisis of truthful narration by tracing the contours of the event where the classical categories of time, truth and world enter into a 'zone of indiscernability,' where these categories undergo a strange reversal and the very 'possibility' of philosophical narration begins to be governed by what Deleuze calls 'the powers of the false.' In this sense, the false becomes a power that orients the thinker's relation to truth and to the world from this point on. As Deleuze argues, 'The power of falsity is time itself, not because time as changing contents but because the form of time as becoming brings into question any model of truth' (N 66).

Before getting too far ahead of ourselves, however, let us first return to our guiding question and ask how is it that time can place truth in crisis? In response, we might notice that there is something in this event which corresponds to the nature of time discovered by chaos theory as a pure force of becoming, and Deleuze and Guattari resort to the figure of chaos in *What Is Philosophy?* to show that it 'is characterized less by an absence of determinations than by the infinite speed by which they take shape and vanish' (42). The figure of 'chaos' that Deleuze and Guattari invoke might give us a modern understanding of the *clinamen* that also appears at the basis of Lucretian physics, which Michel Serres has described by the figure of the atomic 'spiral' or 'cyclone.'[1] Rather than standing in as another form of time – time is fundamentally 'an excessive formlessness [*Unförmliche*]' (DR 91) – its figure marks the event where time 'over-turns' and 'empties out' the simple form which was deployed to represent or contain it. As Deleuze and Guattari write, 'chaos makes chaotic and undoes every consistency in the infinite' (QP 42).[2] At the same time, we must also recognize that the figure of this event is precisely 'nothing new' and cannot completely clarify the qualitative difference that we spoke of above in terms of the crisis of contemporary philosophy that, according to Deleuze's statement, is supposedly caused by an 'irreversible' declension between movement and time. As Deleuze writes in *Cinema 2*, 'if we take the history of thought, we see that time has always put the notion of truth into crisis. Not that truth varies depending on the epoch. It is not the simple empirical content, it is the form or rather the pure force of time which puts truth into crisis' (TI 130). Therefore, following more closely Deleuze's arguments concerning this notion of time in crisis, let us ask 'how,' or rather 'why,' this comes about?

First, according to an argument that appears earlier in *Bergsonism* ([1966] 1988), because time is a constant becoming, which simply means that it refuses to 'be'; the whole of time is never 'given.' Second, because all 'becoming' first appears as abnormal, monstrous and lawless; '[and in its 'becoming,' time] is actualized according to divergent lines, but these lines do not form a whole on their own account, and do not resemble what they actualize' (B 105). Third, because Deleuze (employing Bergson's notion of an *élan vital*) must admit to the existence of 'false problems' or places where the apprehension of time itself gets botched, where its concept loses its way and leads to an impasse. It is the nature of all solutions to be temporary and partial, philosophical solutions included; 'and each time, we will say that the solution was as good as it could have been, given the way in which the problem was stated, and the means the living being had at its disposal to solve it' (B 103).

According to Deleuze one such impasse occurs when time is confused with space, which leads us to think that the whole of time is given at a certain point, even if this point is 'idealized' and reserved for a God or a superhuman intelligence that would be able to see the whole of time in a single glance (B 104). In *The Fold*, Deleuze illustrates this episode with the Leibnizian concept of the monad which, 'having no doors or windows,' proposes an absolute difference (or exteriority) between the luminosity of soul and the visibility of matter, or between thought and perception. In other words, as I will discuss in more detail in the next part, the Leibnizian construction first posits an irresolvable difference or confrontation between two forms of difference, and then, as Deleuze shows, resolves this confrontation in the most bizarre of manners: the creation of God, who occupies the position of the central monad, and of the *a priori* expression of a 'pre-established harmony' (*harmonia praestabilita*) which Deleuze likens to an automaton. In other words, Leibniz solved the problem of time by constructing the series of incompossible worlds where divergent series could be developed without suffering contradiction; he saved truth 'but at the price of damnation' (that is, by creating aborted becomings and cast-away worlds where certain singularities were assigned to spend eternity). However, invoking the third characteristic of time given above, Deleuze asserts that the Leibnizian solution could only have been temporary and 'the crisis of truth thus enjoys a pause rather than a solution' (TI 131). Why?

First, we can say that if the Leibnizian solution gradually led to an impasse and failed to solve the problem of time, this is because he retained the classical function of God (or *Scientia Dei*) and, thus, spatialized time from the point where God could see the whole of time stretched out across incompossible universes in order to choose the world that was the 'most ripe' with possibilities. Second, the Leibnizian solution was still dependent on what can only be phrased as the ethical 'character' of God's judgement; that is, he believed in a God who knew the difference between good and evil, and who could choose the world that exists on the basis of this innate knowledge of 'the best one.' Without this principle of *belief* in the ethical criteria of judgement, of the innate 'good nature' of reason itself (which itself rests only upon the belief that the idea of God contains 'perfect knowledge' and there is nothing unknown or unconscious in the nature of this knowledge), the world that exists would be exposed once again to the possibility of the most egregious 'error' (non-truth, falsehood). In the modern period, when the idea of God becomes predicated on a knowledge of 'History,' there were bound to appear inexplicable accidents, detours, dead-ends and, worst of all, stale possibilities and boring truths; explanations that failed to justify 'what happened,' or 'what's going to happen.' One might conclude that it was only a matter of time before time returned again to place truth into crisis.

Turning now to the second guiding question, in light of the foregoing observations, we must ask once more: What happened? What could have happened to place truth, again, into crisis? Taking our cue from the preface of the second cinema study, *The Time-Image*, we might reply: 'The War!' In its wake, we are all survivors; our memories are stricken by an irretrievable trauma. The earth is laid waste by a paralysis of memory and zones of impossibility: death camps, burned-out cities, atomic sink-holes, summer fields yielding each year a new harvest of corpses. Today, we find ourselves in the age of Auschwitz, on which is superimposed the age of Hiroshima, under the shadow of a horrible decision, a botched and burned-out world. Although I am employing these names in a drastically abbreviated manner – that is, as signs of a kind of universal or world memory – the events they designate remain sombre and cast their shadow over the idea of reason that existed prior (or *a priori*). In fact, they mark a *caesura* or eclipse of reason itself, as a result of which 'before' and 'after' are no longer equal and time undergoes a profound declension and suspense. Certainly, these events were enough to condemn the Leibnizian God for a terrible error in judgement – certainly this could not be 'the best of all possible worlds!' '*We must have taken a wrong turn somewhere!*' If philosophy appears today as perhaps the most impoverished of narratives, it is because its own image of perfect reason ('the true world') ultimately led to its own self-abdication and guilt, a problem exacerbated by the fact that the nature of judgement remains grounded in the classical image of reason. If the modern period has been described an age of 'criticism' (Octavio Paz), it is because all truth must come under the suspicion of harboring an evil genius or another holocaust, and it is not simply by chance that our age has witnessed the countless times when the 'character' of the philosopher himself has been placed on trial. As in the cases of Nietzsche and Heidegger, the philosopher has been brought before his own tribunal of reason to receive judgement. It is as if reason itself suffers a deep splitting (*Spaltung*), and as a result of a primordial cleavage within the 'image of thought,' gives birth to its own double that returns a critical glance against the philosopher's own *logos*.

We might detect this event already in the infamous figure of the *malin génie* (an 'evil genius') whom Descartes conjures up in the *Meditations* in order, finally, to extract the truth of the *cogito* as a foundational ground of certainty. Ultimately, this was a sleight of the hand; by creating its own 'double,' the Cartesian solution already guaranteed its momentary triumph over uncertainty and the problem of error simply by the fact that this demon remained a mere 'fiction' (hypothetically posited at the moment of crisis for the dialectic of reason). Therefore, even behind this phantasm of a 'subject who deceives consciousness,' we can detect the profile of a more malevolent demon, one who can be posed no longer in relation to consciousness, but primarily in relation to the subject of desire or of will. After Nietzsche's concept of 'the will to power' (*Der Wille zur Macht*), at least, we find the possible existence of a subject who deceives not only a rational proposition but, even more, a probable ground of truth and a fundamental cause of uncertainty.

Today, beneath the shadows that are cast by the names of 'Auschwitz' and 'Hiroshima,' philosophy has become, employing Blanchot's fine phrase, 'the writing of a disaster.' If the Leibnizian solution were adequate to determine the best of all possible worlds, then Auschwitz and Hiroshima would have been banished to incompossible worlds, instead of the death-zones that have emerged within our own. Moreover, under its classical image of reason, philosophy would have to assume the task of justifying these as 'the best of all possible worlds,' something it could not do. Rather than offer another 'sufficient reason,' it simply left the stage of history and retired into the silence of pure logic (Wittgenstein), or pure poetry (Heidegger). Can we not read Heidegger's famous statement that 'only a god can save us now' as perhaps the most radical philosophical renunciation of philosophy itself?

Nevertheless, we must admit that the 'end of philosophy' is itself a philosophical moment, since philosophy has risen from its own ashes countless times before. This event of crisis could also signal for us that point where contemporary philosophy folds back and takes itself as an object of the most radical critical operations. Here we could point to the work of French philosophers Emanuel Levinas and Jacques Derrida as being exemplary of this moment of auto-critique. For both philosophers, the classical image of reason and the system of judgement it employed have been found in default, causing the general decline of philosophical sovereignty in the West, since the image of reason can longer be identified with the classical *cogito*, but rather must allow for a radical alterity in the heart of judgement, a 'passive synthesis of the ego' (Husserl). According to Levinas, it does this precisely by situating itself as the subject of time, so that the truth in crisis is the only image of its own transcendence over time.[3] This moment emerges when the symbol of judgement that characterizes the image of classical thought is exposed to the most ferocious self-criticism, whereby the tribunal of judgement becomes a mode of 'hyperbolic doubt' (Derrida) or returns against itself within a discourse of ethics (Levinas). Because the crisis of philosophy marks the default of its concepts of 'identity and 'universality,' it becomes vulnerable to the point of losing its power to identify with the image of 'reason,' which is subordinated to the character of an alterity that animates its history. It is in this sense that we might understand Derrida's ferocious and unforgiving interrogation of the history of philosophy, which also entails a form of its repetition and 'deconstruction.' The Derridean repetition which is different from an Heideggerian repetition of 'ontological difference' since the latter, in the earlier works at least, still holds out a possibility for a 'return' or 'homecoming' of philosophical reflection to a proper form of 'thinking' (*Denken*). Therefore, we should also take seriously Levinas's critique of Western reason, different from but related to Derrida's, which submits the language of philosophy to the primordial critique launched by a discourse of ethics. The radical objective of this gesture must be understood as the 'un-making' and silencing of a philosophical *language of Being*, an unmasking of the transcendental Ego and all its adjacent discourses of knowledge (history, politics, science, anthropology). As a result, the philosophical genre itself undergoes a positive molting of its own image of reason which now appears 'otherwise than being or beyond essence' (Levinas).

A third possibility is represented by the philosophy of Gilles Deleuze where the inability of contemporary philosophy to identify with its classical image of reason is pushed to its extreme, to the point of threatening to silence it altogether. What is this silence that strikes against the very upright and good nature of the classical philosopher's *logos*, if not the logic of reason itself? As Deleuze writes very early on, 'perhaps writing entertains a relationship with silence that is altogether more threatening than its supposed relation with death' (DR xxi). The loss of identity suffered by the philosophical reason and the silence (i.e. 'nonsense') that its language undergoes in the modern period is caused by nothing less than that the very notion of the 'possible' (which marked its relation to the future) has itself become impossible. Contemporary philosophy, in other words, represents the default of the concept of the possible (with which it can no longer represent time, and therefore itself), since the possible has become impossible *a priori*. However, against those who would be inclined to pronounce a death-sentence on the future of philosophy because of its shadowy past, I must underscore the fact that although Deleuze sees the modern predicament as signaling the loss of philosophical identity and the abdication of its classical language and concepts – that is, as having lost the classical 'image of thought' the philosopher no longer knows how to identify the movement of thought with a categorical form of intuition that is equal to the sensibility of time – he absolutely does not renounce its role or its significant importance for the future. This is something that he underlines again and again, particularly in *What is Philosophy?* which returns to the question of philosophy itself to sift through the ruins of the classical picture of reason. The repetition of the 'question of philosophy' now progresses like the 'selective' operation of the dream-work or the powers of discernment that belong to Nietzsche's concept of the Eternal Return. In the wake of a catastrophe, the philosopher moves by a process of decoupage, picking things up along the way, anything that might prove useful to resolving this modern predicament of philosophy. All of Deleuze's work has this fragile and strategic sense of working its way through a fundamental problematic, the default of reason, as if the resort to the expressions of non-philosophy (art, literature and science) was the only way of infusing philosophy with new variables of a future.

Even as early as *Difference and Repetition*, Deleuze speculates on the future of the philosophical genre by stating that its narrative mode must become 'in part a species of detective novel, in part a kind of science fiction' (DR xx). We can immediately recognize here that each of these genres of 'story' is directed toward two regions of temporality: the past, the future. Their object, however, is not the past or the future as such, but rather 'something unknown or unknowable' that takes place in these nebulous zones (or folds) of time. 'What happened? What's going to happen?' These questions are aimed neither at some discrete content of the past, nor at some future state of affairs. Their object is much more fundamental and, therefore, consonant with the philosophical method Deleuze invents to unfold the differential character of temporal events:

> *What Happened?* In other words, what causes the past to become 'the past'? *What's Going to Happen?* 'What are the conditions of an event that causes the future to become 'the future'?

The research of this fundamental duality conditions the description of temporality in the concept of 'becoming' that characterizes the entire Deleuzian problematic around difference *and* repetition.[4]

'To research the conditions of an event whereby the future becomes future' is the principle to which Deleuze submits contemporary philosophy. These conditions can appear in philosophy only by introducing new variations and by launching new connections with the forms of 'non-philosophy.' In this sense, the statement 'time off its hinges' describes the modulation of the philosophical genre itself and underscores the original inter-disciplinary character of a philosophy of difference and repetition. Deleuze had announced this approach as early as 1968 when he wrote:

> It seemed to me that difference and repetition could only be reached by putting into question the traditional image of thought . . . [and] the time is coming when it will be hardly possible to write a book of philosophy as it has been done for so long: 'Ah! The old style . . .'. The search for a new means of philosophical expression was begun by Nietzsche and must be pursued today in relation to the renewal of certain other arts, such as the theatre or the cinema. (DR xxi)

Nearly twenty years later, in the preface to the English edition, Deleuze returns to underscore this task again, this time adding to the semiotic constructions of art (the creation of 'percepts and affects') the 'functions' of science as well:

> Every philosophy must achieve its own manner of speaking about the arts and sciences, as though it established alliances with them. It is very difficult, since obviously philosophy cannot lay claim to the least superiority, but can create its own concepts in relation to what it can grasp of scientific functions and artistic constructions . . . Philosophy cannot be undertaken independently of science and art. (DR xvi)

In the statement, 'obviously philosophy cannot lay claim to the least superiority,' can't we discern the appearance of a new idiom very different from that of Kant, where philosophy claims the supreme right to 'judge' the other faculties, including those of science; or of Hegel where philosophy is responsible for the full deployment of scientific logic through the labor of the dialectic? On the contrary, what is proper to contemporary philosophy is the establishment of 'alliances' and 'nuptials' with the powers of science and art; the princely role of the classical philosopher is subordinated to the mediatory role of the diplomat or the 'intercessor' – in the creation of concepts (of understanding) from the primary materials offered by scientific 'functions' and by artistic constructions of 'percepts and affects' – revealing, finally, a philosophy of conjugations, of becomings effected by a kind of 'passive synthesis' with the forms of non-philosophy.

Having either lost or abdicated its former sovereignty and classical 'image of thought,' philosophy can only appear BETWEEN these earlier forms (which no longer have actuality) and the forms of non-philosophy it is now coupled with: science, technology, literature, cinema, history, ecology, or madness. At this point, we can clearly discern the basis of Deleuze's solution in two senses: first of all, it is not in the sense that philosophy, after the war, itself returns as science, literature, theater, painting, or cinema. Rather, it implies that the thinking of time appears first in these other regions, and philosophy must resort to these 'other planes of immanence and expression' in order to develop its concepts. I cannot phrase this more strongly for the moment than to say that in the contemporary period, the plane of expression that philosophy occupies is no longer immanent to the world *as it is*; the 'questions and problems' that classical philosophy poses (of 'the Good,' of 'truth,' of the 'beautiful') no longer help to clarify the situation at hand. This situation constitutes the 'problem of expression' for philosophy today. In fact, the 'questions and problems' of classical philosophy itself have become too abstract and too general and, in consequence, have themselves fallen into the miserable state of needing constant explanation or justification. As a result, philosophers have become responsible for introducing a *zone of indiscernibility* both with regard to lived experience, but also with regard to the powers proper to philosophy itself. Instead, a traditional understanding of philosophy has limited itself to the formal examination of the problems of logic or to repairing old categories (that is to say, problems that it has some assurance of being solved prior to taking them up or proposing them). The second sense addresses the formula 'everything is impossible *a priori*,' which can be found in the numerous writers Deleuze refers to in the course of his work – but particularly Kafka's 'guilty *a priori!*' Once this is accepted as a 'given,' then everything must follow and this must be understood in an affirmative and Nietzschean sense. If philosophy has abdicated the classical image of reason, then it can only resort to other planes of expression in an effort to escape from its impasse, which is somehow equal to the impasse of the 'world' itself after the events of 'Auschwitz' and 'Hiroshima.' Henceforth, philosophy itself must become a philosophy of 'the event.' The fact that the active powers formerly accorded to the classical *cogito* (judgement, doubt, negation, criticism) are found to be absent from Deleuze's description of the modern philosopher's role serves only to underscore the newness of the situation in which philosophy finds itself after the war, a situation which irremediably alters the 'character' of the philosopher, which is nothing less than the character of truth itself.[5]

3

THE PROBLEM OF JUDGEMENT

'Obviously,' Deleuze writes, 'concepts have a history [*une histoire*]' (QP 23). That is, each concept has a story to tell, although it may be the kind of story told by idiots, 'full of sound and fury.' Understood in this light, we might see that philosophy presents its own history as a narrative of concepts, a fable of thought that must recommence each time from the beginning in response to the innocent and childlike question 'What is x?' For example: 'What is philosophy?' 'A person?' 'An animal?' 'A hero, or a god?' 'A day, or an hour, of the week?' 'What is death?' Or, 'What is an event?' Faced with such questions, the classical philosopher-storyteller might exhibit a kind of blank expression, a gesture of fatigue, or a look of inscrutable mystery, prefacing his response with 'Here begins a long and perhaps inexhaustible story.' This statement introduces the listener to a duration that has nothing to do with the so-called 'age of philosophy.' Although it is as old as the hills, perhaps even as old as 'time' itself, following Kant philosophical knowledge (rigorously conceived) has been divorced from wisdom and gains nothing from an accumulation of experience. The problem of the story's duration is that its episodes are not simply divided between several epochs (the Greeks, the Schools, the Enlightenment), or between several distinct actors or conceptual personae (Plato, Aristotle, Descartes, Heidegger).[1] According to Deleuze, after the philosophy of Leibniz it is also divided between several possible worlds; therefore, in recounting each particular event or episodic encounter in the concept's history ('*Adam eats of the poisonous fruit in the garden,*' '*Jesus Christ is betrayed by Judas Iscariot,*' '*Caesar passes the Rubicon,*' '*Rome falls to tyranny*'), the classical narrator must calculate all its possible versions and variations in order to render to reason the existence of 'the best one,' which is given the pseudo-factuality of the past as well as the quasi-insistence of necessity.

I have characterized the age of our classical narrator only to highlight the sense of fatigue and resignation that inevitably accompanies the evidence of History, which only motivates him to render an account of the reasons that belong to what Deleuze calls the economic or legal connections which come together to form a dominant system of judgement.[2] It was primarily the result of an ancient (mythic) accord between the image of reason and the epic representation of the law that the classical philosophical narrative took on a juridical function and the philosopher himself often appeared as a jurist. (For example, the Platonic figure of the philosopher-jurist is itself derived from the mythic court depicted in *The Meno* and *The Gorgias* where the dead judges appear 'without eyes and ears' and, no longer inhibited by the veil of the senses, can peer directly into the souls of the accused.) The language associated with this function often produced the ethical tautologies and the imperative modes of description with which we are most familiar, as well as a kind of patriarchal and summary conclusion: 'It happened thus and, therefore, it was necessary.' The meaning of an event would be deduced from a system of calculation (or jurisprudence) that handed the real over to the possible by making it a pure expression of what Nietzsche called 'the past and its "It was."' 'Then the sleight of hand becomes obvious,' Deleuze writes concerning this moment in *Bergsonism*: 'If the real is said to resemble the possible, is this not in fact because the real was expected to come about by its own means, to "project backward" a fictitious image of it, and to claim that it was possible at any time, before it happened?' (B 98). For each case there could only be one possible ending: *an Adam eating the poisonous fruit and expelled from the garden, a Sextus dethroned and in exile, a Caesar passing the Rubicon and betrayed by Brutus, a Christ crucified and buried.* After everything is said and done we find that the classical philosopher is after all nothing but a narrator of legal fictions (*les romans policiers*) whose only problem was phrasing a proposition in such a way that it provided an adequate discernment of the principles that would rule the final disposition of each case.

For Deleuze, the fundamental problem of judgement concerns the nature of a certain decision that determines the conditions of any possible world. But what does it mean 'to decide?' What is a 'decision?' Who 'decides?' In response, we should recall that the criteria of certainty, as the dominant characteristic of thinking, commence with Descartes, who invented an 'image of thought' that was itself the symbolic equivalent of an action. As Deleuze describes this moment:

> If I say: Descartes! That's the type of philosopher with a very sober concept creation. The history of the *cogito*, historically one can always find an entire tradition, precursors, but there is nonetheless something signed Descartes in the *cogito* concept, notably (a proposition can express a concept) the proposition: 'I think therefore I am,' a veritable new concept. It's the discovery of subjectivity, of thinking subjectivity. It's signed Descartes.[3]

To decide, to pass judgement, to doubt, is to act decisively concerning the matter to be thought. Within the Cartesian method, this 'action-image' represents the decisiveness of doubt: the power to exclude sensation, belief, understanding and existence in order to arrive at a point of absolute certainty. Yet, how did the criteria of certainty come to resemble the perfection of reason – becoming its aim (*telos*) as well as its ideal image? One could argue that this was itself the result of a certain decision, or action, that bears the proper name of Descartes himself, whose heroic gesture was to create an image of thought that was essentially active (negative, critical) in such a way that, after Descartes, the image of thought itself was represented by Descartes's action-image as dramatized by the *Meditations*.

Here, we have a good example of a series that fails to express the condition of every other series, since the image of thought can exist only if it bears a resemblance to the concept of *cogito* that Descartes created, or invented, to express the relationship between thought (God, or pure Ego) and perception.

In *The Fold*, Deleuze lays down the essential coordinates for responding to this problem in his analysis of the Leibnizian concept of the *vinculum substantia*, which can be defined as a kind of dominant or dominating fold that functions as an 'ideal causality' and defines a substantial predicate, or category. For Deleuze, however, the substance of the *vinculum* cannot be understood as being 'essential' or 'substantial,' but rather as 'sticky' or 'viscous': that is, as a plane of consistency. It is the adhesive that holds everything together and pulls it along – not the center of *envelopment* (world), but all the points of its *ad-hesion* (plane). Because of this, it resembles nothing but a thin and imperceptible film which covers everything and would allow signs to stick to objects, descriptions to individuals, or persons to statements; its viscous membrane does not compose individuals and subjects, but rather encompasses singularities and events. It is in this sense that one could say that a certain function of the fold is 'essential' or 'necessary,' but only under the following conditions: first, that it founds the double articulation of thought to the body and the body to thought; second, that it gives to the body its unity across a flux of the material present and its point of adhesion in sensible space; third, that it functions as the non-localizable connection between a constant and its variables. This is what gives it the ability to disengage from the descriptions of objects and beings in which it is incarnated and which belongs only to the status of events.[4]

In the *Theodicy*, the concept is represented by a God who rules this fold and possesses, in principle (*en droit*), the right to decide upon the series that will 'ripen' into the best of possible worlds (T §218).[5] This is because, at the moment of creation, a decision will have been necessary, a decision that would allow only one possible world to be realized; without such a decision, according to Leibniz, there would only be an infinite number of equally indeterminate points of God's eternal reflection. A universe that was not ruled by the principle of incompossibility would correspond to a chaos or labyrinth in which every point or perspective would be equally indeterminate and every path would lead nowhere, since there is not a series that is actualized and gives order and direction to all the rest. Therefore, the law of necessity, which is expressed here by the requirement that there be only one world that is actualized, appears to be the highest principle (or law), even higher than the Leibnizian God who, in a certain sense, is compeled to choose. (Although in his analysis Deleuze seems to lighten this command by turning the Leibnizian universe into a game of chess in which the laws only function as contractual arrangements between players rather than descriptions of force, or natural laws.) God must decide at each moment on the inclusion or incorporation of one series, and this decision necessarily excludes or disposes of all the others, which fall like the damned into the base of the chosen world to function as its material, 'releasing an infinity quantity of progress' (Fold 74). In order to justify the statement that 'everything real is rational,' then, Leibniz had to posit the existence of a God who calculates while the world unfurls. And because God is not limited by time and space, he would be able to completely follow the full realization of all possible worlds before choosing the one that is best. It is only on this condition that the 'real appears rational,' since everything that happens will appear against the image of this total ratiocination which infuses the real with the appearance of perfect reasoning. The accuracy of God's calculation necessarily presupposes the power of a Reason that is equal to the whole of time and such a presupposition is represented by the Leibnizian certainty concerning the criteria of 'the best.' This criterion must be distinguished from the criteria of 'the Good' of Plato and 'the most perfect of which a more perfect cannot be conceived' of Aquinas. As Deleuze writes, 'the best of all possibilities only blossoms amid the ruins of the Platonic Good' (Fold 68).

Paradoxically, according to Leibniz, the series that God always finds as the best is always the one that leads to death (Sextus Tarquin, Jesus Christ), since a fundamental axiom that Leibniz discovers in the *Theodicy* is that 'a possible world' can constitute its possibility only from the necessary exclusion or murder of certain singularities. This is why, for Leibniz, in each and every world there exists 'a vague and indefinite Adam' who is defined only by a few predicates (to live in the garden, to be the first man); however, there is only one world in which Adam has sinned (Fold 64). Likewise, while there are several possible worlds containing a Sextus Tarquin, a Judas Iscariot, a Julius Caesar, a Jesus Christ, there is only one where Sextus is dethroned and sent into exile, or where a Christ is crucified and buried. There are as many possibilities as there are possible worlds; however, there is only one that is realized. For Leibniz, therefore, creation was a terrible decision, one that placed God in the position of having to choose 'some Thing over against nothing' (Fold 68). In order to justify this terrible act, Leibniz wrote the *Theodicy* where he appears as God's defense lawyer. 'Of course,' he pleads, 'God is *a priori* guilty for the existence of evil, for the suffering of the damned, and for the murder of certain singularities – but, look, he had his reasons! We cannot know what God's reasons are, nor how he applies them in each case, but at least we can demonstrate that he possesses some of them, and what their principles may be' (Fold 59–60). But why does Leibniz choose the word 'ripen' to represent the process whereby a principle is chosen as 'the best one' to rule a given chain of causality that will unfold into a 'world'? Does this also imply that the world is grounded in reason, or that the series that 'ripens into an ideal causality' necessarily expresses the realization of the 'best of all possible worlds'? For example, employing a famous example from the *Theodicy*, the name 'Caesar' is of little interest in all possible worlds; only in the one where he passes the Rubicon does the possible pass into the real as Rome falls into tyranny. This is because in the series that develops into the world that is chosen, the inscription of the predicate 'passing the Rubicon' onto the name of 'Caesar' is over-determined and poses between the event and history (local and global) such a strong connection (or becoming) that it 'ripens' into an ideal causality which appears, *de facto* and *de jure*, the result of divine jurisprudence. We can infer God's unrealized speculations from the point where he assigns each event to its place within a possible world, and discards those that are incompossible to other worlds – that is, effectively banishes them as false and spurious versions, bad copies, as illegal connections, fakes and forgeries.

It is around the criteria used for arriving at such a terrible judgement that Deleuze's response swerves from Leibniz's optimistic assertion that the world that is actualized is the 'best of all possible worlds.' The Leibnizian assertion assumes that the criterion for realizing certain worlds and letting others fall into chaos is itself reasonable, in addition to being 'necessary' (a justification of 'what happened'). That is, this assertion supposes that the decision that causes the passage of this world from being merely possible to being actual and existing is itself grounded in reason, rather than simply being grounded in the world that exists. At this point it may be important to recall that, for Deleuze, nothing is natural or that everything happens either by a species of construction, convention or by some other artificial means – God or the Other, time, the world, you and I. This also applies to the characters of judgement and decision in the above image of thought which touches, too, upon the fundamental conditions of fiction; therefore, 'everything here is purely fictitious (*romanesque*), including theory, which here merges with a necessary fiction – namely, a certain theory of the Other' (LS 318). One explanation for the importance that Deleuze accords to the concept of the Other is because there is a special (or intimate) relationship between the concept of the Other (or God) and the 'image of thought,' as I will discuss in the next chapter. In the encounter with the Other traditional philosophy has attempted to grasp thinking as an object which is said to be either 'innate,' as in Plato, or a common faculty, as in the case of Kant. In either case, thought takes on a fictional or mythic characteristic of something (an idea, a category, a faculty) that is placed 'into' the subject before birth and, thus, the history of thought can be represented as the progression of the dominant fictions that represent the idea of the Other. Part 'story' (*histoire*), part natural history or 'diagnostic novel,' philosophy expresses the Other (as the condition from which it draws its own 'image of thought') by means of the various symptoms which mark definite breaks and ruptures in all of its necessary fictions.

In his account of this pure fiction of a God who calculates while the world unfurls, Deleuze suggests that the original 'character' of judgement is not grounded in reason and may even be formed and 'subsist' by means of an irrational and perhaps most absurd of factors (B 108). In *Bergsonism*, Deleuze addresses this problem under the name of 'virtual instinct,' which he regards as the origin of myth, or 'the story-telling function of society.'

> Take, for example, obligation: It has no rational ground. Each particular obligation is conventional and can border on the absurd; the only thing that is grounded is the obligation to have obligations, 'the whole of obligation'; and it is not grounded in reason, but in a requirement of nature, in

> a kind of 'virtual instinct,' that is, on a counterpart that nature produces in the reasonable being to compensate for the partiality of his intelligence. (B 108)

The 'story-telling function' of society originates on the same surface that conditions the mechanism of thought. This surface articulates a small inter-cerebral interval between society and intelligence, but also an infinitesimal crack that occurs when the surface of sexuality (or instinct) folds back upon the 'first symbolization of thought' producing a doubling effect: on one side of the mirror's surface, a passionate and affective body or emotional thought (i.e. intensity); on the other, a 'virtual instinct,' a fictive and fabulous reason. What is said in this passage concerning the nature of obligation could equally be true for the nature of Leibnizian God. Likewise, we could say the same concerning Descartes's requirement that the most perfect expression of thought must also bear the attribute of 'clear and distinct perception.' This requirement is not grounded in reason itself, but rather in the nature of the *cogito*, that is, the concept that Descartes invents to represent a new image of thought remarked for its clarity.

It was Leibniz, in fact, who accused Descartes of submitting the 'idea of reason' to a partial representation with the requirement that all clear and distinct perception is also certain knowledge. This is because the image of reason must express the 'whole of clarity,' which includes all the degrees of obscurity as well, and this clarity cannot be represented by the clarity of external perception, but must also touch the clarity of the idea itself that arrives through intuition and is not dependent upon any existing object, except the sudden insight that arrives as if from the mind of God. Each monad expresses a certain portion of this intellectual activity that takes place in the brain (*le cerveau*) of God. God's ratiocination spans the entire duration of this world, even accounting for others that do not exist, and his thought and knowledge of everything that happens, has happened already, and will happen encompasses the totality that unfolds the order of the series selected. The relationship between the image of thought that takes place in God's mind and the ideational activity that occurs in the monad is explained by the argument that each thought already bears the signature of God's intellection, as if the thoughts that occur are the works produced by one great artist whose connection and resemblance to the total work of art can be conceived along the lines of its characteristics of expression, style and composition. However, just as the signature does not resemble the work, but only represents the idea of its belonging to the total series of a creator's *oeuvre*, each thought is connected to the 'idea of reason' by an invisible thread that runs through all the monads and links them together in a total expression of a maximal intelligence. The Leibnizian fable of the God who calculates while the world unfurls may represent the purest expression of this virtual instinct 'which will stand up to the representation of the real which will succeed, by the intermediary of intelligence itself, in thwarting intellectual work' (B 108). We can understand this by the way in which this 'conceptual actor' provides the border or guard-rail that protects this world from sliding into chaos by preventing certain singularities and events from becoming realized, excluding others as illusions and simulacra that approach from beneath the screen separating the chosen world from a chaos swarming at its base. In his essay on Pierre Klossowski in *The Logic of Sense*, Deleuze argues that the principle of this God is founded upon the disjunctive syllogism, and all thought that is founded on this principle makes a negative and exclusive use of the disjunctive (Leibnizian 'incompossibility,' Cartesian 'doubt'). In accordance with this principle, it is the philosopher's role to render to reason (*ratio rendere*), since everything that happened, is happening now, and will happen in the future is essentially ordained by God's eternal *de-cision*. We could understand this as the origin of the maxim 'everything happens for the best,' meaning that everything that exists, exists only on the condition and only so long as its existence has been selected according to the criteria that God uses to calculate the world that is chosen. As we noted in the beginning of this chapter, this constitutes the tautological form upon which the classical image of reason is grounded, one which submits all thought to the requirement that it obey the same representation of reason, a representation that is also guaranteed a 'quality' (*quale*) that belongs to the real.

And yet, even by the means of this fiction, of all the classical philosophers Leibniz comes closest to the truth when he shows that 'what is called thinking' does not belong to the spontaneity of the ego, but rather becomes 'subjectivized' – employing Foucault's word – within the human in order to compensate for its partial intelligence. 'Thinking always come from the outside (that outside which was already engulfed in the interstice or which constituted the common limit)' (F 117). Therefore, the capacity to think is always already 'put into' the human as the condition of the mental-object's sociability as well as the objectivity of a common 'Inside.' Within the history of philosophy, the form of thought's 'interiorization' (DR 261) has been expressed in many ways, all of which constitute the essential fictions of the 'eventuation' of thought: the Platonic doctrine of the Ideas and the theory of reminiscence, the Cartesian idea of infinity which appears in the third and fifth meditations, the Leibnizian notion of Pre-established Harmony (by way of the *vinculum substantia*), the Heideggerian concept of an original temporality inaugurated by the event of 'thrownness' (*Geworfenheit*); finally, the concept of the 'Outside' (*Dehors*) as it is conceived respectively by Blanchot (as 'the interiority of expectation'), Foucault (as 'point of subjectivization'), and Deleuze (as 'the fold'). Whatever form this event takes, whatever concept is invented to express or to trace its eventuation, all these fictions share a common presentiment: that what is called thinking embodies the residue or trace – even a 'signature' – of a power that causes the world to unfold and to encompass all beings within a common 'Inside'. And this 'Inside' will bear no resemblance to the subjective interiority of the empirical ego; rather, it is the interior surface of an 'outside' which is folded within the self, and it is only by means of this all-encompassing fold that all the individual monads can be said to include the same world. Hence, the 'outside' is not a place as much as it is a force that is related to the force that causes us to think; 'the thought that comes from an outside is farther away than any external world, and hence closer than any internal world' (F 117).

This last statement is a formula that Deleuze employs constantly throughout his later works – owing to his confrontation with the 'baroque' philosophy of Leibniz in the early 1980s as I will discuss in the next part – in order to indicate the position of the 'unthought' in his own philosophy, but also, as Deleuze claims, the unthought of philosophy itself. 'We will say that THE plane of immanence is, at the same time, that which must be thought and that which cannot be thought. It is the nonthought within thought' (WP 59). Therefore, the concept of the 'outside' cannot be said to belong exclusively to Deleuze's philosophy. Rather, the 'outside' is time itself that no longer forms an interior (of the Subject), nor a common thread of a space *partes extra partes* that can be traced by representation, but rather a force that has creased the Subject of representation in such a way that it can no longer be said to occupy a point of immanence. Perhaps this is why Deleuze describes THE plane of immanence as that which is 'most intimate in thought and yet the absolutely outside' (WP 59).

Although it sometimes appears that 'the outside' and the 'plane of immanence' are two distinct terms in Deleuze's philosophy, following Deleuze closely on this point, the 'absolutely outside' IS 'the plane of immanence' from the position of a subject that is no longer capable of orienting itself in thought, and is exposed to what Blanchot (following Artaud) describes as a radical 'unpower' (*unpouvoir*). 'If there is an "incapacity" of thought,' Deleuze writes,

> which remains at its [thought's] core even after it has acquired the capacity determinable as creation, then a set of ambiguous signs arise, which become diagrammatic features or infinite movements and which take on a value by right, whereas in other images of thought they were simple, derisory facts excluded by selection: as Kleist or Artaud suggests, thought as such begins to exhibit snarls, squeals, stammers; it talks in tongues and screams, which leads it to create, or try to. If thought searches, it is less in the manner of someone who possesses a method than of a dog that seems to be making a series of uncoordinated leaps. We have no reason to take pride in this image of thought, which involves much suffering without glory and indicates the degree to which thinking has become increasingly difficult: immanence. (WP 55)

'Immanence' (= 'the outside') assumes the figure of a strange and contorted fold, of two infinities that run in two different directions at the same time, as the two sides of the chaos that today haunts the possibility of thinking. The bi-directionality of this fold recalls the character of disorientation I noted earlier concerning the relationship between thought and truth; *it is the force of this disorientation that now defines the modern image of thought itself.* 'The first characteristic of the modern image of thought', Deleuze writes, 'is, perhaps, the complete renunciation of this relationship so as to regard truth as solely the creation of thought, taking into account the plane of immanence that it takes as its presupposition, and all this plane's features, negative as well as positive having become indiscernible' (WP 54).

4

THE PARADOX OF CONCEPTS

Yet, Deleuze says, there's a new narrator in the village. He can be identified, in one sense, with the new idiot who appears in *What Is Philosophy?* (with Kierkegaard, or 'a Descartes who goes insane in the streets of Moscow'). In another sense, he can be recognized in the description of the new archivist announced in the opening pages of *Foucault*, 'who proclaims that henceforth he will deal only with statements and no longer propositions' and even, perhaps, with only the most absurd of statements: 'I am a bug or an earthquake,' 'I have an unconscious toothache,' or, 'It is raining. It is not raining' (F 1).[1] For example, Deleuze and Guattari write:

> The ancient idiot [Descartes, for example] wanted the kind of evidence he could arrive at on his own; in the meantime, he would doubt everything, including $3 + 2 = 5$; in this way he would place all the truths of Nature in doubt. The new idiot is not concerned with all the evidence, will never 'resign' himself to believe that $3 + 2 = 5$; he only wants the absurd – it's not even the same image of thought! (QP 61–62)

While our classical narrator was only concerned with rendering each account to reason, our new narrator seeks to multiply each version – that is, to open each 'past' to an infinite number of possible variations – in order to invent new cases previously unaccounted for in the history of philosophy. 'The ancient idiot wanted the truth, but the new idiot wants to make the absurd the highest power of thought, that is, to create' (QP 61). However, because he is still essentially concerned with 'the problem of judgement,' the new idiot often appears in the role of a lawyer for the defence who pleads his case by narrating the story of each victim of History. Here, we might recall in this context the style of Foucault who fashioned his philosophy by narrating the stories of lunatics, criminals, children, animals and bad poets.

One might argue that this role was already prefigured with the appearance of the philosopher-arbiter in *The Republic*, even though Deleuze and Guattari reject this association outright: 'Assuredly, it's not the same character, there has been a mutation' (QP 61). Consequently, in the various conceptual narratives Deleuze invents to illustrate this new image of thought (for example, the conceptual narrative of the Leibnizian Baroque, or the progression and crisis of the movement-image in modern cinema), what is called an 'event' now corresponds to a central problem on the plane of narration, a 'concept' to the differential calculus of partial solutions, and a 'thought' to a jurisprudence in which the cases proceed in a kind of zig-zag fashion and without reflective criteria of judgement. As an example of this new conceptual narrative, let us take up an episode to which Deleuze frequently refers, an episode that is drawn from Borges's 'The garden of forking paths.' In this story, there is a central character by the name of 'Fang,' who has become a 'conceptual character' in Deleuze's philosophy. Unlike the name of Caesar for Leibniz, however, the name of 'Fang' cannot find an historical (public) year, since it refers to the recurrent fragment drawn from Borges's fable. The fable concerns the story of Fang and an intruder, an intruder who is thus named, although still unknown (or anonymous), approaching from the outside, from 'beyond the turn of experience' (Bergson). In the fable the intruder is both inside and outside, in the past as well as in the future. Deleuze establishes these two locutions analogously – signaling an event (a death, a murder) that is for this reason already accomplished, but also predestined and still to come. Fang hesitates and from this hesitation (to kill or not to be killed) several diverse series prolong and can develop to resonate with other series: Hamlet and Claudius, Caesar and Brutus, Sextus and Lucretia, Christ and Judas Iscariot, Robinson and Friday, Gregor and his family, or K. and the Inspectors. '[W]ith its unfurling of divergent series in the same world,' however, 'come the irruption of incompossibilities on the same stage, where Sextus will rape *and* not rape Lucretia, where Caesar will cross and not cross the Rubicon, where Fang kills, is killed, and neither kills nor is killed' (Fold 82). Of course, some might want to localize this fable's 'effect' by proclaiming that it's not much of a problem after all because it belongs to a simple fiction. And yet, fiction offers the occasion for speculation which, in some manner, can be compared to the interval of the brain which cannot be mapped and followed in a concrete duration, but rather spins and bifurcates, synapse upon synapse, path upon path, producing mirroring upon mirrored effect.

As an illustration of this effect, we might further develop this episode of the Deleuzian concept and read it as if it were a cinematic 'shot' – as the 'close-up' of Fang's face filled with pure elements of sound and light, marking the spontaneous instant of association with flashes of insight, memory, association, emotion. As in cinematic space, the longer the duration of the 'shot,' the more the face begins to lose its contours, as if the skin becomes too loose for it, becoming a pure surface of speculation (e.g. 'What can he or she be thinking now?') or the expression of a 'sign' marking the production of a new emotion never before possible (which, for that reason, may not even be human in the strictest sense). In our example, this shot would depict the moment when Fang realizes that the intruder is knocking and this shot is frozen on a close-up of Fang's face, which captures the hesitations that immediately occur in the 'mind of Fang.' Thus, we have the picture of Fang sitting in his room, on the side of the bed (or, perhaps, under the sheets like Beckett's Molloy). Fang is gazing in the direction of the closed door, his attention focused on the stirrings of the stranger on the other side, or perhaps upon the relationship of the secret he holds to the intruder's intentions. (We could study and analyze this shot in this manner.) It is not just a prosaic description of a room, but also a direct presentation of the mind of Fang, full of hesitations: If this, then this or this, but also the possibility that, or perhaps even that as well. 'Nothing happens' except the hesitations that diagram Fang's thoughts while he speculates, and these speculations develop to follow the fractured lines of a crystalline event.

Perhaps the significance of this event can best be explained by referring again to the poetic formula, 'time off its hinges,' which implies that time is no longer connected and resolved through the organic coordination of the motor-sensorial schema. According to Kurt Lewen, whom Deleuze cites in *Cinema 2*, all schema are 'hodological.' In other words, the schema are the 'hinges' of time; they develop and coordinate time by inferring movement from an action that is absent, but which orders and coordinates all temporal events from the point of its beginning or conclusion. Now, it is true that the incident of 'Fang' can be mapped and developed according to a schematic arrangement; however, this would depend on something quite striking since the narrative would be ordered by an action-image that is absent from the fable itself. Consequently, it would only be from the perspective of this 'action' (to kill or be killed, in short, to decide) that several possible outcomes can be inferred. (Of course, this already assumes that only one outcome will have been possible.) The action, then, functions like a 'lever' in the unfolding of the narrative. It pulls and develops the event immediately into denouement, like a cause from which all the different possibilities would crystallize afterward as its unrealized effects. In this sense, the fable presents an indirect image of time than can be inferred from the action that is posited, but not *in-Being*. From this position of *not-Being*, or Non-Being, this action organizes and directs the whole of time. It deploys the possibilities in the image of a certainty that there is a resolution to this crisis and that it has been ordained in advance, that something will have taken place – the intruder will kill or be killed, and Fang will or will not escape with his life.

We can see now why this fable is not just a 'fiction.' Or, rather, we can understand how this indirect image of time is essential to all fiction and occurs within a very Aristotelian determination of tensions and resolutions, whereby space is inferred from the movements that extinguish it, and time is contracted into one duration that pulls everything under its wing. Throughout his work, Deleuze speculates concerning what would happen if a certain decision were no longer possible, that is, when the symbol of judgement no longer had the power to pull everything into its wake, and time no longer rushes for the door, seeks to resolve itself, to 'actualize itself' or become realized in one duration. To rob possibility of its *potentia activa* (that is, the power to actualize itself in a subject or a world) is something that Leibniz accomplished, but only under the condition that all the monads express, or infer from their perceptions, the same 'brand' (or species) of possibility and all include the same world. Of course, this might leave the decision of which brand of possibility up to who-knows-what-God-of-history. After all, someone must decide and, once decided, each decision leads, as every decision eventually must, to a matter of life or death. But something different occurs (as it happens in Borges and not in Leibniz) when the event designated by the above statement introduces into 'the brain' (*le cerveau*) of Leibniz's God a small crack – almost like a stroke – which splinters and bursts on the surface of his reflection. It would change the nature of decision, or 'the image of thought,' which recalls the image of the mirror filled with cracks and splinters; Deleuze often uses this image to represent the mind filled with hesitation, which multiplies possible worlds like the fractal lines of a crystal-event. In this respect, we can now see that, contrary to its earlier determination, the 'close-up' of Fang's mind presents us with the direct image of time as 'the garden of bifurcating paths.'

This image of the cerebral interval constitutes a positive inversion of the earlier schema in so far as the powers of the labyrinth (i.e. the powers of speculation, or 'the powers of the false') are no longer held back in the shadows of decision, but rather given a positive expression of 'actuality.' As Deleuze writes, 'we now find ourselves before another inter-cerebral interval between intelligence itself and society: Is it not this "hesitation" of the intelligence that will be able to imitate the superior "hesitation" of things in duration, and that will allow the human, with a leap, to break the circle of closed societies' (B 109)? The initial response to this question is 'No,' since man often leaps in the name of an essential egoism that he seeks to preserve against social obligation, and the human intelligence often liberates itself from one circle (or closed society) only to find itself the progenitor of another. Yet something positive occurs, nonetheless, which is the appearance of 'something in this interval between intelligence and society.'

In Deleuzian philosophy, this 'something = x' has been given many names – e.g. 'intensity,' 'becoming,' 'the variable' or simply, 'the new.' In *Bergsonism*, for instance, 'what appears in the interval is emotion' (B 110); not the emotion of egoism, however, which is 'always connected to a representation on which it depends,' but rather a new 'creative emotion' which is purely potential (*en puissance*), and 'in fact, precedes all representation, itself generating new ideas' (B 110). In other words, it is not a new image of action that finally breaks the vicious circle of judgement, but rather the appearance of a new 'being' who makes use of the play of circles in order to break into the closed circuit between the dominant image of judgement and the passive nature of intelligence. It is precisely at this point that we might locate the conjugation between philosophy and non-philosophy.

As a result, Deleuze writes, 'the play of the world has changed in a unique way, because it has now become the play that diverges':

> Even God desists from being a Being who compares worlds and chooses the richest compossible. He becomes Process, a process that at once affirms incompossibles and passes through them . . . Beings are pushed apart, kept open through divergent series and incompossible totalities that pull them outside, instead of being closed upon the compossible and convergent world that they express from within. (Fold 81)

In the fifth chapter of *The Fold*, entitled 'What is the event?', Deleuze proposes a concept of contemporary philosophy that corresponds to Borges's labyrinthine construction, which is now defined as a field of bifurcations and divergences in what Deleuze has called in many places the 'ideal game' (*jeu idéal*). The first rule of this game is that there is divergence, rather than opposition, between compossible and incompossible worlds; the second rule is that there is variation, rather than inclusion, of events. As a result, the concept now belongs to an order of events before belonging to a logic of propositions. This becomes a major axiom in the philosophy of Deleuze which he refers to as *the paradox of concepts*: 'the true object of a concept is an idea whose reality cannot be unfolded empirically; an object, consequently, that is both outside experience and can only be represented within a problematic form' (DR 219).

In order to provide an example of this paradox, let us take up one of Deleuze's primary concepts, the concept of the 'Other Person' (*Autrui*), which appears in the final chapter of *Difference and Repetition* ([1968]1994) and then twenty-five years later in the opening pages of *What Is Philosophy?* ([1991]1996). In one sense, the Other Person vividly portrays the problem of an interior that is 'outside' the powers of representation. The Other Person is a surface pushed up against me, a surface that remains nonetheless deeper than any subjective interior and, at the same time, further than any external object of perception. We should recall at this point that the Freudian topology of 'the Unconscious' can be defined precisely as the effect that this interior surface of the other person introduces into the perceptual field of the subject, and, at the same time, as an exterior surface of an object upon which the partial or negative qualities of projection and illusion unfold. The effect of the Other Person, therefore, is that of a distortion within the perceptual field, but a distortion that at the same time takes on the characteristics of the fold whereby the interiority of the other person also becomes, on the other side, the expressed condition of another possible world.

According to Deleuze, the concept of the Other Person is made up from several components that function like the morsels or cut-ups of other concepts, and that must suppose several diverse fields present at each point of the concept's history. However, it is said to have three distinct and inseparable components: a possible world, a face and actualized language (or speech). 'The Other Person is a possible world, such as this world exists in a face which expresses it, and effectuates itself in language which gives it reality' (QP 23). Each of these components, in turn, is drawn from other concepts, cut up from diverse and divergent fields that have intersected around the problem of the Other Person, or are even responsible for its creation as a fundamental concept of philosophy: the phenomenology of Husserl and Heidegger from which the concept draws its distinction between *Welt* and *Umwelt*; the structuralism of Lévi-Strauss and the passage in Sartre's *Being and Nothingness* which is the first to apply the discoveries of a structural science to the appearance of the Other Person in the famous key-hole scene; the psychoanalysis of Lacan with particular attention to the structures of perversion and psychosis; the literary vortices and cartographies of Tournier, Borges, Joyce, Gombrowicz; finally, the philosophy of Leibniz where the concept draws its formula for the expression of a possible world.

In the final chapter of *Difference and Repetition*, on 'asymmetrical synthesis of the sensible,' Deleuze first introduces the Other Person as a 'special object' which cannot be thought according to the requirements of representation, in which the relationship between the Other and a possible world is dissolved and is reduced either to the status of a peculiar object or to the status of a special subject (the 'I'). What is lost or becomes imperceptible (*insensible*) is what Deleuze calls the singular 'expressive value' that defines the relation between the Other Person and a possible world, which instead is erased in favor of a general representational value. In other words, when the positive encounter with the Other Person has already been reduced to the status of another 'I,' it has been stripped of its real expression, which is that of a problem introduced into the field of the subject. As Deleuze writes, 'it is not the other which is another "I," but the "I" which is an other, a fractured "I"' (DR 261). This problematic condition is particularly revealed by the encounter with a lover, or with the lie as the condition of the possibility introduced by the Other Person in language. 'There is no love which does not begin with the revelation of a possible world as such, enfolded in the other which expresses it' (DR 261). The representation of the Other Person as another subject, or of the intention of the other's expression in language by a convention of truth as a shared moral sense, is in fact a foreclosure of the possibility that the existence of the Other Person first introduces. Therefore, we might conjecture that under the requirements of representation, there is no real distinction between others, and thus no differences between one other and the next. What remains 'unthought' and 'outside' representation is precisely the difference that is implicated and enveloped (interiorized) in the idea of another possible world that the Other Person expresses as a *reality*.

Because the Other Person designates the exceptional case of an object whose exterior cannot be fully explicated, of a subject whose interior cannot be enveloped by the 'I,' it cannot be approached by traditional ontology, but only by a special and 'artificial' means. 'That is why, in order to grasp the other as such,' Deleuze writes, 'we are right to insist upon special conditions of experience, however artificial – namely, the moment at which the expressed has (for us) no existence apart from that which expresses it' (DR 261). Here, we might – again – discern the importance that Deleuze accords to the various domains of art (literature, painting, cinema) all of which fulfil these 'special conditions of experience' in a unique way, where the expressed can no longer be separated from its expression. Consequently, it is important to note that Deleuze grasps the position of the 'other person' only from the appearance of the face and from an instance of speech that confers upon this other possible world a reality.

As Deleuze argues in *Foucault*:

> statements are not directed toward anything, since they are not related to a thing any more than they express a subject but refer only to a language,

> a language-being, that gives them unique subjects and objects that satisfy particular conditions as immanent variables. And visibilities are not deployed in a world already opened up to a primitive (pre-predicative) consciousness, but refer only to a light being, which gives them forms, proportions and perspectives that are immanent in the proper sense – that is, free of any intentional gaze. (F 109)

The very possibility of these statements reverses the usual direction of its 'actuality.' Therefore, it is not a question of reading the statement and assigning it to the duration of a fiction, which is to say, annihilating any possibility of expression that is accorded to a face. On the contrary, that it does not face me in someone, does not mean it speaks from nowhere, but rather that it expresses a relation that I am not yet capable of comprehending or expressing myself. In fact, it is sufficient that it is 'expressed,' even though its expression does not yet have existence outside the one who expresses it, in order for there to be 'the expression of a possible world.'[2] Given these special conditions of experience in which the expressed can no longer be separated from its expression, the role of the art as the discovery of new '*percepts* and *affects*' assumes its full sense of non-philosophy, as the new ground for the creation of concepts.

But why are these 'special conditions of experience' necessary for instituting a new ground for philosophy, one no longer determined by representation? On one level, the significance that Deleuze attaches to the concept of the Other Person can be understood as a revision of Kant's formula concerning the 'highest principle of all synthetic judgements' which reads: the conditions of the possibility of experience in general are at the same time conditions of the possibility of the objects of experience. It now reads: the condition of all perception, for others as well as for ourselves, but also the condition of passing from one world to another one, is at the same time the condition of the Other Person as the concrete expression of the possible as such. As Deleuze writes, 'In every psychic system there is a swarm of possibilities around reality, *but our possibles are always others*' (DR 260 – my emphasis).

What is the difference between these two formulations? In Kant's formulation, according to Heidegger's influential commentary in *Kant and the Problem of Metaphysics* ([1965]1990), transcendence is described as the 'act of orientation which lets something take up a position opposite to ... [and] forms the horizon of objectivity in general.'[3] This primordial act or orientation is bestowed upon the Subject of representation, which can be described as a precursory power of 'turning toward ...' and lets something become an *ob-ject* (and therefore must be pre-disposed at all times to becoming an *ob-ject* of representation). Therefore, even though the power of representation is revealed by Kant to be essentially dependent, finite, 'receptive' rather than 'creative,' it is still defined as a precursory orientation 'which alone constitutes the possibility of pure correspondence,' that is, the possibility of truth, provided that truth means 'the unconcealment of' (*Unverborgenheit von*).[4] The crucial significance of this passage, as Heidegger's commentary highlights, is that representation is accorded with a general power of orientation that precedes all empirical truth and renders it possible, as happens when Kant says that ontological knowledge is given an 'empirical use' that serves to make finite knowledge possible.[5]

In Deleuze's formulation of this power of orientation, on the other hand, the Other Person becomes '*the condition of all perception, for others as well as for ourselves*' (WP 18). Under this condition, 'not only the subject and object are distributed but also figure and ground, margins and center, moving object and reference point, transitive and substantial, length and depth' (WP 18). Hence, the primordial act of 'orienting to,' which functions as the condition of truth as well, is no longer accorded to a transcendental structure of representation, but rather to the reality of the effect that is introduced into the perceptual field of the subject by the Other Person. If it did not function, as Deleuze says, transitions and inversions would be abrupt and we would always run up against things. In short, there would be no breadth or depth of the perceptual field, and therefore, no possible world. Perhaps this is why Deleuze reasserts at several points that 'the concept of the Other Person ... will [also] entail the creation of a new concept of perceptual space' (WP 19). In contrast to the Kantian formulation, the power of orientation is '*derived*' from the empirical plane, which is then given a transcendental use – 'we will consider a field of experience taken as a real world no longer in relation to a self but to a simple "*there is*"' (WP 17) – and it is from this use that the perceptual field (and by extension, the world) is OPEN to redistribution, each time, as to its margins, its center, its length and its depth. There is no longer an *a priori* or transcendental perspective from which a world is *given* from an ideal perspective that totalizes all other perspectives and orients them. The famous transcendental unity of space and time is derived from an empirical plane, not from the transcendental unity that belongs to a subject of representation. Therefore, the Other Person is given the status of 'an *a priori* concept from which the special object, the other subject, and the self must all derive, not the other way around' (WP 16).

Although we have explained the 'reversal' of the conditions of experience introduced by the concept of the Other Person, one last problem concerns us, which is why the conditions introduced by the Other Person are always described in terms of a 'multiplicity.' This question immediately returns us to perhaps *the* problematic of contemporary philosophy: the existence of multiple worlds, since 'we are dealing here with a problem concerning the plurality of subjects, their relationship and reciprocal presentation' (WP 16). For his part, Deleuze locates the origin of this problem of multiplicity precisely in the baroque period, when the principles that organized the world were shattered to bits and philosophy itself suffered a schizophrenic episode. (It is interesting to note that Deleuze defines the period of philosophy that followed under the term 'neurosis,' particularly with regard to the philosophy of Kant.)

> We can better understand in what way the Baroque is a transition. Classical reason toppled under the force of divergences, incompossibilities, discords, dissonances. But the Baroque represents the ultimate attempt to

> reconstitute a classical reason by dividing divergences into as many worlds as possible, and by making from incompossibles as many possible borders between worlds. Discords that spring up in a same world can be violent. *They are resolved in accords* because the only irreducible dissonances are between different worlds. (Fold 81–82)

It is precisely the creative or productive nature of the baroque solution that marks Deleuze's definition of philosophy as 'the creation of concepts.' However, from the passage above, we are perhaps also in a better position to understand Deleuze's constant demand for a thought of multiplicity. As Deleuze once said regarding the Leibnizian statement concerning the principle of sufficient reason, 'the real is rational,' it would be wrong to understand this as a proposition. Rather, it was Leibniz's cry. It was the Leibnizian demand that everything be rendered to reason, at the point of philosophy's greatest crisis when the world itself was being threatened by disillusionment and the principles were about to be toppled. Creation, therefore, is an action always taken in the last resort, as a kind of scream. As Deleuze remarks in a seminar on Leibniz:

> In some ways, the philosopher is not someone who sings, but someone who screams. Each time that you need to scream, I think that you are not far from a kind of call of philosophy. What would it mean for the concept to be a kind of scream or a kind of form of scream? That's what it means to need a concept, to have something to scream! We must find the concept of that scream. One can scream thousands of things. Imagine something that screams: 'Well really, all that must have some kind of reason to be.' It's a very simple scream. In my definition, the concept is the form of the scream, we immediately see a series of philosophers who would say, 'yes, yes'! These are philosophers of passion, of *pathos*, distinct from philosophers of *logos*. For example, Kierkegaard based his entire philosophy on fundamental screams. But Leibniz is from the great rationalist tradition. Imagine Leibniz, there is something frightening there. He is the philosopher of order, even more, of order and policing, in every sense of the word 'policing.' (In the first sense of the word especially, that is, the regulated organization of the city.) He only thinks in terms of order. But very oddly in this taste for order and to establish this order, he yields to the most insane concept creation that we have ever witnessed in philosophy. Disheveled concepts, the most exuberant concepts, the most disordered, most complex in order to justify what is. *Each thing must have a reason.*[6]

Perhaps, by analogy, we can now understand Deleuze as 'the thinker of multiplicities,' as a different cry – everything is multiple, everything must be different, and only in this way can it also be found to be in accord – posed today in a world that is on the brink of being swallowed by difference understood as irreducible divergence, opposition: a world fashioned by the negative and by representation in which real differences are fated to annihilation, and all that remain of these differences are the various ghosts and phantoms.

In conclusion, therefore, let us try to formulate a provisional axiom from the above observations. *For Deleuze, it has never been a question of 'breaking out' of the world that exists, but of creating the right conditions for the expression of other possible worlds to 'break in' in order to introduce new variables into the world that exists, causing the quality of its reality to undergo modification, change and becoming.* The discovery of this 'something = x,' in other words, engenders the condition of 'the new': the various concepts that Deleuze has invented in order to excavate the 'outside,' the sensible surface from which he will extract new assemblages of visibilities and statements that combine to create new 'signs' that have never before existed on the face of the earth (a process that is illustrated in the frequently cited Proustean signs of 'madeleine' and 'Combray'). Consequently, the domains of literature (with its esoteric word and its paradoxical statements), cinema (with its images of movement, action and time), and finally the architectural fragments of the Baroque (with its internal, monadological spaces and its infinite façades) provide material for the production of new surfaces and new sensible signs that diagram an essential 'indecision' in the mind of God, a 'hesitation' in the nature of movement, and a 'stammering' in the proposition. Indecision–hesitation–stammering – these are the special forces that are combined to introduce a new brand of repetition into time, a species of repetition that will find its source in new arrangements of possible intuitions, a poetics of chaos.

PART TWO

ON THE (BAROQUE) LINE

AN EXPOSITION OF *THE FOLD*

5

'THE MIND–BODY PROBLEM' AND THE ART OF 'CRYPTOGRAPHY'

Ecrire et dessiner sont identiques en leur fond. (Paul Klee)

Obviously, the highest, if not the final, aim of philosophy is absolute knowledge. Yet, this means something very different in its Platonic, its Epicurean and, finally, its Hegelian epochs. After Descartes, at least, a certain tradition of contemporary philosophy has understood 'absolute knowledge' as the subject of 'representation' (*Vorstellung*), although this only fulfills and exacerbates a certain Platonism and perverts the very sense of knowledge by misrepresenting its essence as *adequatio* (truth as certitude, rectification with 'a state of things or affairs'). In taking up the critique of Western philosophy after Descartes, Deleuze is not that far removed from Derrida, although each expresses the critique of representation in radically different terms. For Deleuze, any critique of negativity (for example, 'deconstruction') still grasps the question of knowledge from extrinsic and, therefore, representational terms. On the contrary, absolute knowledge – if it is to become adequate to a knowledge of the process of creation – must be understood from a creator's point-of-view. (This remarks the strange alliance between Leibniz and Nietzche.) According to this view, the final goal of knowledge is the discernment of the principle by which 'life' is *implicated* with matter; knowledge is the discernment of the method by which the soul is folded with an animal's body. Thus, the fields of embryology and cryptography may offer a better image of the Leibnizian philosopher's *logos* than mathematics. Moreover, this principle of discernment has a practical and ethical outcome as well, since all knowledge must have a practical application in that it guides us in discerning the best principles for determining 'how one can live.'

In *The Fold* ([1988]1993), this method is presented as 'cryptography.' Deleuze writes: 'A "cryptographer" is needed, that is, someone who can at once account for nature and decipher the soul, who can peer into the crannies of matter and read into the folds of the soul' (Fold 3). Here we might discover the allegorical significance of baroque architecture for Deleuze, which takes the crypt as its foundation and *prima principia* of construction and gives a different notation to the function of a 'key,' which I will address below. Deleuze presents the concept of the 'Baroque' in the same way that he might present a problem in architecture; that is, where the formal possibilities of the design are inseparable from the possibilities (and 'incompossibilities') enfolded within each material component. Specifically, the problem of design issues from the existence of two distinct kinds of infinities that make up the universe, which Deleuze describes as two heterogeneous and irreducible types of fold ('*entre les plis et les replis*') that run through the baroque construction. In turn, this problem is further complicated by the presence of a third term which exhibits a tendency to 'fold between these two folds,' a tendency that Deleuze identifies with the Leibnizian concept of the monad. What occurs under the term 'baroque,' therefore, no longer refers in its essence to an historical and epochal concept, but rather to a process (*operatio*): to something that expresses this proclivity to fold and un-fold, or to 'endlessly create folds.'

In so far as cryptography is 'the art of inventing the key to an enclosed thing,' Deleuze refers to the baroque line as the problem of what is called a 'crypt,' as well as to the proliferation of its random combinations that are like the twisted coils of matter surrounding the living beings that are caught in blocks of matter. However, if the crypt holds the key for deciphering both Leibniz *and* 'the Baroque', it cannot be understood as a content, or an essence, but rather as a dynamic instability produced by the scission that runs between mind and body: 'a scission which causes each of the two split terms to be set off anew' (Pli 40–41). This entails a notion of the fold that runs between the mind and the body that can no longer be figured in terms of opposition and, thus, is much more complex than that of Descartes. As Deleuze argues, Descartes was unable to reconcile the body and the soul because he was unaware of the body's own inclination and 'tried to find content's secret running along straight lines and liberty's secret in the uprightness of the soul' (Pli 5).[1] Deleuze locates the principle of this scission in the monad itself, and the problem of architecture refers to complete construction of the concept from its initial premise, 'no doors or windows.' This unfolds the autonomy of 'an interior without exterior,' which can be figured no longer as the result of a simple opposition, but as the distinct product of the two infinities that run through the living being and which separate the absolute interiority of the monad from the infinite exteriority of matter. (This division also results in the creation of the two façades of Leibniz's philosophical system, which comprise independently of one another the metaphysical principle of life and the physical law of phenomena.) In other words, this forms a 'distinction in kind,' following Bergson's phrasing of the distinction between matter and memory, a distinction that figures prominently in Deleuze's reading of Leibniz. And it is by means of this distinction that Deleuze locates in both Leibniz and 'the Baroque' a nearly schizophrenic tension between open façade and closed chamber; specifically, the absolute scission caused by the incommensurability and incommunicability of two kinds of fold that require, in order 'to trace the thread through the labyrinth,' a more distinctive order of procedure (or *operatio*) than has been represented either by mathematical clarity, or by the distinctness of the object as it appears to the senses.

On the conceptual plane shared between philosophy and mathematics, this solution will require a new division of labor other than the one, still present in Kant (at least, the Kant of *The Critique of Pure Reason*), which relegates to philosophy the use of concepts and their regulation through a process of jurisprudence, even though reason draws the construction of concepts from mathematical knowledge.[2] Although the concept of the fold in some ways resembles the problem of inflection in mathematics, it cannot be reduced to a mathematical problem, since it concerns many other fields as well including biology, economy, language and the arts (hence, Deleuze's kinship with the problem faced by Leibniz concerning the new ground of philosophical concepts, the ground of 'non-philosophy').[3] As a result of this diversity in relation to the genesis of ideas, according to Deleuze, what is required is an 'entirely new regime of light' (Pli 44), that is, a philosophical construction drawn from the possibility of its own art of creating concepts, using whatever light can be fabricated without reference to any objective façade, or the profile of a contour.[4] Here, the notion of the problem that Deleuze employs in order to read this central proposition of Leibniz also finds an analogy to a problem of contemporary music in its search for new harmonies by means of an extended range of dissonance. It is Leibniz, according to Deleuze, who 'makes Harmony a basic concept' of philosophy (N 163). We might immediately add, however, that harmony can only be understood as a solution to the problem of multiplicity, or, in Leibnizian fashion, the problem of multiple and potentially incompossible worlds.

The thematic of dissonance is treated in *The Fold* as indicating the horizons of incompatible worlds encrypted within the monad; thus, Deleuze imports its concept from the domain of musicology in order to account for the use of the crypt within a baroque architecture and to decipher the problem introduced by the Leibnizian notion of 'incompossibility.' There is a cryptic dissonance within the monad, caused by the horizons of 'incompossible worlds,' which will allow Deleuze to problematize the notion of harmony within a Leibnizian construction that is founded on the propositional identity. Instead, Deleuze employs a more modern conception of harmony that is present in certain modern writers, 'like one finds with Joyce, or even with Maurice Leblanc, Borges or Gombrowicz' (Pli 111), in which several divergent series, or incompossibles, can be traced within the same virtual '*chaosmos*,' rather than excluded to entirely different worlds. As a result, the Leibnizian notion of a central harmony (or principle of sufficient reason) undergoes a fundamental change that is best exemplified in the domain of modern literature: in place of the subject as identity of the proposition we have the subject as an *envelope* of the type 'Finnegan' (Joyce), or 'Fang' (Borges); in place of the predicate as attribute, we have the event: to wake, to attend one's own funeral, to mourn and be mourned, to shed a river of tears, to sing a lullaby, or 'to have a secret,' 'to kill or not to kill the stranger.' This will become an important consideration when we analyze below the role that Leibniz assigns to the concept of God within an absolute order of inclusion (or compossibility).

According to both notations of the problem outlined above, the Leibnizian proposition 'no doors or windows' functions as a central contradiction in a philosophical system whose newly invented task will no longer be the suppression of the dissonance it produces (as, for example, what happens in Aristotle who reduces it to a species of contradiction, or Hegel to the negative), but rather the multiplication of its principle. According to Deleuze, this proposition will also function as a 'wild-card' that Leibniz draws from his sleeve in order to effect a complete change in the rules of the game. This is what Deleuze refers to as the Leibnizian revolution, which is the transformation of the concept of Right into a universal jurisprudence, whereby principles are given a reflective usage, and the philosopher will have to invent the principle that rules a given case (Pli 91). This accords to the philosopher a new distinction, never known before Leibniz, from which he derives his concepts by a method of *inventio* and no longer *adequatio*. It is at this point that one understands the importance of this transformation for the new role of philosophy defined as 'the artful creation of concepts'; after Leibniz, the philosopher must invent the 'best conditions' in order to justify any presentation of truth. Since principles are no longer given, nor do they fall ready-made from the sky, they must be created, which is to say they must be fashioned by hand.

Returning to the question 'What are crypts for?' – moreover, against the usual notion that crypts are used for hiding, for repression or exclusion – Deleuze often defines the crypt by the special type of reading that occurs within the monad. The crypt designates both the place of reading in the monad (the reading-room sealed up in light, or the book) and an *operatio*, that is, the 'act' of reading itself (the art of cryptography). In short, it is at once crypt and cipher, secret passage and 'the shortest path through the labyrinth.' This movement creates what the poet Yves Bonnefoy once described as the integral 'movement of interiority' within the Baroque, and signals a point of light that is both infinitely divided shadow and light rising up from an obscure background within the monad itself, a light defined by its damp luminosity, like the glow of large animal hides or the skins which drape the walls of the crypt and provide whatever light there is for reading. At the same time, we should recall that the crypt accounts for the creation of the concept in Leibniz's philosophy as an extreme movement of scission by which he encrypts all perception, that is, the force engendering the subject of perception along with the unity of the perceived, within the monad in order to follow its principle 'fold after fold, fold upon fold.' According to Leibniz, because they are finite, all monads must unfold their own predicates according to a prior order laid down by God's point-of-view (*Aügenblick*). However, Deleuze often employs the poetic statement, 'fold upon fold, fold after fold,' to show what happens when the vertical series of folds stacked on top of one another, representing the scholastic conception of God (*Scientia Dei*), fall back upon (*se rabat sur*) the horizontal series formed by the monads – like 'a dance of particles folding back on themselves' (N 157). By constructing the relation of these two series via the concept of the fold, Deleuze improves upon the Leibnizian construction by effectively creating a 'diagonal line' in order to avoid the vertical line of transcendence. (In short, Deleuze renovates '*la maison baroque*' in order to make it follow more modern principles, even tastes, which would include the rejection of the transcendent as a dominant factor.) As for the vertical line, it is curved to echo 'the pleats of matter.' Thus, what Deleuze refers to as a 'cryptography,' and Leibniz simply as 'the act of Reading,' is a new method invented to discern the process by which the life is enfolded/unfolded within the body of the monad, thus forming an analogy to the tensions that make up the scission between exterior and interior, between perception in matter and reading in the soul. As an aside, Deleuze gives the relevance of this method of 'reading' for our contemporary situation in *Negotiations*, where he says the following: 'The move toward replacing the system of a window and a world outside with one of a computer screen in a closed room is taking place in our social life: we read the world more than we see it' (N 157–158).

Figure 1 Diagram of the interior and exterior of the monad

In order to better comprehend what Leibniz understands by an 'act of reading in the monad,' and Deleuze by 'cryptography,' therefore, it will be necessary to follow the various diagrams that Deleuze develops to theorize the baroque construction of the conceptual pair: *reading–seeing*. The first diagram offered by Deleuze, '*la maison baroque*' (an allegory of the monad), presents us with a building that is comprised of two levels: above, a closed private room, draped with cloth 'diversified by folds' lit from below, where we find a common room that receives light 'from a few small openings' that designate the five senses (Pli 7).

The problem of the upper room, in which all luminosity has been sealed in, can be posed in terms of the classical relation between natural perception and the source of light to which Plato responded with the doctrine of the Ideas. Here, there is no such continuity and the direction has been reversed. It is no longer a matter of forming any continuity between perception and the ideational, since there is no relation between the two; neither is it a question of light raised to the level of the idea, nor of the idea descending to a level of a common perception, or *doxa*.[5] Consequently, there is not a difference in degree between the two lights, nor even an opposition, but rather, 'a whole new regime of light.'

As Deleuze recounts, the second figure (or diagram) that was created to explore the interiors of the baroque construction is the *chambre obscure*, which functions like the small chamber in the apparatus of a camera, and is linked in the process of photography to the dark-room where an image is developed.[6] At first, the dark-room has only a small, high opening through which light enters, passing

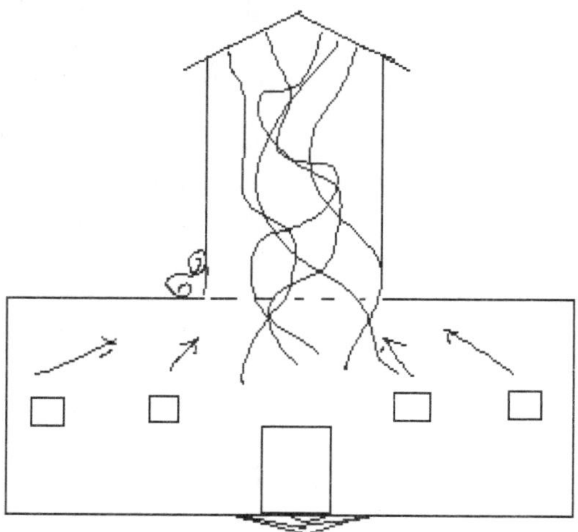

Figure 2 'The baroque house' (an allegory)

through two mirrors, the second of which is tilted to follow the page upon which light will project the unseen objects which are to be drawn. And yet, as Deleuze argues, this schema will not prove adequate for an explication of the baroque line, which, first of all, necessitates the separation of the line of light from an optical diagram. Leibniz, according to Deleuze, is the first to liberate the fold as a pure formal element: 'a fold that unfolds all the way to infinity' (Pli 5). Perception is grasped from a point where it is no longer dependent upon the metaphor of light, which effaces the importance of contour. The point of light will no longer be situated as the cause of perception, and the monad is not to be confused with a surface onto which an object projects its shadow, nor somewhere beneath this first surface, with the shadow of an internal space for mental representation. Concerning these shadows, Michel Serres writes:

> My knowledge is limited to these two shadows; it is only a shadow of knowledge. But there is a third shadow of which the two others only provide an image, or a projection, and which is the secret buried deep within the volume. Now it is probable that true knowledge of the things of this world lies in the solid's essential shadow, in its opaque and black density, locked behind the multiple doors of its edges, besieged only by practice and theory. A wedge can sunder the stones, geometry can divide or duplicate cubes, and the story will, inevitably, begin again; the solid, whose surfaces cannot be exhausted by analysis, always conserves a kernel of shadow hidden in the shade of its edges.[7]

Contrary to this infinite analysis of shadow and the kernel of shadow, the superficial shadow (or edge) and the shadow of depth (interior of a solid), in the case of Leibniz the subtraction of the 'point of light' from the external world of objects corresponds to the new determination of the *realitus objectiva* (or *ob-jectum*, in the sense of what stands opposite, or over against, as pure possibility) that, for Leibniz, is merely passive. In *Theodicy*, Leibniz writes:

> It is true that Form or the Soul has this advantage over Matter, that it is *the source of action*, having within itself *the principle of motion or of change*, in a word, *ta autokinaton*, as Plato calls it; whereas matter is simply passive, and has need of being impelled to act, *agitur, ut agat*. But if the soul is active of itself (as indeed it is), for that very reason it is not itself absolutely indifferent to action, like matter, and must find in itself *a ground of determination*. According to the system of Pre-Established Harmony, the soul finds in itself, and in its ideal nature anterior to existence, the reason for its determinations, adjusted to all that shall surround it. That way it was determined from all eternity in its state of mere possibility to act freely, as it does, when it attains existence. (T §323)

What is important to note from the above passage is that Leibniz makes the distinction of possibility–actuality derivative of what he calls *vis activa* (power), which designates the pure capacity of the soul for some act, as well as its capacity to undergo becoming, or to allow something to be made out of itself. The *vis activa* thus corresponds to what Deleuze will later define as 'the virtuality of the idea' (inclination), that is, the power that belongs to the soul and is expressed by its tendency to action and by the act itself as the ultimate actualization of the action.[8]

As Leibniz writes, 'Aside from this interior principle of change within the monad, there must also be a particular trait of what is changing, which produces, so to speak, the specification and variety of monads ... and within each monad, a plurality of affections and relations, [even] though it has no parts' (M §11–13). Leibniz's statement that monads are simple, 'meaning, they have no parts,' implies that the relation part–whole cannot be predicated to them since predication entails the possession of an attribute. Yet, because monads possess no parts, they cannot enter into aggregation or composites *as* parts, or be determined from the perspective of a whole as a portion that is interior to the whole. Hence, 'there is nothing that might be transposed, nor can there be any internal movement which could be excited, commanded, or diminished between monads' (M §7). But how, then, do monads communicate with one another? This immediately poses the critical problem of the communication between monads in terms of the movement between apartments, or the passage between the compossible and incompossible worlds that each monad includes at its base. According to Deleuze, the passage between monads can only be deciphered by the operations of allegory and by the forms of secrecy that are particular to the baroque artifice.

Both the allegory and the secret are founded upon the condition *that no direct communication is possible.* It is precisely in response to this incommunicability (which Leibniz calls 'incompossibility') that allegory and secrecy attain communication by an indirect means. Allegory is constituted on the principle that there can be no direct presentation, or transposition, of the perceptual; therefore, perception itself must become a sign, and the sign must become a text that must be read, deciphered. The secret is constituted on the condition that no direct discourse is possible, and so communication must take place in relation to a certain 'absence of a Third,' which (as linguist Emile Benveniste reminds us) founds the distinction between language and code that determines the particularity of human language as 'free indirect discourse.'[9]

But something quite striking occurs in this composite of the allegory and the secret, which corresponds to the formation of the crypt in architecture and the cipher in language, that is, the composite of *écrire–dessiner* (writing–designing) in the baroque artifice. In the absence of light, perception takes place in the design, and must be constructed, piece by piece, apartment by apartment. This allegory of perception corresponds to the function of the crypt as topological region in the monad and is defined by the activity of reading. The monad is a book or a reading-room. But the visible and the legible, the exterior and the interior, the façade and the room are not two different worlds, because

> the visible has its own way of being read (like the newspaper for Mallarmé), and the legible has its own kind of theater (its theater of reading). Thus, the combinations of the visible and the legible constitute the emblems or the allegories that were dear to the Baroque . . . and we are always being led back to a new correspondence or mutual expression, 'inter-expression,' 'fold following fold.' (Pli 44)

If we have found that the secret indicates the situation of light as a 'problem' within the monadological construction, it is precisely the sense of a crypt placed in perception and of a type of incorporation (or inclusion) which is not as much an enclosure of the thing, but rather a process which turns perception itself into an allegory.[10]

There is a danger here of perceiving both too little and too much from this state of affairs. For instance, there is a danger of reducing allegory to the composites made up of the emblems and small interior decorations that are fabricated to replace an external view. This is the case of the newspaper, in which the interval between perception and memory is founded on the analogy with perception in only one of its aspects: brevity. On the contrary, in its very act of encryption, the secret indicates a point of perception that is not continuous with its 'figure,' and a limit that cannot be resolved by perception (or the understanding associated with it), but rather by a formal power to extend itself infinitely. It is for this reason that perception is not capable of deciphering (unfolding) a secret, and it is a pure prejudice that the understanding takes the secret to be a content corresponding to its own formal limitation. In turn, this immediately leads us to a second danger, referred to above under the function of a *doxa* (the origin of common sense and opinion) that makes the secret an expression of ideology (an allegory of power). However, this conception of power would violate the sanctity of the crypt, which cannot be thought of on the basis of the inclusion of a foreign idea or perception, since the monad contains the whole world immanently, and since Leibniz outlawed that anything could pass between monads in the form of influence (*Einflüss*). This is explicitly stated in the following proposition:

> It is impossible also to explain how a monad can be altered, that is, internally changed, by any other creature. For there is nothing in it which might be transposed, nor can there be conceived in it any internal movement which could be excited, directed, or diminished. In composites this is possible, since the parts can interchange place, but monads have no windows through which anything could come in or go out ... In consequence of what has been said, the natural changes of the monads must result from an internal principle, since no external cause could influence their interior. (M §7 and §11)

Here, the notion of the crypt evoked above cannot be reduced to an already constituted notion of the Unconscious: as a closed and sealed-off room, or a variable key invented by an alien occupant. In place of this, Leibniz constructs a topography where room and occupant, world and monad, would be entirely inside, and the door would be on the outside, and would shut only from the outside. In other words, the Leibnizian crypt is utterly, one might even say infinitely, *open*. Thus, it follows that there is no need of doors that lock or invite, of windows that shut out or illuminate.

But how can we account for this apparently bizarre and ludicrous description, this topography for lunatics – all background, as if forming a *there* without a corresponding *here*, a front without a back? Nevertheless, this would be necessary deduction of the statement, 'no doors or windows.' In effect, this would entail a conception of the monad as cryptic enclosure, the crypt being both the supreme 'contradiction' and the founding principle of the *Monadology* because it produces the very form of the scission referred to above. Consequently, it is not a matter of a representation, because the monad can never come to its own limit, but falls from level to level, by occupying a present that consists of a contracted point and an infinitely dilated bottom section, or a basement 'hollowed by other basements' (Pli 6). What is missing is precisely the foreground, the object of consciousness. The monad never becomes an object *to itself*, and does not represent itself objectively, but rather becomes an *objectile*, the material support or canvas. In this way, the body serves as the base for drawing up the shadows that emerge with greater intensity from an even-more obscure background, since whatever light there is plunges ceaselessly into shadow.

Returning to Deleuze's diagram of the monad (or 'baroque house'), the lower levels are 'pierced with windows' or small openings, while the upper level is 'sealed and sightless.' At the same time, the upper room is described as being 'resonant,' a sounding box that will 'render audible the visible movements coming from below' (Pli 7). The attribute of the crypt belongs only to the upper level 'sealed in whiteness,' while the lower level remains infinitely open, both divided and infinitely divisible. The monad is that infinitely contracted point which is differentiated from an infinitely divided space. Hence, the concept of closure must be revised. We cannot say, for example, that the upper level is closed off from the other, since the attributes of closure ('doors and windows') are said to be completely lacking within the monad. Thus, Leibniz's concept of an interior can neither find analogy with a content of perception (or a psychological datum), nor be based upon the composition of geometrical solids in which content is also what lies behind the representation of three facing sides, as the fourth side which can be extrapolated only as an geometrical solution of the first three. Therefore, what I referred to above as 'shadow' is composed neither of light nor of darkness, but rather by the movements of the visible that oscillate or vibrate from the matter below; it is by a process of resonance in the monad that the visible movements in matter become audible. This is why there is no analogy of perception between the soul and matter, since there are two very different kinds of receptivity involved: the receptivity of matter to the visible movements created by the light streaming in from small openings, producing movements that spiral upwards, becoming audible, resonating within a new series that has its own material consistency. What is perceptible on one level becomes legible on another through a melange of different material, and only by an essential 'graphism,' or a diagram of light that is made completely from movement, can there be anything like communication between the two levels.

The crypt functions as the echo chamber by which the visible movements in matter are converted into an audible series without any notion of projection or any continuity established between the two levels. Any communication between interior and exterior must pass through the crypt which *resonates* with the visible movements which take place below in matter. The crypt remains a breach, or scission, nonetheless, and there can be no isomorphism established between what is visible in matter and what is readable in the soul. It is important to see the combination of two different aspects in the process of perception illustrated in Figure 3: at one end, that of blurred vision caused by movement, sometimes

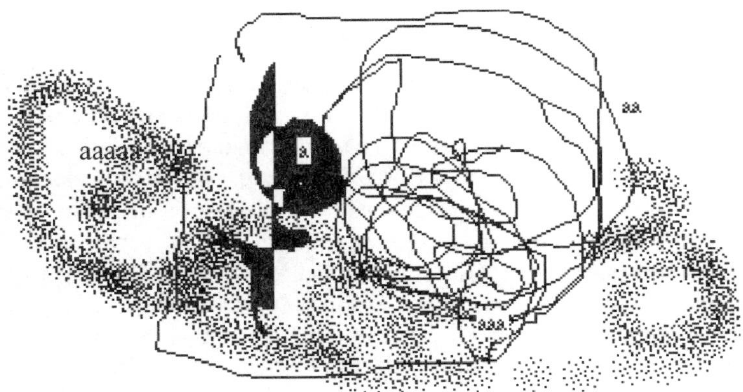

Figure 3 Resonance in the monad

creating a series of images, like the movement of an athlete in slow motion; at the other end, the point where a clear sound trails off and is obscured by dissonance, or emerges from a background of noise. Light is not a cause of perception because perception is essentially constituted by the fuzzy, the opaque, the indeterminate or the blurred motion occurring in matter. Neither is it the question of a clear and distinct note in the soul that would produce an echo, because the monad can already be described as a chamber full of echoes and it is from this cacophony of echoes that the possibility of a single note first arises. (This is simply because a single note never occurs without the series that conditions it.) Both aspects, lacking in the distinct clarities of the visual field and the audible field, seem to blend and indicate how there is communication between the two levels of the monadological construction through a process of reverberation.

We already commented above on the construction of perception in the Baroque as profoundly allegorical. Suffice it to say that the figure of the crypt that Deleuze detects in the *Monadology* allows him to enlist the Leibnizian philosophy within a certain logic of sense inspired entirely from the domain of empiricism, 'which knows how to transcend the experiential dimensions of the visible without resorting to ideas' (LS 32). Consequently, Deleuze sees in Leibniz's philosophy the onto-genesis of ideas by means of the function of allegory, ideas being only the macro-hallucinations that are produced and animated by the micro-movements that occur below in matter. This does not mean that the visible movements in matter are the cause, since reverberation describes more the proclivity of the interior to resonate with itself, that is, its capacity (*potentia activa*) to fold, re-fold, mani-fold. Therefore, ideas can only be shaped from the resonance of a thousand tiny perceptions, and it is because of this that their contours appear fuzzy or vague, or can be described as without contour since they are entirely without an object, but instead are only composed of smaller folds 'right down to the minuscule folds of the atom.'

6

THE RIDDLE OF THE FLESH AND THE '*FUSCUM SUBNIGRUM*'

In the *Monadology* the problems as well as the possibilities for the construction of the monad, or 'the baroque house,' are derived from a melange of two distinct materials: the number or algebraic function inscribed on papyrus, and the heavy blocks of marble and stone borrowed from the geological strata (representing the resistance of materials in an architectural construction). Matter resists infinity according to its own material 'consistency,' which in turn, produces the characteristics that are particular to it (M §7). In order to solve 'the riddle of the flesh' (or animal body), Leibniz chose to combine the heaviness and density of a geological stratum with the fragile exoticism of papyri, which even after the writing has been rubbed away still bears an impression. He did this, according to Deleuze, in order to avoid the Oriental line that constructs an infinite and empty space from a simple paper fold – a fold that could be seen to influence the Occident via the Platonic doctrine of Ideas, or Cartesian Geometry. The baroque Leibniz, however, did not believe in emptiness, and according to Deleuze, 'it is profoundly characteristic of the Baroque to set itself in confrontation with the Orient' (Pli 51). Consequently, the singularity of the monad, its tensions, as well as its politics, is inseparable from the object-matter (*ob-jectile*), and the way in which this matter undergoes folds that constitute its textures, and give rise to the resistances that are peculiar to the living body. It is owing to this principle that in Leibniz's writings, particularly the *Theodicy*, the most unassailable structures appear to tremble, or seem to be on the verge of toppling, either as expressing a central 'imbalance' that could be considered the result of a flaw or error in the design, or as expressing their perfection, even their 'glory,' depending upon one's perspective. This is particularly true within the domain of baroque sculpture, which offers Leibniz the greatest quantity of examples, apart from architecture, where apparently intractable figures always seem to be falling or getting up, or otherwise appear to be suffering from spells of dizziness and vertigo (*l'étourdissement*). According to Deleuze, this 'trembling' (either out of intense joy or extreme suffering) expresses the state of 'crisis' that marks the baroque period in particular. Deleuze writes: 'The baroque itself already marks a crisis in theological reasoning – a final attempt to reconstruct a world that's falling apart' (N 161).

The book of the idea forms the common walls of the monad, or baroque house, and the façades themselves are unearthed from their strata through a process of leafing. The monad is both book and reading-room, paper and stone, as well as the rumour of *a life* that takes place between the two, in the fold between the two other folds. What constitutes the specificity of this fold can be enumerated under the problem of the flesh, which is why light is not adequate to the 'luminosity' of an interior that it cannot reach to unfold. In other words, the flesh is presented as a 'problem' that cannot be explicated by too simple a notion of light, or by mathematical extension, since it encompasses the meaning both of a crypt, the architectural motif, and of a cipher, which is difficult to discern without knowing the 'key.' The 'act of reading,' introduced above, corresponds to what life ciphers in the body, to the riddle of life itself, which can only be deciphered in each individual by following all the predicates (perceptions) that belong to it, and each monad can possess these predicate-perceptions only to the degree that it can express them clearly.

To illustrate this, let us take as an example the problem of 'having a body,' which Deleuze treats in Part Three of *The Fold*. It is normal to express one's relation to one's own body as a form of 'possession' and, therefore, to define the body as a form of 'property.' However, as Deleuze argues, the 'right to possess my own body' is an order that is in no way 'natural,' but is rather a 'moral requirement' (Pli 113). On one level, it is an order articulated by a social typology of statements which condition the form this right will take as well as the constraints and limitations that qualify this right due to the demands of social and cultural institutions (e.g. childhood, gender, ethnicity, class and economy). Second, this right 'to possess' is an order that results from a command that in no way can begin with the individual. What is only apparently the most intimate and 'natural' of liaisons is itself the issue (*pragma*) of a command: 'I must have a body, it's a moral necessity, a "requirement"' (Pli 113). In the form of 'having,' of possessing, which radiates into all the sensible predicates that I can associate with my body (its shape and feeling, its movement, its sensorial perceptions, its age and sex), are all the secondary predicates of a primary order that has been folded upon me and that allows me to possess them as *mine* – that is, to possess them, but also to express and articulate them in a series of perceptions that trail in and out of consciousness. It is only because of this primary order that I am capable of having a body.

And yet, precisely because the condition of my 'having a body' first arrives to me in the form of a command, it somehow also distinguishes me from my body – which is both 'mine' and 'not mine' – and thus makes 'me' responsible for 'it.' Consequently, because my relation to my body is given in the form of a command, I can possess my body only in as much as I obey this command, and so long as I follow this order which, in turn, is linked to the forms of law and social institutions that articulate it historically (definitions of property, legal and illegal appropriations, the forms of domination, usury and theft). Without this distinction, there could be a confusion of the two determinations of 'property' and this would lead to the most dreadful consequences: cannibalism, necrophilia, slavery, molestation, rape, self-immolation. Therefore, it is not merely by accident that the two fundamental prohibitions that Freud found at the base of civilization (incest and cannibalism) are both determined by this fundamental distinction, which is why he saw those neuroses that exhibit a 'primary narcissism' as a collapse of this distinction. Eating one's own faeces is cannibalism or the eating of a corpse; masturbation is symbolically a form of incest with oneself, or a member of one's own family.

Does this mean that I possess my body, so to speak, passively? Am I possessed by it in possessing its attributes (such as my hair, the color of my skin, my sex)? Yet, 'I must have a body.' Why? This could be phrased as a tautological command that lies at the origin of the notion of property and, in a fundamental way, echoes the tautology of instinct. I must possess my own body because I (as a subject) must be able to *possess,* pure and simple, that is, to possess something rather than nothing.[1] Deleuze describes this tautology by the degree of 'obscurity' that it presents to our consciousness and he portrays the fundamental gravity and density of our feelings of anxiety concerning the possession of our own bodies. According to Deleuze's formula of this anxiety, 'I must have a body because there is an obscure object in me' and not the other way around: that because the body is obscure, I must possess a more clear and distinct perception of myself as a subject.

What is the source of this obscurity? Earlier we discovered that the notion of the crypt designates a region of the monad and 'cryptography' describes the activity of reading that takes place there, as the manner by which the monad takes possession of the predicates, or events, belonging to its substance. At this point we discover that there are secrets only to the degree that every monad must possess a body, and that predicates circle around the attributes of possession in the sense that they pose a problem of *having* rather than *being*. The monad does not *have* an outside as predicate, in the sense that 'every perception must have a relation to the body,' and what is 'outside' expresses no such relation of necessity to the interior of the monad. The façade, even pushed up against the monad, does not express a relation or have the same formal properties that belong to that entity which is in every case mine. It is in this sense that the body becomes the cipher by which the monad reads the world it includes. It turns the statement around and expresses a positive condition of possession, of 'having a body,' which it possesses to the degree that there is 'an inside' that remains obscure. The image of the body as a kind of container is here replaced by an obscure background, *fuscum subnigrum,* where the events form a series from a present whose line goes in both directions, both toward the future and toward the past. Consequently, the body corresponds to this moral exigency, this task, for each monad to develop all its perceptions. Deleuze writes:

> In a certain sense, one that is more restrained, more intrinsic, one can say that a monad, when it is called upon to 'live,' or even more when it is called reason, unfolds within itself this region of the world that corresponds to its

> own interior zone of clarity: it is called to develop all its perceptions, that is its task. (Pli 101)

Or, as Leibniz writes:

> It is necessary that entelechies (monads) differ from one another or not be completely similar to each other; in fact, they are the principles of diversity, for each differently expresses the universe from its own way of seeing. And precisely this is their peculiar task, that they should be so many living mirrors and so many concentrated worlds.[2]

For Leibniz, therefore, the body is more than a simple crease in the skin, a hem-line, sutured with organs, and perhaps the entire *Monadology* is constructed to account for it. If we have posited a relation to the body as exemplary, perhaps it is because that it is folded by another distinction that cannot be exposed by light without destroying its true nature. The very notion of a 'content' implies a space that is coextensive, even though it remains hidden, or unexposed. Yet, what we have discovered is a measure no longer continuous with perception, or with the profile of an object (the destruction of all contour, the subtraction of the point of light). The body does not correspond to its objective or physical representation, but rather to 'a pure feeling': it is the form under which the datum is folded in a subject. For this reason, it may even be misleading to refer to this 'image-matter' as body, since this would be a body without façade; that is, without *ob-jectum*, which bears no relation to the body that can become object (the other's body, or the body as object of knowledge, or the body as component of the mass in politics). In this sense there is an extreme disassociation of the body from the space it occupies, which in turn can be represented and coordinated with other spaces by becoming a location, a point, a numerical sign which can be easily tabulated and manipulated by representational systems. Hence, the concept of the crypt represents the very solution to the problem of freedom in the *Monadology*, a solution that even approaches the meaning of 'liberation.' It refers to the formal power, or tendency, by which each monad steals away by means of the crypt that it includes, foiling every attempt to grasp 'its own relation,' and only to the degree that the monad is able to maintain possession of its own body. And yet, the body is not the monad either; rather, it is a riddle (or cipher) extracted from a background that lies somewhere at the interior of the monad in which there remains something obscure.

If to live is to fold, to decipher the imperative to unfold all of one's perceptions, and if the secret is defined by the pure affirmation of 'having a body,' then how can we account for its negative representation, as the anxiety surrounding its loss, as the shadow of 'what one does not possess,' but is possessed by others? According to Deleuze, this corresponds to the image of container, which we have interpreted simply as a type of fold that remains imprisoned in a rigid materiality, unable to grasp its own formal element. Although the *realitus objectiva*, as defined above, corresponds to pure possibility, it would be a contradiction to the first principle of the *Monadology* to bestow upon it the power to 'enfold itself,' or to encrypt itself in the interior of the monad, since it does not have this formal attribute of power (*vis activa*) which belongs only to the soul. Thus, we might account for the negative representations as the various phantasms that assign an 'un-real' attribute of power to an external agency, even a non-existent one, and this will be the entrance of evil into Leibniz's system. Here is Leibniz's puzzling axiom: the monad contains the entire world within it, and there can be no exercise of influence, power or 'possession' between monads; yet, even so, between monads there is only a relation of exclusion, or resistance, as if each monad is haunted by the secret of all the others that it carries somewhere within itself. These 'others' can be expressed in several ways. They might appear as expressions of bifurcation and divergence ('I have multiple pasts'), as the plenitude of possibilities that the monad must choose from at each moment ('I am pregnant with future selves'), or as the self that it includes but leaves 'unrealized' ('I am another'). In a sense, in each moment all others appear as variations of a past or a future that the monad cannot unfold. Here, in this sense of temporal divergence or the multiplicity of selves (which appear as others), we are perhaps approaching the purest source for the conception of 'the unconscious,' one even envisioned by Freud as Deleuze himself remarks, prior to allowing this concept to be occulted by 'familial' personalities and by infantile politics.[3]

If I have referred to the 'shadows' traced in the monad by all the others that make up its open base, it was only in order to extend the vertigo (*l'étourdissement*) of inclusions that make it difficult for the monad to unfold the predicates that belong to its own special region and bring them to expression. We might also extend the definition of these shadows in order to account for chaos-cacophony of voices, stray thoughts and the interior poly-logue that always bubbles up from its obscure base and seems to threaten consciousness from an indeterminate point that is felt to be somewhere on the inside. As an aside, we might identify this interior cacophony as the absolute condition of speech, and it is important to note that there is neither *a* voice belonging to the monad, nor anything like *silence* in the interior. The monad is already a chamber of whispers, and expression occurs then only as the synthesis of these whispers into a chorus in which the monad itself might appear like a conductor. What this dissonance represents is nothing less than the ceaseless activity of expression by all the other monads, that is, the joy of possessing their own attributes and developing their own perceptions which constitute the various movements and vibrations that form the somber background of the monad itself. At the same time, it is also from this background that it draws its own hints and clues to deciphering all the signs that swirl up from its obscure base.

The monad *perceives* with and by means of the act of folding, by drawing perception out of its obscure background, a process closely approximating hallucination. Again, this does not imply that it perceives by means of projection, since the monad itself is entirely without surface, while perception, almost hallucination, remains without an object.[4] Thus, according to Deleuze, the Baroque replaced the operating distinction, form–content, with that of form–material (form being understood here as the infinite potential which the very concept of the fold implies). Here, Deleuze is very close to Heidegger's reading of monad as drive (*Drang*), which also bears a relation to 'trigger,' or the 'bent bow.'[5] The fold refers to primary form in the soul, to the *vis activa*, and the form being the actuality, which is the 'material expression' shaped by the singular characteristics that the fold takes up. The fold describes the power to maintain the fold while folding, and at the same time taking up new materials that will form the characteristics and textures specific to the variety within each fold.

On the other hand, the fold then must also be understood from its passive, or material, aspect, and not simply relegated to the status of a verb (that is, to refer its figure to language alone).[6] Texture is also active, but in a sense its 'act' is also a passion (a *potentia passiva*), since the act of folding is conditioned just as much by the material that submits to this operation and, at the same time, gives to the fold its own characteristics, its singular tensions and vibrations that create the texture of the living body. In this context, we might recall that the specific matter that composes the body determines its capacity to be folded by language or permeated by light. This would also apply to the matter of the secret as well, whose different figures could be understood as being caused by the matter of expression, since there is no secret in general; each and every secret is both formed and limited by the material in which it is embedded ('Origami, 'Embryology,' 'Geology' = paper, flesh or tissue, stone or strata), since each will be constituted by the folds proper to it. Resemblance does not result from the same fold that runs through each unfolding them as the contingent predicates of one infinite fold; rather, it is the divergence, the material difference, that will allow one fold to be captured within another, creating a resonance that is the condition of harmony.

Finally, *resonance* (or what Leibniz calls Harmony) returns us once more to the 'communication' between orders or levels, that is, between two different types of folds: between the coils of matter, which correspond to a multiplicity of materials (as many as there are folds), and the folds themselves, which correspond to the variable of powers in the soul. Resonance is already a rhythmic shadow produced in matter and corresponds to the very problem of expression by liberating expression to another plane. This is the distinction that Deleuze refers to with the two phrases that are repeated throughout his study: fold following fold, and a fold between the two folds, '*entre les replis et les plis.*' The case of resonance here is thus between two systems – between paper and flesh, between the flowing mane of a horse and the crest of a tree-line seen from the distance of a observer – in which a variation in one system finds itself becoming a variable of another. However, the relation is still not one of identity, since paper will not bleed when it is cut and the mountain will not shake blocks of ice from its mane. Rather, there is simply a resonance (or harmony) between the two systems, or series. In order to illustrate this, let us return once more to the diagram of the 'baroque house' with its upper and lower levels. The upper level sealed in whiteness, which could be expressed as simply an absence of color (since the folds in the soul are immaterial folds composed of power); while below light spreads out, becoming dimmer, invaginated by shadow (*fuscum subnigrum*). It is not a matter of the absence of light, but rather an excess of color, movement and depth. It is for this reason that Deleuze identifies Klee, Fautrier, Dubuffet and Bettencourt as baroque painters, since they follow the same fold, or method, of beginning with a dark canvas and adding texture, density, adding color as if through mixed media (cloth, metal, wood, hair, teeth, shit = pale mauve, rust, blond, hazel, green, brown). If white is seldom used, it is because it is the most difficult color to reach, since one would have to pass through all the materials to liberate the immaterial fold. White, therefore, does not express the absence of color, since nature abhors a vacuum, but expresses the immaterial vibrations of all the folds, or what Paul Klee has referred to as a 'gray point.'

As Klee defines it, the 'gray point' is the 'conception non-conceptual of the non-contradiction' between that which becomes and that which dies; 'gray because it is a non-dimensional point, a point between the dimensions and at their intersection, at the crossroads.'[7] Contrary to philosophy up to Hegel, which motivates the dimensions by the relations between point, line and plane, Klee sees them motivated by three series of polarities: a temporal dimension expressed between white and black, a tonal dimension expressed between height and base, and a caloric dimension expressing all the degrees between hot and cold. Thus, temperature and degree of imbalance caused by the center of gravity upon an affective body must be taken into account within any abstraction of perceptual space-time.

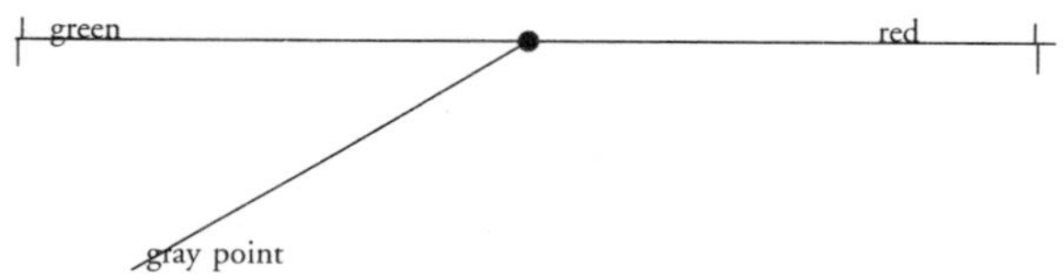

Figure 4 Illustration of the 'gray point' (PS 61)

In the above diagram, the gray point corresponds to a mobile equilibrium, a center of balance, suspended over a veritable chaos of sensations. For Klee, this balance or pendulum is nothing less than the symbol for the unity of time.

In constructing the concept of the 'gray point,' Klee first abandoned any linear conception of color (represented by the natural phenomenon of a rainbow) and with it any pathetic conception derived from the domain of the human, the higher animal, with its tragic struggles between the body and the soul. In place of this, Klee constructed a series of six colors, grouping them in three couples, or opposing diameters, running back and forth from red to green, from blue to orange, and from yellow to purple, all three diameters fixed at a point (the center of the chromatic circle) which expresses the gray point. Klee proved his theory of color by conducting two experiments, as described below.

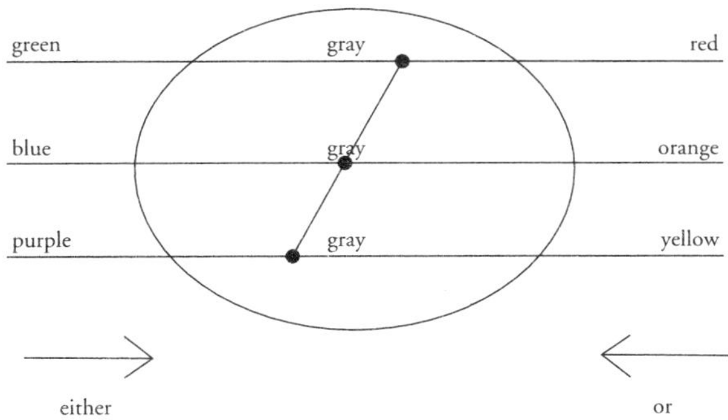

Figure 5 The 'gray point' and a series of colors (PS 61)

The first experiment observed that the effect left upon the retina by the sudden withdrawal of red after a long exposure was not red, but green (hence the couple red–green will constitute one of the three diameters), thus proving that there are two complementary colors alternatively engendered in the eye, and between them, the point gray where they are equally mixed. Gray is not a color, then, but the expression of the principle of homeostasis and represents the balance movement and counter-movement along each diameter.

The second experiment is where we find the monadological construction of color. It consists of a piece of paper folded into seven compartments with gradations from pure red to pure green, in 'movements and counter-movements.' This causes a center to appear: the central gray, compartment four. Klee writes:

> The reciprocity or alternation of the scale red–green returns us to the pendulum between movement and counter-movement. It also recalls the mobile balance which will finally immobilize itself at the intersection of the gray. This in no way signifies that red and green are captured in a static representation, with all the red on one side and all the green on the other. Such a representation would not suggest the simultaneous alternation, since it would be necessary to pass by leaping from one term to the other (construction).[8]

Here again, we must hold onto the diagram at the point of its extreme contradiction where the body can be described as a shadow, or point of adumbration, even though the conditions that normally determine the possibility of shadow are lacking. It is neither a shadow of an object (the interior not perceived by the senses), nor projected by a point of light. Hence, the quality of shadow does not refer to light but to color – as gray as granite, an uncarved block of marble, or the flesh. It is from this point that Klee motivates the entire spectrum of color and his construction of the gray point resembles the process of perception within the monad and must, as Leibniz says, be differentiated from apperception and consciousness. 'The passing state which comprehends and represents multiplicity in the unity or simple substance is nothing but what is called *perception* ...' On this point the Cartesian doctrine has been defective (M §14).

If we discovered a determination of the object above as *objectile*, or the 'material support' (*fuscum subnigrum*), perhaps here we discover a new determination of the subject as the mobile unity of a passing state, as a point of equilibrium between movement and counter-movement. As in Klee's diagram above, the gray point is a 'mobile balance' between two terms that must be *constructed* by a process of leaping from one term to the other. The subject now designates the temporal unity of a 'point-of-view,' but only on the condition that every point-of-view is centered on variation, as in the examples offered by Klee. As Deleuze writes:

> The status of the object has profoundly changed, so also is that of the subject ... Such is the basis of perspectivism, which does not mean dependence in respect to a pre-given or defined subject; to the contrary, a subject will be what comes into view, or what remains in point-of-view. That is why the transformation of the object refers to a correlative transformation of the subject: the subject is not a sub-ject, but as Whitehead says, a 'superject.' Just as the object becomes objectile, the subject becomes superject. A needed relation exists between variation and point-of-view; not simply because of the variety of points of view ... but because every point-of-view is a point-of-view on variation. (Fold 20)

In Leibniz's system, therefore, the point-of-view can no longer be conceived as a static center in a configuration of perspectives, but rather is described as a problem of expression: the need to find the best point-of-view 'without which chaos would reign' (Fold 22). Consequently, if the world can be described as an infinite number of perspectives in variation, approaching chaos, then point-of-view would correspond to the secret order of these perspectives that, according to Leibniz, each monad includes. Ultimately, this is why Deleuze refers to perception in the monad by the art of cryptography, since each monad includes a unique variable (a key, or cipher) whereby the labyrinth can be ordered from a single point-of-view, and this point-of-view will have important consequences, finally, for the role played by God in Leibniz's system.

7

ON GOD, OR THE '*PLACE VIDE*'

One final problem concerns the role assigned to the concept of God, or 'the central monad,' in Leibniz's philosophy. This is important for our overall argument, since Leibniz's concept will prepare the way for Deleuze's later treatment of the problem of transcendence, which I outlined earlier, and even provide him with the principle for solving this problem, and precisely by means of the concept of 'the fold.' Despite the supposed importance that God plays in Leibniz's system, it may well be that what distinguishes Leibniz's philosophy from everything that has preceded it is that the concept of God is relegated to a pure function. This is a particularly modern characteristic and prepares the way for a notion of structure, although here we are speaking of an infinite structure of inclusion (or compossibility), rather than a certain image of structure that derived from a linguistic model. Here, the notion of a 'function' essentially follows Frege's argument on the cipher which can be formulated by the following proposition: there is something of the order of the function only where there is not, or not yet, something of the order of an object, since the expression of the object bears no relation to a *place vide.* The function, then, is the purest expression of a *place vide*, and here, as Frege remarks, 'we touch on something so simple that it permits no logical analysis.'[1] God can therefore be defined as the most indeterminate element that belongs to all possible worlds, as the most dilated and de-contracted state of the monad; he can also be likened to a continuous note of an organ with a punctured valve (also called a cipher), which becomes the key by which all the monads harmonize. Concerning this condition of harmony, Deleuze writes, 'At its limit the material universe accedes to a unity in horizontal and collective extension, where melodies of development themselves enter into relations of counterpoint, each spilling over its frame and becoming the motif of another such that all of Nature becomes an immense melody and flow of bodies' (Fold 135). Some might immediately object that this would reduce God again to pure spirit; on the contrary, Leibniz reduces the concept of God to pure possibility.

The *place vide* can in no way be defined as empty, a null set, or even 'the set of sets'; rather it designates an 'undefined or indefinite space,' not because it is empty, but because it is full of all possible determinations. As Deleuze notes, it is a space replete with multiple definitions and types of multivarious folds.[2] This essentially concerns Leibniz's argument with Descartes who defined all space negatively as the projection, the outline, of the most indefinite object equal to consciousness. In this sense, all space is literally cut from the same mold, made-to-order, or as Heidegger posited, 'ready-to-hand' (*Zuhandeldt*). Yet, for Leibniz, space cannot be determined from its limit (*extensio*), but only by its tendency to remain indeterminate and infinite, always productive of more and more, always in surplus of its most minimal determination. Thus, the *place vide* is another name for the pure 'background' from which the monad will draw all its determinations in order to decipher its own obscure depth, or to distinguish itself from all the others that populate it. In other words, Leibniz designates space not by its form, but by its pure proclivity to fold, in-fold, un-fold, mani-fold (which, in turn, must be distinguished from the particular infinity that belongs to matter, which can be sub-divided, as Leibniz says, *partes extra partes*). And yet neither infinity succeeds in attaining the interior principle, the formal dimension of the fold that comprises the soul, which is 'unable to unfold all at once all its folds, for these go on to infinity' (M §61). Leibniz designates this interior principle by the function of the central monad, or God.

At this point, Leibniz's argument becomes rather difficult, even treacherous, since one could easily comprehend a space that is replete with all possible determinations by an image of 'latency,' in which every possible determination is 'already installed' and 'ready for use' (in the same manner that a mainframe is installed with certain programs that can be operated according to a given application or problem of calculation). This is an error that often happens when the function of the central monad, or the principle of God in the *Monadology*, is conceived on the basis of its resemblance to the Scholastic notion of the *Scienta Dei*, where God represents the highest of totalities and can synthesize every perspective in a static unity of the One. Thus, the Leibnizian God is often represented as the 'wealthiest' of all the monads, and every other monad can only possess its own perception as a representation of what, from time immemorial, will have already been preordained (and previewed) in the mind of God. It is in this way that Lyotard, for example, still understands Leibniz's conception of the central monad, according to a static synthesis of possible perspectives that founds every system of representation, which is why he so quickly dismisses the *Monadology*.[3]

Beginning with Leibniz, however, infinity no longer corresponds to eternity, but only to the indefinite, the variable. Therefore, according to Leibniz's description, it is important to see that the central monad is perhaps the most improper of all the monads: poorer than the poorest of the poor, but without an accompanying state of suffering derived from the loss of possessions; and wealthier than the wealthiest, but without ever having possessed anything of its own. This is due to the fact that 'God alone is entirely bodiless' (M §72). If we have already discovered that each monad is defined by a necessary relation to its own body, to its own perception (from which it receives the imperative to develop its perceptions following the world it includes and according to the cipher, something like a singular point-of-view that it extracts from its base), then God can have no such relation of necessity to *a body*. It is by the metaphor of 'nudity' that Leibniz described the poorest of the monads, and while God expresses the very possibility of 'nudity,' he cannot possess this nudity as his own; that is to say, he cannot realize it. *This is why he remains an expression of pure possibility within all possible worlds, a beautiful and alien thing.* However, it would also be a mistake to conclude from this that God is therefore without time (or duration), since this would simply confuse, as Leibniz often says, 'a long swoon with death.' God suffers the longest duration of time, brought about by vertigo and the fainting-spells he gets from spinning around in all directions and all perspectives of all the possible worlds and in all times. There is a certain diabolical humor in Leibniz's description of God, who appears in a state of constant intoxication, always suffering from a little too much of time in its pure state.

It is important to recall here that this resembles the anxiousness that afflicted the man-of-the-Baroque, and which accounted for his allegorical constructions. Here we might recall a similar expression of dizziness and vertigo (*l'étourdissement*) that is suffered by the individual monads. If we were to describe this state of dizziness, it might be perceived as faint 'Brownian motion,' a blur, or as Leibniz says, 'a squirming of fishes.' The monad already encounters this feeling of vertigo from an indeterminate point that is already located in its interior, even though this interior is also identified with the interiority of the world it includes. However, this feeling is what appears to threaten it with the loss and dispossession of all its perceptions, of its 'own relation' to this world; and in response, it must, if it is to live, develop all the infinitesimal perceptions into a perception that is ordered by what Deleuze calls a *crible* (a screen, or a filter), and what I have been calling a 'cipher.' If this dizziness is the effect of what was referred to above as the *place vide*, then this indicates that the point of 'indetermination' is where the monad and the world are related through the function of the central monad to an inside in general, to time in its longest duration. This duration (or 'Inside') would necessarily include the entire range of intervals or perceptions, from the smallest to the largest, which constitute infinity, or time in general. We can see here that the principle of inclusion follows precisely the proportion of the fold by which the furthest dimensions converge; where the molecule is equal in proportion to the whole of the universe, and a single moment is equal to the whole of time. In fact, Leibniz considers the moment itself as equal to time in its longest duration, as only the most contracted point, which is why, given enough time, the monad can unfold (that is, express) all its predicate-events to a degree of perfection: 'Consequently, every body experiences everything that goes on in the universe, so much so that he who sees everything might read in any body what is happening anywhere, and even what has happened or will happen. He would be able to observe in the moment what is remote in time and space, *sumpnoia panta*' (M §61).

Returning to the notion of 'cryptography' posited in the beginning of my exposition of *The Fold*, we can now see why the notion of the crypt represents this point of indetermination in Leibniz and the Baroque, as the expression of a moment stacked with other moments, piled up like shelves in a columbarium, or opening through a trap-door into a basement 'hollowed out by other basements.' It is only due to this structure of inclusions that it could be said to be virtually bottomless (*Abgrund*) – that is, constructed upon a principle that is without grounds, a fantastic premise, a fiction – so, for instance, it could be speculated that one could travel through the interior of the moment without ever attaining a surface, that is, the limit of a façade that would close it off. In so much as this is a fiction, however, it must be relegated to the order of fictions that Kant would call 'necessary'; if there is to be anything like time at all, then there must be such a moment. In fact, this moment is the pure function of time and I have already compared it with the valve of a cipher that is stuck in its open position, or the mouth-point of a bladder – blown out, so to speak – one that fills all the monads with a long and continuous note like the thread they all share, the base upon which they harmonize. Its function is to release the pressure of time within the monad; it is the means by which time becomes sensible and this pressure is the cause of the activities of folding (reading) and unfolding (perception).

What Deleuze calls Leibniz's 'liberation of the fold' is nothing less than the release of the pressure of time within the monad. Leibniz effected this liberation by a radical means, which again concerns the concept of God. He did it by the splitting apart of the two senses of cause that belong to the principle of God up to this point, but are particularly determined by Christian philosophy: God as 'efficient cause' (*causa efficiens*), and God as 'final cause' (*causa finalis*). Leibniz encrypts the efficient cause on the inside, as the interior principle of the crypt, and protects it from any undue influence by the final cause. Again, this transformation concerns what Deleuze calls the new usage that Leibniz accorded to the role of principles, and here corresponds to the splitting (*Spaltung*) of God into two distinct entities in the *Monadology* (and also later in the *Theodicy*): God as efficient cause (the principle of architecture), God as final cause (the principle of law). The latter represents the principle of clarity that is already built into the establishment of the sign, that is, an already established order of signification that would prohibit *a priori* an expression of indetermination by reducing it to a form of nonsense (which becomes the obscene, the derogatory and offensive within an existing order of significations). The danger that Leibniz perceived in a system that was ruled by an exclusive use of this principle was what he referred to as a 'system of extreme Vengeance'; such a system would conceive of any vagueness as the absence of meaning, as an offense that could be restored by a system of writing, that is, by a disciplinary order that incarnates these moments of 'nonsense' within determinate and identifiable subjects, which can then be persecuted or even annihilated.

Leibniz showed that the experience of what would provisionally have to be called 'nonsense' was, in fact, the expression of an *event* that could be reflected by these divergent principles, or two different expressions that bear on the same point of non-determination. Referring again to Frege's definition of the *place vide*, since all signs comport some definition and a definition associative of a meaning or denotation, where meaning and denotation are totally in default, 'then one can no longer properly speak of a sign or definition.'[4] This can be illustrated by using two mirrors, or a double-sided mirror interposed between words and things, since there are no things without perception, and perception is often likened to a mirrored thing. Each side reflects this space according to its own principle: one from the perspective of *causa finalis*, which finds a definitive object lacking and the destruction of the conditions of the sign; the other from the perspective of *causa efficiens*, which discovers in this non-determination a background 'that causes the entire world of series to communicate in a "*chaosmos*"' (Pli 111). Leibniz discovered in the direct confrontation of these two principles an expression of extreme antagonism and a tendency, expressed by opposition, to annihilate one another. This is the regime of 'representation' evoked earlier on, which can be characterized as the type of repetition in which two doubles enter into the destruction of each other by their very resemblance. Thus, representation is linked to the realization of a system that persecutes all nonsense as contradiction, and through opposition reduces all difference to identity, to the repetition of the same. This can be vividly illustrated by what happens when two mirrors face one another vertically: there is neither space nor time in either mirror, only the event of their vanishing – the point where both mirrors explode into pure nothingness or emptiness. What remains is only the point of their infinite absence, like an empty image of eternity (*nunc stans*), or of an indefinite set (perhaps even 'the set of all sets'), both of which have been introduced into the world by the logic of representation as purely 'negative states.'

Leibniz's solution, therefore, was the turning or tilting of each mirror horizontally to follow the principle of the fold, which sets the destructive violence of opposites apart into the division between the two levels (upper and lower, the soul and matter) as a way of balancing this scission through the creation of a mobile point of equilibrium, or what Klee called a 'point of non-symmetrical balance' (PS 44).

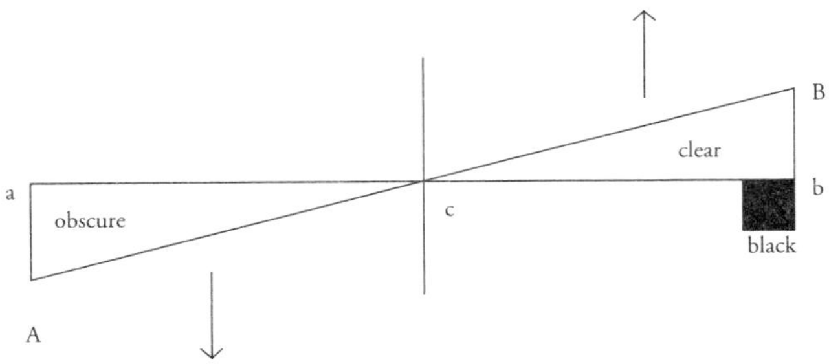

Figure 6 Illustration of 'non-symmetrical balance' (PS 44)

Of course, the precedent for this distinction is already found in *Genesis* 1:2, which describes creation of these two levels by God's face moving over the surface of the waters. He laid the mirror flat, like a tableau or a surface that reflects, above and below, like air and like water, two completely different folds. This very movement, or proto-movement, follows the curvature of the distinction between the two folds, between the act of reading and the receptivity of perception, since all perception must be developed, must be read, must be deciphered in relation to the individual concept. As Deleuze writes, 'The Divine Reader is a veritable passage of God into the monad (a little like what Whitehead described as a passage of Nature into the place).' Moreover, each monad is a passage of God: each monad has a point-of-view, but this view is the 'product' of God's reading or view-point, which passes through and coincides with that of the monad (Pli 99). In turn, the monad draws something like the shadow of God's passage from its obscure base in order to differentiate something from the nothingness that haunts it, the chaos that seems to press up from underneath. In much the same manner, God created the world by moving across the face of the waters, separating the upper and lower realms, which distinctly echo the two levels of the baroque house. In this way, Leibniz portrays the God of creation, the architect, in a schizophrenic accord with the God as legislator – and according to Leibniz, 'the former must "satisfy" in all respects the latter' (M §89). *This is the precise meaning of the function of Harmony in the Leibnizian system; the pair higher–lower resolves the tension introduced by the scission between inside and outside, since there is no longer a content of perception, but an image-matter, and no longer a form, but a formal power, an operatio, namely, a 'process.'* Moreover, it was by means of this creative process – of tilting transcendence (represented by a purely vertical line) in order to harmonize with immanence (represented by a purely horizontal line) – that Leibniz overcomes the crisis of theological reason, as Deleuze writes, 'giving way to human reason pure and simple' (N 161).

Concluding our commentary on *The Fold*, if we have discovered a strange and even bizarre logic that comprises the fold, or the baroque line, this is because what Leibniz calls the soul actually represents an infinite dilation of the fold, which has often been confused with the representation of a pure empty space, or the eternity of a *nunc stans* (hence, all the misconceptions of God as an entity who contains the totality of perspectives, such as in the School's conception of *Scientia Dei*). On the other hand, matter represents what is actually a pure façade, although because it is composed of infinite textures, it might offer the illusion of an infinite, dark cavernous depth (something that Deleuze sees in the block of marble with its flanges, its swirling crests, like the surface of a great ocean). There is a danger, however, of reading the soul, or time, as a pure vertical line, and the façade, or space, as a pure horizontal line. Rather, the vertical is precisely what is presented as time's greatest temptation – and perhaps here we might discern a few brush-strokes of Leibniz's Christ, afflicted by the intoxications of helium.

Phenomena, according to Leibniz, may be a pure façade, but a surface is already a torrent or swirling of points, even though it is without depth. And it is from this proposition that the entire ocean can be distilled from a single drop of water. One can trace the profound and 'diabolical' humor in Leibniz by noticing that the principal characteristic of the monad is an extreme vertigo, or dizziness, brought on by extreme heights even though it lives in a room located on the second floor, one without any windows. Perhaps the innate knowledge of its position makes the soul want to climb down from its podium, and this forms the attraction to all the obese bodies below which are coiled up and sleeping encompassed by thick blocks of matter. Deleuze constantly refers to this virtual state of suffering within the monad as a potential counter-point to the Heideggerian concept of *Geworfenheit* as well as the feeling of dread that accompanies it. By contrast, here the state of the soul's 'throwness' is nearly identical to the physical description of its beatitude, or state of blessedness as a feeling of vertigo like a physical phenomenon of weightlessness. This characterizes the baroque conception of 'Glory,' a term used by Germain Bazin to characterize the state of anxiety particular to baroque constructions and also the atmosphere from which Deleuze will draw the philosophy of Leibniz. Thus, it is not a division of the body and the soul that is the cause of suffering, but rather the expression of the soul's 'inclination' to fall upwards, to lose itself infinitely – *something that it must resist at all cost*! In response to this temptation, the soul would desire matter, color, movement, in order to escape from its own 'line of abolition,' which is represented by Leibniz as the Cartesian line of the Orient. It is for this reason that the soul could be said to lie on the floor of its small chamber, with its ear to the floor, listening hard, trying to decipher the stirrings that are going on below.

I will not digress further into the *Theodicy*, but will end by noting that there is something particularly modern in all these figures; it concerns an extreme resistance to verticality, a tendency one can also find in many commentaries concerning the influence of the Baroque on a modern sensibility.[5] As Deleuze writes concerning a formula that is drawn from Beckett: 'it's better to be sitting than standing, and better to be lying down than sitting. Modern ballet brings this out really well: sometimes the most dynamic movements take place on the ground, while upright the dancers stick to each other and give the impression they'd collapse if they moved apart' (N 53). Thus, verticality is presented as one of the most difficult problems for a modern sensibility to confront, something that can be confirmed by a major proposition by Paul Klee concerning the origin of human tragedy: 'It is this contrast between power and prostration that implies the duality of human existence ... TO STAND DESPITE ALL POSSIBILITIES TO FALL.'[6]

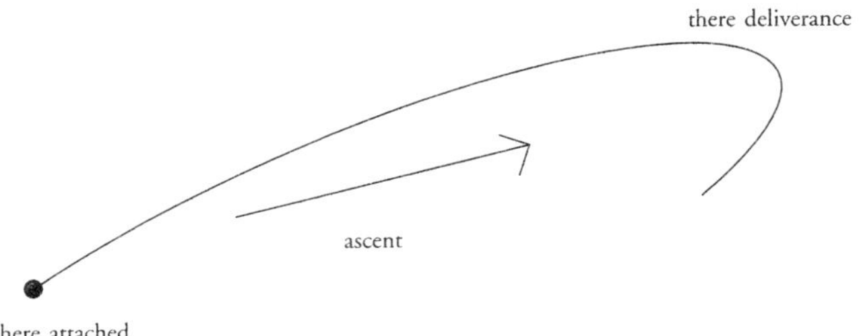

Figure 7 The soul's temptation (from Klee's diagram: PS 54)

Perhaps the origin of this problem can be found in the singular constructions of allegory, a problem whose solution the Baroque maintains as its own secret, since it is precisely in the invention of a secret as its highest problem that the Baroque can be said to have chosen 'something over nothing.' That is, hopelessly wrecked by identity, at the point of losing his very objectivity in a vague mist, the man-of-the-Baroque renounces his search for his essence; 'incapable even of seizing its existence, he seeks to apprehend the object, no longer by its resemblance, since he has ceased to believe in this possibility from the perspective of the real, but by its detour of the double, the analogy, the metaphor, processes proper to poetry, as well as rhetoric.'[7] This suggests that the Baroque refers no longer to the limited determination of a historical concept, but to a cryptic solution whose principle continues to distort the fields of perception-consciousness of the modern, which continues to be founded on the representation of the clear and the distinct.

It may sound somewhat 'fantastic,' even grandiose, to suggest that the secret of the fold is nothing more than a baroque cipher encrypted within the perceptual field of the modern; however, Deleuze himself suggests this as well when he says that the problem that often goes by the name of the Baroque is our situation too if we take account of the new way 'things are folded with matter' (N 157).[8] This makes the situation confronted by the 'man-of-the-Baroque' exemplary for our current situation today. It is as if by renouncing his own identity and the truth of the object, by the detour of allegory, the man-of-the-Baroque can make a little headway through the chaos that threatens him on all sides: from the deepest point of his own interiority to the most remote distances of the universe, from the world itself which is made up almost entirely by the noise from all the other worlds that are pressing up underneath it. He does this by means of a secret – a secret so perfect, so glorious, that he must even keep it from himself – if only so that he might be able to hang onto the world *as it is*. Of course, this does not concern all secrets, or the secret in general, which the Baroque itself destroys in favor of the minimal secrets of the fold.

Following Leibniz, we have been able to identify this secret as the multiple, the possibility of multiple worlds, each of which *must* have its own reason. Here, in the invocation of the Leibnizian cry '*Everything must have a reason!*', we might hear an echo of Deleuze's own cry, '*Everything must be multiple!*' However, it is not at all the case of each philosopher (or rather, both philosophies) 'saying the same thing,' since I have already shown that although Leibniz affirms the possibility of multiple worlds, of multiplicity *per se*, he still resorts, at least in principle (*en droit*), to justify a God who chooses one world over an infinite number of others, and who condemns difference to suffer under the requirements of representation (under the principle of incompossibility), even though this regime of judgement now allows for the existence of evil as well. Thus, even though both philosophies can never be heard in unison around this point, it is precisely here that we might discover the condition by which both philosophies can be said to harmonize, and I might even venture that it is through the repetition of Leibniz's philosophy that was effected by Deleuze in *The Fold*, that the Leibnizian system has, in a certain sense, been redeemed. Here is a case, as Deleuze described this method very early on, of 'the *pure* repetition of the former text and the present text *in one another*' (DR xxii), of the fold. It is by means of this repetition that Deleuze takes up and re-fashions Leibniz's 'basic concept of Harmony' as the supreme justification of the principles of difference and multiplicity which he has sought ever since first announcing this goal in the opening pages of *Difference and Repetition*. From this point onward (but then, which point?), the highest task of philosophy becomes 'the production of harmonies,' and what is the goal of the activity defined as the creation of concepts if not creating harmony, as it is also with music? 'Music – are philosophers friends of music too' (N 163)?

PART THREE

ON THE POWERS OF THE FALSE

8

THE BAROQUE DETECTIVE
BORGES AS PRECURSOR

In 1988, Deleuze published *Le Pli: Leibniz et le baroque* which I have argued signals a radical turning point; at least a 'solution' had been found concerning a problem that had preoccupied him for more than twenty years since the publication of *Différence et Répétition* in 1968. The problem can be posed in the following manner: How does one live in a world without principles, a world in which all principles have been shattered to bits? Another way of posing the same question, although more in the terms of classical or Platonic philosophy, is how does one live in a world amidst the ruins of 'the Good'?[1] In other words, the problem that preoccupied Deleuze during this period concerned nothing less than the default of 'the Good' as the highest principle of Reason – something that can be situated under the modern critique of the Enlightenment – in the sense that the 'Good' by a kind of default can no longer function as the highest principle of reason and that the nature of reason itself is suspected of harboring a much more malevolent nature which would include the possibilities of treachery and deceit, a suspicion that today can be ascribed to the concepts of 'Ideology' and 'the Unconscious.'

'But what happened in this long history of "nihilism,"' Deleuze asks in 1988, 'before the world lost its principles?'

> At a point close to us human Reason had to collapse, like the Kantian refuge, the last refuge of principles. It falls victim to 'neurosis.' But even before, a psychotic episode must have been necessary. A crisis and collapse of all theological Reason had to take place. That was where the Baroque assumes its position: Is there some way of saving the Theological ideal at a moment when it is being contested on all sides, and when the world cannot stop accumulating its 'proofs' against it, ravages and miseries, at a time when the earth will soon shake and tremble . . . ? The Baroque solution is the following: we shall multiply principles – we can always slip a new one out from under the cuff – and in this way we will change their use. We will not have to ask what available object corresponds to a given luminous principle, but what hidden principle corresponds to whatever object is 'given,' that is to say, to this or that 'perplexing case.' . . . A case being given, we shall invent its principle. (Fold 67)

In order to understand this passage, we need to define what Deleuze means by a 'principle'; perhaps the best way to define a principle is to say that it is a rule not unlike those found in games. Let us take the example of chess, which Deleuze resorts to many times in order to address the function of principles. Chess is defined, literally carved out of time and space, by the rules of play; as a result, 'the play not only internalizes the players who serve as pieces, but the board on which the game is played, and the material of that board' (Fold 67). At the same time, all of the little pieces that serve as players have been endowed with singular characteristics. (We might even call them personalities.) A knight can only move two squares forward, then one square left or right. If it moved any differently, then it would no longer be a knight. It would be a bishop, a pawn or a queen. Here, we can see that the clearest definition of a principle, or a rule, is what provides the possibility of identity, that is, for a knight to be a knight. Therefore, a rule cannot be understood as a kind of command, or coercion, which would force each piece to correspond to its identity, which would put into these little pieces of wood a kind of homunculus, a subject of desire, a relation to freedom which is strictly impossible for wood.

From this example, we might begin to infer why the loss of principles would signal the 'end of the game': the inability to make a move, the sudden or stupefying moment when everything is frozen in a terrifying death grimace. Not only would the game stop, the board itself would become incomprehensible, and the differences would cease to signify the possibilities of play. Applying our analogy to the foregoing problem, for philosophy to lose its principle of Reason would imply that it could no longer go on being itself, but rather would turn into something else such as literature, poetry or ethics. Here, the 'end of Metaphysics' is no longer such a lofty and impenetrable concept, but rather the simplest thing to understand: the moment when philosophy lost the rule of reason and could no longer go on playing the 'game of truth' according to the same old rules. At this point our aging philosopher was faced with a stark alternative: either invent new ones, or abandon the game altogether. Briefly put, this is the fundamental problem that Deleuze's work addresses throughout his entire *oeuvre*, or at least from the first pages of *Différence et Répétition* to the publication with Guattari of *Qu'est-ce que la philosophie?* in 1991.

From the period of *Difference and Repetition*, Deleuze's earlier solution to this crisis was to couple himself to Nietzsche and to Mallarmé, for whom the end of the game is affirmed in a 'throw of the dice.' The solutions offered by Nietzsche and Mallarmé, Deleuze reflects later in 1988,

> have rewarded us with the revelation of a Thought-World that throws dice. But for them the world lacks principle, has lost its principles. That is why the throw of the dice is the power of affirming Chance, of thinking of chance in sum, which is above all not a principle, but the absence of all principles. Thus Mallarmé gives to absence or nothingness what issues from chance, what claims to escape it all the while limiting it by principle: 'The world is the anonymous domain of absence, from which things disappear

> and into which they appear . . . The apparition is a mask behind which no one exists, behind which nothing really exists other than nothing.' Nothing rather than something. To think without principles, in the absence of God and in the absence of man himself, has become the perilous task of the child-player [the little demiurge, or infant God] who topples the old master of play, and who makes incompossibles enter into the same world, shattered (the board is broken to bits . . .). (Pli 67)

This solution represents what Deleuze earlier calls 'the Ideal Game' (*le jeu idéal*), but it is also a solution that could be said to belong to the long history of 'nihilism.' In order to understand why this is so, it is necessary to be clear concerning the meaning of nihilism that is given in the above passage. Nihilism is what happens when the subject encounters a loss of the highest principle and 'Nothing' is affirmed in its place: *nothing is affirmed in place of something*. This can be taken as the formula for nihilism. With both Mallarmé and Nietzsche, for example, the affirmation of the 'empty space of nothingness' is itself the space of freedom that is left open to Chance – to the terror of absolute play, on the one hand, or to the freedom of an absolute automaton, such as language, on the other. For Mallarmé, we might think of this 'empty space' as what the absolute poem introduces into Language; for Nietzsche, the 'empty space' inserted into time is the affirmation of the Eternal Return. Yet, by affirming chance in each instant, the board (that is, the world) is also exposed to being shattered, sending all the pieces flying into chaos, which is why Deleuze would later abandon this solution as potentially false and inherently risky.

Here is how Deleuze described this moment in 1968:

> To every perspective or point-of-view there must correspond an autonomous work with its own self-sufficient sense: what matters is the divergence of series, the decentering of circles, 'monstrosity.' The totality of circles and series is thus a formless ungrounded chaos that has no law other than its repetition, its own reproduction in the development of what diverges and decenters. (DR 69)

The above passage should immediately recall Borges's description of 'The library of Babel' (1962). There we find a series of hexagons; each containing twenty shelves, five shelves to a side except two where there is a hallway (with two small closets to the left and to the right, one for sleeping and the other for depositing 'one's faecal necessities'), leading to the next hexagon which has the same exact dimensions, contents and facilities. As if this horrible symmetry is not enough, Borges adds that each shelf contains thirty-five books, each book is 410 pages long, each page contains forty lines and each line is eighty characters in length. In his account, Borges also mentions a spiral staircase that rises and descends from each passage, so that when one of the occupants of the Library dies, he is simply tossed over the rail into the void that surrounds each staircase where his body falls through an infinite and groundless space, until 'it will gently decay and dissolve in the wind generated by the fall' (BR 52). Here, we see many of the same elements that appear above in Deleuze's affirmation: first, a series of divergent units (circles or hexagons, the architectural details do not matter); second, a certain groundlessness (or the dissolution of all content into a great nothingness), all of which is summarized by the following principle: 'The Library is a circle whose exact center is any one of its hexagons and whose circumference is inaccessible' (L 52).

Yet, there is also a fundamental detail that distinguishes between Borges's confrontation with the problem of repetition and Deleuze's early allusion. In Borges's description of 'The Total Library' (absolute knowledge), the architectural details form a kind of monotonous 'Eternal Return of the Same' which seems to strike everything with an unbearable evacuation of difference. (After all, what other purpose is the installation of toilets in each cell if not to signal for us the principle of evacuation of all content?) In the final paragraph of 'The Total Library,' however, we find a new principle expressed in the statement that 'The Library is unlimited and cyclical.' That is, 'If an eternal traveler were to cross it in any direction, after centuries he would see that the same volumes were repeated in the same disorder (which, thus repeated, would be an order: the Order)' (L 58). We must ask what has just happened? That is, what is the difference between the classical principle of architecture, 'the Library is a circle whose exact center is any one of its hexagons and whose circumference is inaccessible' (one might also say 'impossible'), and the new principle announced by the second statement that 'the Library is unlimited and cyclical.' The difference emerges, according to Borges, when we understand that the second principle offers a determination of the 'infinity' that now belongs to the Library. If in the first proposition, the exact center of the Library is any one of its chambers, then we might speculate that the whole (the circumference) is present but in a manner that is infinitely remote or even 'inaccessible.' In the second, the whole is defined as 'disorder' (which is still a kind of order, and perhaps even the Order), one that suddenly causes the Library to become de-centered and without circumference. In a footnote that Borges adds to this final sentence, he remarks that this in effect qualifies and completely changes the architectural principle of the Library, since the entire edifice could in principle be compressed into a single volume, containing an infinite number of infinitely thin leaves (which a seventeenth-century writer described as 'the superimposition of an infinite number of planes'), each page unfolding into the next, although the inconceivable middle page would have no reverse (L 58). Here, we might already see that Borges has prefigured the solution that Deleuze later discovers in *The Fold,* since the circumference has disappeared and in its place we have the principle of the *Zwischenfalt*, the middle fold, or a fold in between folds in such a way that the principle of the fold (*le pli*) becomes inseparable from the species of repetition that is deployed by a process of reading that now belongs to the concept of modern literature.

In his famous entry on 'The analytical language of John Wilkins,' Borges reveals the presence of an ideological flaw or error that structures the former library in the arbitrariness of all universal schemes: 'obviously there is no classification of a universe that is not arbitrary and conjectural. The reason is very simple: we do not know what the universe is' (BR 142). Still, this last statement does not cause Borges to capitulate to the position of 'nihilism,' which again is the affirmation of *Nothing* in the place of *Something*. In this case, we might see that the principle of a correspondence, which relates a system of classification (the library) with the organization of the real (the universe), is broken by the declaration of a purely arbitrary or chance relation. This is the same crisis of principles that Leibniz had also encountered in the seventeenth century, which is why the Leibnizian solution holds a privileged place in Borges's reflections as it does for Deleuze. If this correspondence is purely arbitrary, then nothing could be affirmed in the real that would henceforth be the condition of any possible knowledge; the order of language and signification would simply close upon itself as a universal automaton, a labyrinth which shares no corresponding principle that would refer outside itself to the order of nature or the universe. (To even refer to 'an order' of the universe would already be a false ascription of a notion of 'order' that refers only to the closed system of classification.) Here, we have a profound expression of schism, since if there is no rational element in the real, then every system of classification that pretends to find a correspondence is a simple 'fiction,' an 'artificial universe' which would be foreclosed from the real. If we take up one of Borges's primary metaphors to describe this relationship, we would have the Library, and outside the Library, the universe; between them, there could be no unifying principle, no possibility of reference, no possible truth as correspondence.

To illustrate this point, we might recall a similar crisis in Saussure's announcement of the 'arbitrariness that determines the relationship between the signifier and signified.' In the wake of this announcement, this led many to proclaim that the relation is total and all-encompassing in the sense that every order of the signifier is completely arbitrary; therefore, every relation is potentially false, and the signifier itself despotic. Such a view led to many exaggerated and naïve statements concerning 'the arbitrariness of the signifier' that has recurred often in the history of postmodernism, and has evolved into similar statements concerning 'text' and 'textuality' by those associated with deconstruction early on (i.e. 'there is no signified,' 'no meaning,' 'nothing outside the text,' etc.) most of which betrayed a certain manic polarity between jubilation and despair. Yet, much of this exaggeration might have been avoided if these same critics had chosen to read Saussure further on this point; they would discover that while the relationship between signifier and signified was '*arbitrary in principle*' (my emphasis), it was at the same time 'absolutely necessary.'[2] Here, at this moment, Saussure affirms Something over Nothing, which takes the form of 'necessity,' that is the historical unfolding of a signifying chain through time, so that 'the community itself cannot control so much as a single word; it is bound to the existing language.'[3]

Taking up Borges's commentary on this same crisis nearly two centuries before Saussure, it is interesting that he immediately turns to the somewhat gnostic solution by one of his baroque contemporaries, David Hume. 'This world', wrote Hume,

> was only the rude essay of some infant deity who afterwards abandoned it, ashamed of his lame performance; it is the work of some dependent, inferior diety, and is the object of derision to his superiors; it is the production of old age and dotage in some superannuated deity, and ever since his death has run on . . . (Hume quoted BR 143)

In the above passage, we might notice a contradiction in Hume's description of the little demiurge who is simultaneously described as an infant and as 'the production of old age and dotage.' This is because Hume still holds out for the possibility that the order of knowledge can be likened either to the mental production of an infantile and primitive consciousness, or to a product of senility and old age; in other words, he still leaves room for the advent of a development of reason that would be corrective and diagnostic – in a word, perfect. If there is a perceptible derision in Hume's tone, this can be likened to gnosticism, to a spirit of criticism of and hatred for the world *as it is* (as a botched or 'bad' creation), and to an 'other-worldly' idea of reason as perfect – a pre-sentiment of idealism is already present in Hume's scorn. As Borges says, however, we must go further than the solution that is offered by gnosticism, or its contemporary avatar, idealism. The baroque solution still retains the minimal criteria of a rational element in the universe. To put it differently, faced with the monster of chaos, the baroque solution still chooses Something over Nothing, and this 'Something' can be defined as something of a secret. Thus, Borges goes further than the gnostic solution in that while he completely rejects the notion of the universal 'in the organic, unifying sense that is inherent in that word,' he still retains the idea of a hidden order that takes the form of God's secret dictionary. Thus, contrary to the sentiment expressed by the statement 'Everything is arbitrary,' or by the gnostic sentiment that everything is botched and corrupted, Borges holds up the example of Wilkins's analytical language that does not rest upon 'stupid, arbitrary symbols.' Rather, every letter is meaningful, as the Holy Scriptures were meaningful to the Cabalists. To summarize, while the divine scheme of the universe is impossible, says Borges, 'this should not dissuade us from outlining human schemes, even though we are aware they are provisional' (BR 143).

In the last statement, perhaps we have the most direct example of affirming something in place of nothing. For Borges, this something takes on the order of a secret, of a secret that is not divine but rather a purely human design, which is to say, something that is produced by the arrangement of little letters in a signifying series. Because there is something of a secret, which is at the same time purely historical, the universe retains a relationship to truth that avoids the chaos ushered in by the statement 'Everything is arbitrary,' or the nihilism of the underlying assertion that reality is generated by stupid, arbitrary symbols. For

Borges, on the contrary, the exemplary system of Wilkins refers to this moment when the arbitrariness of the 'system of grunts and squeals' is nevertheless affirmed as capable of a relation of truth; that is, despite its complete arbitrariness, Wilkins produces his system of classification in the 'belief that an ordinary civilized stockbroker can really produce out his own inside noises which denote all the mysteries of memory and the agonies of desire' (BR 143). Therefore, what was originally the profound defect of language turns out to be its condition of possibility: the possibility of expression which is only possible, finally, from the arbitrariness of its initial principle that the relation between the signifier and the signified is not fixed, not even in the mind of God, but is only provisionally determined and thus open to new expressive modulations through time. Even though this system assumes the nature of a labyrinth that is made up by the infinite combination of twenty-six letters, it is a labyrinth whose possible combinations can never be totalized, and must admit the constant quantity of new passages and new signifying relations.

Perhaps the best exemplar of this process is the figure of Pierre Menard, whose affirmation can be read in the context of the following sentence: 'He dedicated his scruples and his sleepless nights to repeating an already extant book in an alien tongue' (L 44). The principle that governs Menard's process, which Borges comments on in detail, is neither translation nor copying, but rather corresponds to the creation of what Deleuze calls a 'simulacrum.' What differentiates the simulacrum from the simple copy or the translation is a principle that returns to the Leibnizian axiom that only what differs can begin to have a resemblance. The 'difference' one finds in the tale of Menard is the following: 'To compose the Quixote at the beginning of the seventeenth century was a reasonable undertaking, necessary and perhaps unavoidable; at the beginning of the twentieth, it is almost impossible' (L 41). However, the difference that governs and determines the undertaking for Menard is defined as 'impossible.' 'Impossible' in what sense? The answer to this question is given earlier in the sentence which describes the composition of the *Quixote* at the beginning of the seventeenth century as a natural act, perhaps even one that was 'necessary and unavoidable.' At the beginning of the twentieth century, however, we must determine this act to be something unreasonable, that is, completely avoidable. Menard's gesture is an act that runs against the grain of his time – it is impossible *a priori*. On the other hand, according to Borges, Cervantes's 'genius' was something thoroughly inscribed in the possibility of his time, almost to the extent that this negates Cervantes's singular importance as the author of the *Quixote*, since if he didn't write it then someone else certainly would have, by necessity. Thus, we can take the comparison of the two passages that Borges gives us to substantiate his claim of their fundamental difference, passages that on first inspection are exactly identical:

> ... truth, whose mother is history, rival of time, depository of deeds, witness of the past, exemplar and advisor to the present, and future's counselor

and:

> ... truth, whose mother is history, rival of time, depository of deeds, witness of the past, exemplar and advisor to the present, and future's counselor. (L 43)

Upon first glance, both versions appear identical; however, Menard's version highlights the importance of history as the mother of truth. In other words, in Menard's version history is identified not with what happened, but rather with what we judge to have happened. As a result of this change of emphasis, the difference between Menard's passage and that of Cervantes is profound; they don't say the same thing! Between them, something has changed and this change of 'origin' is historical, 'the mother of truth.' What is different for us is that, today, there can be no *Quixote* without Menard; this could be said to be Borges's relation to the 'tradition of all of Western literature,' which is established by the principle of repetition. No *Quixote* without Menard!! That is, only what differs can begin to have resemblance, but this 'resemblance' will only appear from the second instance that repeats the first. That is, *Quixote* will resemble Menard, more than Menard will resemble *Quixote*; or 'Cervantes' text and Menard's are verbally identical, but the second is infinitely richer' (L 42).

Here, I want to suggest that we find the same principle that motivates Deleuze's solution to the loss of principles, to the shattering of the tables of representation, in his turn back before this moment to the philosophy of Leibniz, although in a manner that was strictly possible for someone from our time, and this would necessarily entail both a repetition and a difference inserted into his reading of Leibniz. In short, Deleuze abandons the 'ideal game,' the game of chance; instead, he affirms the principle of creation, which he later with Guattari infuses in *What is Philosophy?*, with the definition of philosophy itself as a creation of the first order, a creation of concepts. The relevance of Borges is that Deleuze himself solves this problem by turning to Leibniz in a manner that closely follows Borges's own solution, even though Deleuze himself would not see the correspondence exactly in these terms. Borges also turns to the seventeenth century in a manner that prefigures and anticipates Deleuze, so much so that I would define Borges as precursor in the same sense we find in 'Kafka as precursor' and 'Pierre Menard, author of the Quixote.' The above can be described as the doctrine of repetition that founds Borges's literary process, and can be discovered to underwrite every individual reflection or plot. For example, we find it again in his note on 'Kafka and his precursors,' where we have another version of this uncanny repetition of 'Kafka' in such figures as Aristotle, Kierkegaard, Leon Bloy and the English poet Robert Browning. 'In each of these texts,' writes Borges, 'we find Kafka's idiosyncrasy to a greater or lesser degree, but if Kafka would have never written a line we would not perceive this quality; indeed, it would not exist' (L 201). Hence, this proves that by a kind of repetition that appears only in what essentially differs, 'his work modifies the conception of the past, as it will modify the future.' Moreover, it is this theory of repetition that Borges shares with Deleuze, or which Deleuze lifts from Borges as early as *Difference and Repetition*, which cites Menard in the preface as a supreme justification to his philosophy of difference and repetition.

Like Kafka, Borges's signature underwrites philosophical projects of Deleuze, Foucault (hence the citation which occurs in the preface to *The Order of Things*) and Derrida (can one even conceive of the process of 'deconstruction' of the text of Western Metaphysics without the precursor of Borges's 'total library'?). Restricting our comments to the understanding of Borges's process, we should not underestimate its importance for the situation of the post-colonial writer in relation to the literature of the West, and those who have entered into the field of culture too late, due to some historical accident or political fatality. However, for Borges, this subject occupies the privileged position of being the 'second.' This is why Borges finds the representatives of this position less in the personage of the author than in the figures of the critical reader, the scholar or the baroque detective – that is, those figures who always arrive on the scene of knowledge second and who are, for that reason, superior to the author (in the case of the book) or the criminal (in the case of crime).

In 1937 Borges was employed as a first assistant in the municipal library, where he spent 'nine years of solid unhappiness,' until 1946, his 'season in hell' as he would later describe it. In the account from which I read this information, the biographer quickly adds some Kafkaesque brush-strokes.[4] Above him, he had not only the director but three officials. In due time, 'Borges would ascend to the dizzying heights of the third assistant' (BR 346). The other assistants were only interested in 'pornography, rape and sports,' according to the biographer; and to avoid their hostility, Borges had to agree to catalogue no more than 100 titles a day. (On the first day, he had ambitiously catalogued more than 400, and received rage and enmity from the other clerks.) Borges only acquired some status from 'the women who worked there and who were interested in society gossip,' when it was soon discovered that he was a friend of Elvira de Alvear, 'a beautiful and despotic woman whom he loved hopelessly and who was at that time in Buenos Aires an arbiter elegantiarum' (BR 346).

When I first read this, I was immediately suspicious of all the Kafkaesque flairs: the director and the three assistants; the vulgar tastes of the assistants for 'pornography, rape and sports'; the gossip of the women co-workers; the phrase of a 'beautiful and despotic woman'; and finally, the phrase 'hopelessly in love' (which, to my mind, is too much of an instance of the 'Kafkaesque' to be believed). At the same time, there is other evidence to support the assertion of Kafka as precursor to this period. It was during this time that Borges read Kafka, and even edited and prefaced an edition of his stories in Spanish. It is also said that Borges, during his days in the Library, would sequester himself in the basement or on the roof to write, and in this period some of his best stories were produced including 'Death and the compass,' 'The library of Babel' and others in the collection of 'The garden of forking paths,' and finally, the two drafts of 'The (new) refutation of time,' which he penned in 1944 and 1946 respectively.

Borges himself, we might conjecture, could not have failed to notice the uncanny repetition of certain details from Kafka's work in his own experience and this must have shaped his understanding of the singularity of his own experience as precisely having the strange character of a repetition that he will pursue throughout his entire body of work. It is a species of repetition that he demonstrates in the above stories as well as in the famous 'Kafka as precursor' and 'Pierre Menard, author of the Quixote,' which were also written during this same period. However, one conclusion that we might draw from this analogy, according to Borges's own theory of repetition, is the identification of the Library as a problem that bears (and precisely due to its difference) a repetition of the same problem that determines the position of the Court in Kafka's own work. This assertion, although obvious, is still undefined; and in both cases, the court and its officers, apparatus of the Law, and the Library, and its personages, apparatus of knowledge, are shrouded in a certain 'mystery' – this is the exact word used by both writers to describe their respective objects of interrogation – that is, by a certain secrecy that they both attempt to resolve in the most direct of manners, by the means of the most precise analytical instrument each has forged in his own way – the instrument of a fiction, of literature.

Like the court, the Library is an infernal machine. Borges himself describes it as a kind of 'minor hell.' All that is required is a series of little letters, of signifiers, to generate an infinite space and time. To illustrate this possibility, we might use the following formula that Borges cites from Leucippus: 'A is different from N in form; AN from NA in order; Z from N in position' (BR 94). Thus, following this postulation of three series of differences (that of form, order and position) we can construct an infinite library from twenty-six letters. A universe can be generated from this simple formula, since each species of difference can include others: an elephant is different from a bird or a fish in form; the relation between today and yesterday is different from the relation between today and tomorrow in terms of order; and finally, noon is different from midnight in terms of position. As Borges recounts, the Library (as some call it, the universe) includes the total combinations possible, so that in the modern period, Huxley conjectured that six monkeys with typewriters could, given a few eternities, reproduce all the volumes in the British Library (although Borges provides a notation that in principle only one absolute monkey would be required). At the same time, we find another series in Borges: the series of four letters that make up the unspeakable name of God; each letter will signify a certain point in time, a place, the first letter in the proper name of a victim, a position in the zodiac calendar. These are the four letters that Erik Lönrott traces from the pages of ancient volumes in the library of one of the victims, through the streets of Buenos Aires, to the exact point of his awaited death. Or, in 'The garden of forking paths,' it is the secret name of 'Albert,' which also signals the target of a German bombing raid during the war. The second series is set in opposition to the first: in the first we have an infinite number of combinations which makes each seem purely arbitrary and insignificant; for the second, there is a singular combination, a 'secret' series of letters, for which there is only one possible solution. Or rather, there is a singular arrangement of three letters, which is punctuated by a fourth, which completes the series and marks the exact and indisputable solution of a mystery. This could be the axiom of Borges's process, the baroque detective, to resolve the mystery by the most direct of means. I would not be the first to suggest that human beings, for example, are composed of three letters as well; however, what is remarkable is that for each there is only one possible solution, or cipher. The mystery is one of singularity, which causes *a* life to diverge from all the others. At the same time, because God is unconscious of this perspective, a point-of-view which is that of the Library itself, he necessarily 'misses' the singular – by default. It is through this gap in the architecture of knowledge that the unconscious of God enters the universe at the same time that it is from the 'absence of the singular' from his point-of-view or perspective that disorder or difference is introduced into the Library.

In response to this problem, Borges deduces six axioms or codes which function as the principles of the detective genre, and in turn, applies these codes to his investigation of the European library. In other words, it is by the application of this literary machine (or process), which very much resembles Kafka's discovery of a set of similar codes which will function to distinguish the solution of the shorter works (the letters, the animal stories) from the novels, that Borges invents a discrete formula by which all of knowledge (that is, the library itself) can be submitted to an ongoing interrogation, or investigation. This investigation of the Library may well be interminable, just as Kafka's investigation of the Court, its anterior and adjacent bureaucracies, its agents and its victims, which seem only to multiply and proliferate until, in the end (which, I remind you is only the end of 'K.' in *The Trial* and of a certain abandonment by Kafka himself in the case of *The Castle*), the court is revealed to be total. In a similar manner, for Borges, the investigation in the total library will always unearth new investigations that will later be abandoned in course, or punctuated by the mystery of a given solution (e.g. 'Death and the compass'), and like Kafka's juridical apparatus, also reveals itself to be somewhat of an infernal machine.

Every instance of accepted knowledge can, through Borges's literary machine, become an item for the investigation; all that is required is the purely formal subscription to the following five axioms: (1) a discretionary maximum of six characters; (2) the resolution of all loose ends to a mystery; (3) a rigid economy of means; (4) the priority of how over who; and finally, (5) necessity and wonder in the solution (BR 72). There is no reason to believe that Borges could not have invented more principles (or laws) to rule on this or that occasion or in this or that story according to his needs, but here I highlight only these five in order to underline the character of what Deleuze and Guattari define as 'a literary machine.' What we are dealing with here is the creation of a purely formal and somewhat arbitrary series of codes that determines the conditions of enunciation from one occasion to the next. Once this series is established, however, to violate it would result in the loss of form and, at the same time, would produce the conditions for judging the outcome as somehow botched or a failure. Therefore, each of these laws must be rigorously followed, and for each there is always a notation of illegal or bad moves, as in a game of chess. (Examples of the various illegal solutions, for instance, include the uses of 'hypnotism, ingenious pseudo-scientific tricks, and lucky charms' [BR 72]). The fifth law is the most interesting one to comment on for our purposes, since it demands two things simultaneously: first, that the mystery is determined (that is, it is fit for only one possible solution) and; second, that the reader must marvel over the solution without resorting in any way to a supernatural explanation. When this law is set within the Library, the fifth law gives us a key to understand Borges's theory of ideology: the agent, or criminal, must be found to be of purely terrestrial, one might say 'historical,' origin (which, after Menard, is 'the mother of all truth'). In other words, the solution itself must never take the form of (a Universal) myth or superstition to solve the problem of the 'mystery.' (Consequently, Borges's solution would be different from Freud's.)

If we apply the fifth axiom to one of Borges's most famous stories, 'Death and the compass,' what do we find? That the solution is determined, following the first of the criteria, in that the solution arrived at is the only one possible to resolve this mystery; at the same time, we might notice with marvel that the detective's solution to the mystery of the murders at the same time means his own. It is almost as if the detective sacrifices himself to such a perfect criminal design in order to guarantee that his solution will remain that much more something to marvel at, as if the perfection of his knowledge of the mystery must make of his subject its final and summary execution. Thus, the mystery which is traced through four letters of the unspeakable name of God, in the end becomes the bullet from the revolver that finds its target at precisely that point in space and time where his solution of the mystery and the path of the bullet meet at the bull's-eye of Lönrott's body. What it is crucial not to miss (no pun intended) in this perfect conjunction of the detective's intellectual process and the unfolding of process that is located in the real is that they are, even for a second, perfectly symmetrical and that one proves the accuracy of the other. In other words, there is nothing arbitrary in the order of signifiers that the detective follows, but that it allows him to trace a commensurate path in the real. In short, the detective saves the truth and certainty of his 'reading,' even if he achieves this truth at the price of his own death; the detective Lönrott critiques the deadly mystery that was created by Scharlach. It is not perfect enough, he announces, looking straight into Scharlach's eyes. He utters the now famous line: 'In your labyrinth you have three lines too many' (L 86).

At this point, some might be reminded of Kafka's solution at the end of *The Trial*, where K.'s investigation of his own guilt or innocence ends with his execution. In this case, I think there is something different from what takes place in Borges, since while the 'sentence' finally lands on K., nothing is determined by this, K.'s death appears like something completely arbitrary, and the law itself is still wrapped in a cloak of mystery. Thus, Kafka's solution is indeterminate, and the reader is left not feeling 'marvel,' but disgust and dread at the fact that K. dies 'like a dog.' This gives us a clue concerning the nature of the 'secret' in Borges: first, it must be entirely terrestrial (which is to say 'hellish' or 'infernal'); second, it leads, as in 'Death and the compass,' straight to the death of the subject, although in a manner that does not leave its shroud of mystery intact.

If the literary machine that Borges created has often been likened to a game, this is because it violates this order of death in a very special way. A game, by contrast, is infinitely reversible; thus it is a special case of exception that is created in time. This is what gives a false and pathetic character to all games. (For example, Baudelaire observes that gambling emerges precisely in order to restore to the game its temporal nature, which is that of irreversible loss.) In a letter to Rémond (January, 1716), Leibniz rejects games of chance for the sake of chess or checkers; games of position and games of emptiness or 'void' for the inverted games of solitaire; and finally, games modeled on battle for the sake of the Chinese games of non-battle (consequently, the game of Go is preferred over the game of chess) (quoted in *The Fold* 152*n*). In turn, we find the exact preferences repeated by Borges who, as we know, found both the game of lottery, or the principle of chance, to be indeterminate and abysmal, leading to an annihilation of the subject. Concerning the game of chess, we find this stanza in the poem of the same name:

It was in the East, this war took fire.
Today the whole earth is its theater.
Like the game of love, this game goes on forever.

And finally:

God moves the player, he in turn, the piece.
But what god behind God begins the round
Of dust and time and sleep and agonies. (BR 280–281)

Borges' preference for the solitaire of the detective and the scholar expresses the principle of a duel with an absent player, an intellectual process that must assume the position of the 'Other,' whether the mind of the criminal or the figure of the author-God. Following Deleuze's observation we can easily detect in the labyrinthian and divergent series, as well as in the line of the Orient that runs through Borges's entire work, a preference for a Chinese principle of non-battle, 'this network of times which approached one another, broke off, or forked, or were unaware of one another for centuries' (L 28), a game which embraces all possibilities at once, and different futures, where in one you are my enemy, and in another, my friend. As Deleuze writes, if Borges invokes the Chinese philosopher-architect Ts'ui Pên rather than Leibniz, it is because he wanted 'to have God pass into existence all incompossible worlds at once rather than choosing one of them, the best' (Fold 62). And yet, Deleuze here would have Borges violate one of his own rules, perhaps the most important as we have seen, which is that there be only one possible solution to 'a mystery,' the solution that leads most directly (one might say singularly) to the subject's own death. How do we account for this discrepancy? That is, Deleuze makes Borges affirm Nothing over Something, even though here Nothing takes the form of all incompossible worlds, whereas Borges affirms just the opposite. Deleuze either refuses or fails to recognize that in turning back to the solution of 'a certain baroque Leibniz' Borges had already been there before him, that Borges is now in a certain sense a precursor to Leibniz. In other words, no Leibniz without Borges! This could be the fundamental axiom that will determine the entire argument concerning the seventeenth-century philosopher in *The Fold*.

In *The Fold*, Deleuze defines the Baroque as a kind of schizophrenic order of creation (the multiplication or invention of principles) that resolves the crisis of theological reason in his reading of Leibniz. What marks the definition of a schizophrenic order of creation for Deleuze is a litigation, even a war, over the principle of reason; the schizophrenic rages against the order of God's creation, the closed universe of the symbolic order. Thus, Deleuze outlines the following problem as the fundamental basis for the Baroque: 'How to conjoin freedom with the schizophrenic automaton's inner, complete, and pre-established determination?' (Fold 69). We might see this as the same problem that Borges takes up with regard to the determination of the Library. Yet, although I noted the passage of time, I want to underline the fact that this question was possible only in the seventeenth century; whereas its reappearance in our twentieth century bore something new, a character of repetition that will necessarily diverge from Leibniz's solution. In a manner similar to the baroque solution that is discovered by Deleuze – that of multiplying principles, one for each case, inventing new ones for exceptional cases – we might think of Borges's solution to the problem of the Library (i.e. the architecture of knowledge).

Borges seems to move through the European library, inventing new editions (so-called fictitious volumes) whenever he runs into an impasse. It is this movement, this process of invention, or creation, that defines the concept of literature in Borges. Thus, the procedures of archivization and critique that an act of reading entails constitute the architecture of Borges's work; by which the 'Library' becomes, under the axiom of Borges's solution, a labyrinth. Here, we have two readers which are opposed in a direct confrontation: God, the author, who sees everything at once through a giant telescope and gathers all perception into a central eye, and the reader in the labyrinth who follows a trail that may eventually lead through the labyrinth, but must also necessarily include in his/her trajectory points of impasse, detours, traps, blind alleys, wrong turns and failures. This is an important consideration, since 'knowledge' – both in the form of its pre-supposition and in the material organization or architecture of the 'Library' which classifies, separates into distinct locations, and creates a taxonomy of memory traces that have a pure and non-individual repetition to insure that they can always be found by everyone – must now include the points of confusion, the misunderstanding and the formal 'blindnesses' that are the result of what the God-reader misses, and which constitute his profound unconscious. It is the Unconscious of God that, in turn, forms the architecture of the Library.

As Deleuze shows, Leibniz creates in *The Theodicy* a trial in which a lawyer defends God's principles against the evidence of reality, which can be summed up in one simple word: 'misery.' However, as more recent and less pious scholars have observed, to 'defend' God's principles is not the same thing as defending God. In *Leibniz et Spinoza* (1975), Georges Friedman insists on Leibniz's philosophy as a thinking of Universal anxiety: the Best is not a 'vote of confidence in God; on the contrary, Leibniz seems to be defying God himself' (Fold 152*n*). O. J. Simpson was not the first defendant to go down in history as an ambiguous client for the defense; Leibniz had already laid the precedent, by separating the character of God from the principle of law (i.e. what is really at issue). Consequently, today in crime dramas on TV, we often witness a scene in which the defense lawyer knows his or her client to be guilty of the prosecution's complaint – guilty to the teeth! – but must present a case to the best of his or her ability in order to salvage something from the loss of the 'Good.' What is salvaged is the principle of law, that is, to save its possibility for the future. This marks what Deleuze calls Leibniz's cry, that 'Everything must be rational.' That is, for each event there must be a principle, and his entire philosophy proceeds from the insane demand that the real be rationalized, that Something rather than Nothing must be affirmed for each event and being, that in cases where the principle is not known it be created and adjudicated right down to the smallest molecules.

I want to call attention to the fact that we can find exactly the same cry in Borges, although it is no longer issued by a philosopher but by a 'man of letters' (in every sense implied by this phrase, including, I might add, 'a true man of the seventeenth century'), that is, a being who emerges in the heart of the Library, who spends all eternity there, who rages against its imperfect order and who dreams, deliriously, of perfecting it in the following statement:

> In adventures such as these, I have squandered and wasted my years. It does not seem unlikely to me that there is a total book on some shelf of the universe. [Borges adds the following axiom: 'it simply suffices for such a book to be possible for it to exist.'] I pray to the unknown god that a man – just one, even though it were thousands of years ago! – may have examined and read it. If honor and wisdom and happiness are not for me, let them be for the others. Let heaven exist, though my place be in hell. Let me be outraged and annihilated, but for just one instant, in one being, let Your enormous Library be justified. (L 57)

In this passage from 'The library of Babel,' we can detect the cry of a man of faith, even though his place be in hell. Like Leibniz, his cry is that there is one creature – who may have existed thousands of years ago, or who may not yet exist (although this doesn't matter, since the Library contains all possible times and it is sufficient to posit his existence for all these times, regardless of past or future with respect to the present) – who has read the book and for whom the universe is completely and perfectly justified.

Here, again I want to be clear, it is as if the whole universe (the Library) receives its entire justification in this one moment, in this one being. This is astounding, that the whole universe, in principle, can receive its justification in one singular reading; that, in principle, it is this event that becomes the condition of its possibility – even though this total sense, which excludes me (that is, Borges, Leibniz, Deleuze, you and I), assigns us all to an eternity of waiting, of leafing through all these dusty volumes in hell. The game of knowledge exists only to be completed in this one moment; in the meantime, God can be condemned a thousand times over, history can be discovered to be a farce or a nightmare, Borges, you and I can dissolve into night or be revealed as imaginary beings, simple fictions like in the dream of Chuong Tsu and the butterfly. This does not matter, because the game may not be for us, but, as Borges writes, 'for the others.' (In a certain sense, this might recall for us the statement that Kafka once made to Max Brod: 'There is in the universe something like hope, an infinite amount of hope, but not for us.') What is interesting, however, is that Borges, following this pious declaration, refers to an 'other,' the impious and reasonable. He writes:

> They speak (I know) of 'the feverish Library whose chance volumes are constantly in danger of metamorphosizing into others and affirm, negate, and confuse everything like a delirious divinity.' These words, which not only denounce the disorder but exemplify it as well, notoriously prove their author's abominable taste and desperate ignorance. In truth, the Library contains all verbal structures, all variations permitted by the 25 orthographical symbols, but not a single example of absolute nonsense. (L 57)

It is, of course, interesting to note for the record that the impious and reasonable author whom the narrator at this point cites and rejects as a person of 'abominable taste and desperate ignorance' is none other than Borges himself, who penned these very lines a few years earlier in the essay 'The total Library.' It seems clear from the above passage that we have found the principle that Borges struggles for: the 'sense of sense,' or the 'secret order of disorder.' To salvage something of a 'sense,' if not something of an 'ultimate meaning' from the arbitrary and ignorant combinations of the signifier – that was the hidden principle in Borges's struggle! – since for him, every signifier is filled with both tenderness and fear, and every word is, in some language, the name of God. (Thus, every word, in as much as it is expressed, is at the exact center of the universe. It necessarily supports the universe, in the same way that for Saussure each instance of speech [*la parole*] supports the whole of Language.) It is this hidden principle that gives him the faith and the courage to go on, even though he spends his time in hell, outraged and annihilated by the order of knowledge that exists, and which condemns him to his artificial and fictional interventions, to merely 'literature' (and this, I remind you, was often Kafka's despair as well).

The principle that Borges discovers is that of 'repetition,' a repetition that he creates and that must be understood as an artificial creation that is inseparable from the technique of literary creation or process he forges, whereby the library is opened to an infinite number of various readings that diverge and bifurcate. It is by means of this creation that Borges can descend into the seventeenth century, that he can correct the imperfections of Berkeley and Hume, in other words, that he can avoid the errors and false solutions of Idealism (which leads straight to Hegel) and of the subject of nihilism that comes after, perhaps in a way that prefigures something that is now possible for us as well.

In my discussion of Deleuze and Leibniz, what I argued is something so simple and at the same time Borgesean, that in conclusion I want to return to emphasize it again: that Borges is the precursor of Leibniz; that it was not possible for Deleuze to read Leibniz without Borges. This is something so simple and yet evident, that Deleuze himself did not often see it, or did not choose to see it exactly in that way, perhaps due to an anxiety of influence, and this caused him to locate Borges still in terms of his own earlier reading of Borges as a player in the absolute game of chance, 'the game without rules' (Fold 63). However, this claim does not prove to slight Deleuze in any way, since he could only claim that he was not Borges, and could have seen the exact same thing in his own way. At the same time, returning to this subject of Borges himself, let me remind you that we are talking about a man, a Jew, who received a little notoriety as an Argentinian writer of the Spanish literary tradition, whose own relation to this tradition was marked by the nebulous situation of what today is called 'the post-colonial.' However, even despite this situation (and not, I would argue, because of it as with so many others who are defined by this situation in the Library today) it also describes the infamy of an author whose few books (or rather fictions) have been worthy enough to claim a place on the shelves of the Library for posterity (although we must state categorically that the name of Borges may be forgotten at some point, and necessarily so). All of these things are true and could be defined as the predicates of 'Borges'; however, these are not encompassing, since there is this 'other' Borges as well. It is this one who 'went further' than the former, who claimed that there was one and only one solution to the problem of the universe, that there was in other words a straight line that ran through the labyrinth, and who took it upon himself to seek this line, and most of all, to claim that he had a right to solve the mystery of the universe. If we compared these two beings, Borges and his double, there would be nothing that could account for or justify such a delirious desire (except, that is, the somewhat arbitrary, on first glance, principle that is the condition of the Library as well). This form of repetition he creates is absolutely simple, and yet by means of it, he can make all the difference; so that we can say that Menard is the precursor to Quixote, or that today, Borges is our only true precursor. In different universes it may be possible to imagine a Library without the name of this other 'Borges,' but I want to remind you, not for us. Therefore, our only consolation is that the Library that exists (for us) – or as some call it, 'the universe' – is infinitely richer.

9

HOW THE TRUE WORLD FINALLY BECAME A FABLE

Deleuze argues that the world had to wait for Borges who corrected the Leibnizian solution and rectified time. However, if the Leibnizian solution saved the world for truth at the terrible cost of damnation, it is Borges who saves time, but at the cost of dispensing with truth. This produces a fundamental paradox in the history of the concept of time. Consequently, we could say that the Borgesean solution is not a philosophical one, but rather 'non-philosophical,' and belongs to the field of modern literature. Borges proposed two things. First, he constructed a labyrinth that is composed of a single straight line; however, as the force of chaotic time, that is, as paradoxical, '[the straight line] is also a line which forks and keeps on forking, passing through incompossible presents, returning to not-necessarily true pasts' (TI 131). Second, Borges replaces the fictional identity of a God with the conceptual personage of the 'forger.' Both of these elements, according to Deleuze, signal the emergence of a new status of narration, whereby 'narration ceases to be truthful, that is, to lay claim to the truth, and has become fundamentally falsifying' (TI 131).

> This is not at all the case of 'each has his own truth,' a variability of content. It is the power of the false, which replaces and supersedes the form of the true, because it posits the simultaneity of incompossible presents, or the co-existence of not-necessarily true pasts. Crystalline [or 'falsifying'] description was already reaching the indiscernibility of the real and the imaginary, but the falsifying narration which corresponds to it goes a step further and poses inexplicable differences to the present and alternatives which are undecidable between true and false to the past. The truthful man dies, every model of truth collapses, in favor of the new narration. (TI 131)

Taking up this Borgesean fragment, which Deleuze uses to signal a partial solution to the crisis of philosophy, the fact that the philosopher can no longer identify with himself may underscore the appearance of the 'forger' as the avatar of the 'last man.' Deleuze writes in the original preface to *Différence et Répétition* (1968) that the forger signals a form of repetition which is 'identical' although much more rich.

> It should be possible to recount a real book of past philosophy as if it were an imaginary and feigned book. Borges, we know, excelled in recounting imaginary books. But he goes further when he considers a real book, such

> as *Don Quixote*, as though it were an imaginary book, itself reproduced by an imaginary author, Pierre Menard, who in turn he considers to be real. In this case, the most exact, the strictest repetition has as its correlate the maximum of difference. (DR xxii)

Thus, the Deleuzian philosopher as forger repeats by treating the 'history of philosophy' as an imaginary novel; this constitutes a certain categorical imperative at the basis of Deleuze's work: 'Write as if the past itself was a supreme fiction. How then would you make it more usable for the future?' It is in copying this novel (the virtual) that richer details are incorporated and new variables are introduced. ('Cervantes' text and Menard's are verbally identical, but the second is infinitely richer.') This solves the problem we began with, that of 'time off its hinges,' since it signals the advent of multiple pasts, new variables, and a new regime of narration under 'the powers of the false.' Philosophy becomes its double: 'the pure repetition of the former text and the present text in one another' (DR xxii).

In order to give this new species of narration its full conceptual force, it will be necessary for us to locate the personage of the 'forger' who occupies the moment when narration ceases to be truthful and becomes fundamentally falsifying. According to Deleuze, the forger appears precisely at that moment when the philosophical pretension to 'truth' (i.e. will to truth), on the one hand, is revealed to harbor within itself another hidden motive (i.e. will-to-power) and, on the other hand, when this discovery of the form of truth and the philosophical personage who embodies its force of identification was, in fact, itself simply a species of 'falsehood' (a discovery which inevitably must pass through its nihilistic stages). 'Even "the truthful man ends up realizing that he has never stopped lying," as Nietzsche said' (TI 133). Finally, this leads to the positive discovery of a notion of the false beyond its moral-juridical determination which belongs to the system of judgement this new narration has displaced; 'the power of the false exists only from the perspective of a series of powers, always referring to each other and passing into one another' (TI 133). Consequently, if the philosopher is revealed to be in reality a forger, then 'the forger will thus be inseparable from a chain of forgers into whom he metamorphoses' (TI 133). However, recalling our previous discussion, this second revelation can happen only as the result of an event which makes the idea of the 'true world' impossible *a priori*; at the very least, making its concept 'useless' for distinguishing the imaginary and the real with regard to perception, or for discerning the true and the false with regard to the past. In other words, the concept of truth is itself found in default, 'out of use,' failing to clarify the future and the past both of which remain equally impenetrable and indiscernible. A new method must therefore be sought, signaling a new clarity and a form of discernment. Yet, this task does not necessarily entail the creation of a new model of truth, as we will see below.

Although Borges occupies the episodic moment of the appearance of the forger, in point of fact it is actually Nietzsche who first gives this moment its critical acumen:

> We have not mentioned the author who is essential in this regard: it is Nietzsche, who, under the name of the 'will to power,' substitutes the power of the false for the form of the true, and resolves the crisis of truth, wanting to settle it once and for all, but, in opposition to Leibniz, in favor of the false and its artistic, creative power . . . (TI 131)

Deleuze ends this statement elliptically, which is characteristic of his style in those passages where the thought is interrupted and remains in need of further clarification. In this case, we might infer that in another context the Nietzschean desire to settle the crisis of truth once and for all would itself be scrutinized by Deleuze as an expression of a 'will-to-power' that violates the two fundamental axioms in Deleuze's philosophy concerning the nature of problems and resolutions: (1) that all resolutions are necessarily partial and cannot be taken as final; (2) that time returns constantly to put the concept of truth again into crisis.

The entire argument contained in the chapter 'The powers of the false' in *Cinema 2* is, in fact, narrated through Nietzsche's aphoristic fragment from *Will to Power*, 'How the "true world" finally became an error.' Deleuze situates the full development of the Nietzschean concept of will to power within the domain of cinema, recalling the relationship between philosophy and non-philosophy discussed earlier, thereby substituting for each stage in the Nietzschean commentary a particular director – e.g. Welles, Robbe-Grillet, Lang, Godard, Cassevetes, Perault, Clark, Passolini, Jean Rouch and Alain Resnais – who works over the concept of the 'will-to-power' under the name of the power of the false. Thus, the directors themselves appear as 'forgers' who participate in narration of the concept of truth as the history of an error. The domain of cinema with its production of movement- and time-images, its creation of perspective or 'point-of-view,' and its invention of story with its objective and subjective façades are taken up by Deleuze as the place where the problems of truth and falsehood are equated to the technical problems of narration in cinema: What is a story? What is character? What is the real? What is the past? Or rather, how can the past be represented as being also substantial and a force of causality (whether from the perspective of subjective character, or from the perspective of world-memory). All of these questions appear as problems that are resolved, each resolution being only partial, each director and representative body of work passing into relationship with the other directors and works that add a new approach, element or technique to resolve the crisis of truth that seems immanent to the history of cinematic narration.

In his aphoristic account, Nietzsche shows the stages that the concept of truth undergoes to reach its penultimate modern expression of nihilism, representing that stage where the true world is vanquished but drags in its wake the world of appearances as well. He shows the progression from its origin in the identification with the truthful man, represented by the Platonic world and corresponding to the natural figure of the sage-philosopher. Truth is accessible to the sage, the virtuous and religious man; 'it lives in him, whose figure is identical to the true world *qua* expressed: "I, Plato, I am the truth."' This stage is then followed by the several avatars (or forgers) who substitute for this original identification of truth with the 'character' of the sage-philosopher, the truthful man. In the second stage, represented by the Christian world which succeeds the Platonic world of ideas, the 'true world' is inaccessible in the present, but is permitted to the sage and virtuous man through suffering and penance. (Augustine would be the corresponding image of thought.) In the third stage, the 'true world' becomes both inaccessible and undemonstrable; it cannot be promised – even in the after-life – although it can be imagined, and this in itself becomes a kind of consolation. (The philosopher and image of thought that corresponds to this stage would be the Kantian wisdom where 'the Good' can only have an analogy and the product of the faculty of the imagination.) In the fourth stage, the inaccessibility of the 'true world' becomes itself open to question, and philosophy immediately finds itself offended by the idea that the source of obligation and truth would derive from an unknown and unconscious source. (The conceptual personage would be the philosophy of Locke and Hume, the 'birds of positivism.') Finally, in the fifth and sixth stages, the idea that was found offensive and contradictory in the fourth stage, now appears useless and no longer bears any power of obligation; it is no longer worthy of belief or of faith. It is Nietzsche himself who represents both these moments under the name of Zarathustra, a moment which bears a Janus-face that casts a glance both forward and backward and encompassing the entire unfolding of 'truth as a history of error.' Thus, the character of Zarathustra represents the twilight of the concept of truth, the death of the 'truthful man,' and the collapse of every model of truth (that is, the entry into the long night of insomnia, pessimism and even nihilism); however, on the other slope, his appearance also marks the dawn that breaks into a long night of insomnia and promises the return of good sense and a spirit of happiness and joy (that is, the affirmation of this world which comprises the meaning of the Eternal Return). The apparently contradictory senses that can be ascribed to these last two stages – or rather, this last stage split into two aspects – are summarized in Nietzsche's final aphorism that with the vanquishing of 'the true world' the world of appearances vanishes as well.

If Deleuze adopts this Nietzschean account to narrate the history of cinema, it is not to develop the relationship between the concept of truth in philosophy and its representation in cinema by analogy or metaphor; rather, cinema takes up the problem of truth and attempts to resolve it by purely cinematic means and Deleuze simply traces its 'problem-solving' faculty step by step. What is cinema, after all, but a world constructed by pure appearances? However, it is precisely the relation between this world of pure appearance and the so-called 'real and true world' that recapitulates the philosophical problem recounted above in a striking way; each director and 'film-maker' must, therefore, take up and resolve this problem in a singular manner, although using the materials and technical means that are made available by others who have preceded him or her. According to Deleuze, it is precisely at that moment in the history of cinematographic narration when the movement-image is abandoned in favor of the time-image that cinema resolves the problem of its dependence upon the 'the real and true world.' That is, cinema no longer seeks to represent the latter through the movement-image, which 'is linked to (real) sensory motor descriptions,' or through truthful narration, which is 'developed organically, according to legal connections in space and chronological relations in time'; but rather, as in Godard, 'moves from pure descriptions to falsifying narration from the point-of-view of the direct time-image' (TI 132–133). As Deleuze writes: 'Here is the essential point: how the new regime of the image (the direct time-image) works with pure crystalline optical and sound descriptions, and falsifying, purely "chronic" narration. Description stops presupposing a reality and narration stops referring to a form of the true at one and the same time . . .' (TI 134–135).

From the above statement we might establish a direct connection between the time-image and the concept of the forger. Post-war cinema resolves the problem of truth by purely technical means, that of no longer positing a 'true world' as the basis of its narration; at this point, as Deleuze writes, 'description becomes its own object and narration becomes temporal and falsifying at the same time' (TI 132). The representation of a truth in itself is revealed as a purely conventional means of establishing the relation between terms or elements of a given narration. In other words, it can be seen as the formal perspective of an elsewhere which is posited as being exterior to the plane occupied by appearances, and which sets all appearance *qua* appearance in movement around its position which remains virtual: '[T]he elsewhere may be close to a here, and the former of a present that is no longer' (TI 132). From this topographical perspective the 'truth' could be seen as a vectoral dimension which coordinates all appearances and causes them to unfold according to an order of time that is laid down in advance, coordinating every there with a corresponding here and every present with a formerly that is absent as a content of narration but reappears as either its term or its referent. However, in the absence of this elsewhere, cinema discovers a new means of producing description that, although it unfolds in the proximity of 'a world' or a 'subject,' does not find itself organized and coordinated by the terms that are located there, as if cinema has found the means of disconnecting itself from this 'true world' and becomes immanent to itself, a world of pure appearances.

Perhaps this corresponds to the exact meaning of Nietzsche's earlier discovery, since when the 'true world' is no longer posited as the point external to the plane occupied by appearances, as either their real term or their point of reference, then the notion of appearances themselves no longer bears a secondary and derogatory value of them as 'unreal' or 'false.' Consequently, at the very same moment that cinema is disconnected from 'the true world,' the notion of the false itself is 'disarticulated' from its moral-juridical sense.

Deleuze addresses this relationship between these two events in the following manner:

> The formation of the crystal, the force of time and the power of the false are strictly complementary, and constantly imply each other as the new co-ordinates of the image . . . Narration is constantly being completely

> modified, in each of its episodes, not according to subjective variations, but as a consequence of disconnected places and de-chronologised moments. (TI 133)

We might assume from this description that, initially, a certain 'dizziness' results from the loss of the 'true world' as the anchor and referent for 'the world of pure appearances,' the shattering of the cardinal points of space and time upon which the elements and terms of classical narration were coordinated and ordered, and finally the collapse of the sensory-motor schema which oriented a description of the world that unfolded in the proximity of the subject – in short, all the traits or characteristic attributes that Deleuze finds operating in the new type of narration-description of post-war cinema with its 'irrational cuts,' 'hallucinatory perceptions,' 'false movements' and 'crystal-images.'[1]

Would this not constitute a vivid illustration of the statement, 'time out of joint,' which corresponds to the adventure and crisis of contemporary philosophy? '[I]n becoming, the earth has lost all center, not only in itself, but in that it no longer has a center around which to turn' (TI 142). More specifically, we might refer to what Deleuze calls the 'spontaneous Nietzscheanism in Welles,' which is nothing less than the radical change to which the very notion of center is subjected: 'Welles, through his conception of bodies, forces and movement, has constructed a body which has lost all motor center or configuration – the earth' (TI 142). Yet, as Deleuze cautions more than once – 'Pay attention! This is cinema!' In other words, it would be a mistake to conclude that cinema has solved the crisis of representation, since it has only solved the crisis of 'movement-image' in cinema with the invention of a new means of narration, new characters and new technical procedures for producing images and story. Moreover, each solution that a given director achieves is partial and must be taken up again by other directors, or even by the same director in later productions (as in the case of Resnais, or even Welles), because the problem of representation is never settled 'once and for all' (which already characterizes a certain 'action-image' which proceeds from the judgement of the 'past and its "it was" '), but rather each solution is given immanently and leads only as far as the next move.

At the same time as cinema discovers the new narrative possibilities that belong to what Deleuze calls 'crystalline description,' it also finds in the characters of the 'man who lies' and 'the forger' its own double; that of the artificer, whose account is therefore not simply a variation or even betrayal of the constant and immutable version of the 'real' implied by the presence of the truthful man, but rather the 'nth degree' of a power of fabulation which must be at the origin of every possible story. Deleuze's statement regarding Robbe-Grillet's *The Man Who Lies* can, thus, be accepted as a general description of the significance of this character for cinema itself: 'this is not a localized liar, but an unlocalizable and chronic forger in paradoxical spaces'; and it is only on the basis of this strong identification that Deleuze's statement that 'the forger becomes the character of the cinema' (TI 132) can be properly understood. What are directors, after all, but the forgers of characters who, in turn, are the forgers of stories (excuses, accounts, alibis, treason)? In this regard, we might think of the recent film *The Usual Suspects* (Bryan Singer, 1995) which has for a central character the nefarious Kaiser Sozja, who is completely forged from the various scraps and posters on the wall of the interrogation room where the film's central plot is spun. Consequently, the descriptions that Deleuze offers of the narration specific to the forger, or the metamorphosis of specific characters into a chain of forgers, or rather 'the perspective of a series of powers always referring to each other and passing into each other,' can be taken as immanent to the movement of narration that cinema discovers as its own 'story-telling function' (TI 133).

As Deleuze writes, 'perspectives and projections – these are neither true nor false' (TI 144). Therefore, the false can no longer be understood simply as a 'modification' of a truth that is limited to subjective variation or 'point-of-view.' Returning to the history of the crisis of truth which passes between Leibniz and Borges, post-war cinema can also be situated within this same problematic, which it has resolved to some degree by discovery of an 'irreducible multiplicity' as the condition of each character, each perspective, or 'point-of-view.' If time is described as the force which enters to throw truth into crisis, each stage or passage then implies a point where a 'character' of truth failed to resolve this crisis either in terms of perception or in terms of action (decisive will); but in each case, this impasse is revealed from the perspective of another, more powerful character who can project its own version across the state of things and affairs. The force of time is in each case equal to the power of a narrative that binds truth to the identification with a certain perspective and gives this perspective the positive expression of a character. It is for this reason that the forger implies multiple worlds (perspectives), even though these perspectives cannot be understood as simple variations of the same world, organized and coordinated around a common center. Why? As Deleuze responds to this question, it is because 'the forger exists only in a series of forgers who are his metamorphoses, because the power itself only exists in a series of powers which are its exponents' (TI 145). The answer to this question simply corresponds to the situation of the concept of truth already outlined, since if man will always already have discovered the truth to be lying from a certain 'point-of-view,' then every truthful narration must in turn be discovered to be falsifying from another perspective which, in turn, is capable of being betrayed by a third and a fourth perspective. Yet, the classical representation of a truth that is 'in itself' cannot exist in a world where everyone must be discovered to be lying from a certain perspective; in short, its concept suffers a fatal contradiction and finally becomes useless. The truthful man invokes a true world, but the true world in turn implies the truthful man. 'In itself, it is an inaccessible and useless world … Thus it is not hidden by appearances; it is, on the contrary, that which hides appearances and provides them with an alibi' (TI 146). Again, we come back to the situation when the truthful narration ultimately fails to discern the relationships between the real and the imaginary, or to resolve undecidable alternatives and inexplicable differences between true and false perspectives; in a world already full of lies and treason, falsifying narration may be the only mode that is adequate to time.

In order to illustrate this last statement, I would like to show how the collapse of truthful narration and the positive emergence of the powers of the false are vividly dramatized in the Alain Resnais production of Marguerite Duras's *Hiroshima Mon Amour* ([1960]1963). To begin, it is important to see Duras's story as a certain 'war-text' that is launched against a certain type of truthful narration: 'to have done with the description of horror by horror' (H 9). This attack can be discerned on three distinct levels. On the first level, Hiroshima has been chosen as an exemplary sign of a past that has been reduced to a banality – it is a monument of emptiness. Thus, it is not a special or rarefied sign, but rather indicates a certain class of signs: the classification of the signs 'Hiroshima' and 'Auschwitz' as signs of history which designate their characteristic function of globalized or epochal representation. It is this global character that underlines the species of 'recollection-images' that appear in conjunction with these signs, as if these images were themselves the memory associations of a certain 'age of the earth' (Resnais) or a vast 'world-brain' (Deleuze). Banality expresses the kind of repetition which occurs when something is repeated a thousand times a day all over the world in which what is repeated bears both a minimum of difference and a maximum of amplitude. Therefore, banal repetition, or the 'description of horror by horror,' sees nothing since it represents a kind of representation that is too general, vague and amorphous. From the technical perspective of 'story,' Duras strategically chooses the place of Hiroshima as a means of reviving the most exhausted and fatigued of plots or the most conventional and artificial repetitions of a certain tale of love and traumatic memory. *Hiroshima Mon Amour* is, after everything has been said, simply a 'love-story.' It is important to see, however, that Duras inserts another banal repetition on the level of plot ('the one-night affair'), but the fact that this affair takes place at Hiroshima implicates one level of banality in another, producing variations within each order of repetition, and causing an entirely different series to unfold around the name of Hiroshima.

On the second level, the place of Hiroshima can be characterized as a 'monument of emptiness' (as Duras describes it in the prologue to the script) in the sense that its place-name designates the purely conventional and artificial forms of historical representation that have come to determine it as a sign. Here we might even discern a resemblance between the representation of the past that characterizes Hiroshima in Duras's description and in Nietzsche's 'monumental form,' except that there is also the presence of a negative function of monumentalizing that is specific to the 'age of Auschwitz and Hiroshima,' and which Nietzsche himself could not have foreseen. In the beginning of the film, Resnais utilizes the documentary footage and still-shots of the horrors of Hiroshima within the convention of the 'flashback' (as if from the psychological viewpoint of personal memory) to underscore the impasse of this artificial construction as well as its global character as a perspective or point-of-view which belongs to world-memory. Thus, the opening dialogue that takes place between the French actress and the Japanese man presents us with the collapse of a certain kind of truthful narration in the series of opposing statements made by each character – specifically, the failure of the 'recollection-image' to adequately present 'what happened' at Hiroshima.

> HE: You saw nothing in Hiroshima. *Nothing.*
> ...
> SHE: I saw everything. *Everything.*
> ...
> SHE: Listen ... I know. *I know everything.*
> ...
> HE: No. *You know nothing.*

Within this series of declarative statements that threaten to annihilate one another, which are spoken over the series of 'recollection-images' (the documentary footage, some of it fictionalized, of days that followed the atomic explosion, the archival records contained at the museum at Hiroshima), we are directly confronted with a situation of inexplicable differences concerning imaginary and real (She: 'I didn't make anything up'; He: 'You made everything up'), and non-decidable alternatives between true and false pasts (She: 'I saw everything'; He: 'You saw nothing'). Consequently, the character of Riva, the French actress, can be understood as an avatar of forger: she has 'forged' a direct relationship to Hiroshima (for example, by occupying the position of an eye-witness), but only through the most indirect of means, a fact which is made all the more scandalous in view of the way that she has made her presence to Hiroshima, in a certain sense, absolute. Could we initially ascribe her motivations to the role of an actress who has come to make an 'enlightening film' (Duras) on peace at Hiroshima? After all, do not all actors lie? This would be one possible interpretation, of course, if we were not also immediately presented with the traces of a more profound causality that motivates her desire to forge a direct experience with 'what happened' at Hiroshima.

The statements of the Japanese man initially function to negate her attempts of appropriating the 'past of Hiroshima' for her own line of flight (i.e. as a means of escaping her own past at Nevers) and serve to foreground this dilemma by opening her character to a certain suspicion of impure motives behind her attachment of personal memory to the name of Hiroshima. In a certain sense, they function to place her character on trial, in the minds of the spectator, as an incredible witness whose testimony must be discovered as falsifying. Yet, are we to infer from the negative judgements of the Japanese the presence of the 'truthful man,' thereby ascribing to his perspective the truth of 'what happened' at Hiroshima? Not necessarily, since such an ascription would be prejudicial and even moralistic in two senses. First, it would be a prejudice to confer a privileged 'point-of-view' and true knowledge of the past to his character simply by the fact of his national identity (an identity, moreover, which the spectator has no knowledge of in the first scene, and which, thus, could only be assigned retroactively). This kind of inference represents a symbolic, or even an allegorical, projection of a species of the past that is both singular and non-presentable, being the equivalent of a 'true world' that becomes inaccessible since any possible relationship that approaches it through the present has been singularized and belongs to the individual notion that expresses it as one of its attributes (for example, 'my past,' or the organic unity of a past that belongs to a particular 'people'). In the second sense, the Japanese offers no positive representation of the past that would correct her 'inauthentic,' and possibly deceitful, private appropriation; nevertheless, his negative and 'unbearably impersonal' (Duras) statements serve to deny the access of all appearances to the true perspective of 'what happened' at Hiroshima. In other words, through the purely formal judgements made by the Japanese, the truth of 'what happened' at Hiroshima is projected elsewhere than on the plane occupied by appearances, or recollection-images, as being a past that is in itself inaccessible and unknowable in the present. Resnais uses the formal and negative to introduce a crisis in the representation of the past by means of the 'recollection-image,' since her statements are accompanied in a contrapuntal manner by the images from documentaries and archival footage which are immediately negated by his statement 'You see nothing.' Consequently, this general crisis or dilemma of representation is shared by the spectator who also sees and knows nothing, even in the very act seeing the series of images that unfold against the characters' dialogue, or knowing what these images signify by referring them to the artificial conventions of the recollection-image deployed by the 'made-to-order documentary' (Duras) or historico-dramatic film.

At this point, we must turn to a general question concerning the recollection-image itself. How does this mode of representing the past participate in the crisis of truthful narration discussed above? In his discussion of the problem of the 'recollection-image' in *Cinema 2*, Deleuze regards Resnais as the purest disciple of Welles; it is Resnais who resolves the problem of the 'recollection-image' which was only given as a certain direction in Welles. Thus, Deleuze recounts the different stages of Resnais's solution where each film is grasped only from the function of providing more data to resolve the mechanism of the 'time-image,' which ends in the solution of finally doing away with the recollection-image altogether and the discovery of new techniques for presenting the pure recollection of the past. However, as Deleuze writes concerning the abandonment of the recollection-image, 'this inadequacy of the flashback does not stop his whole work being based on the co-existence of sheets of past, the present no longer even intervening as center of evocation' (TI 122). But we must ask why the 'recollection-image' ('the flashback' in cinematic technique) emerges as the fundamental problem in the discussion of Resnais and Welles? First, because the recollection-image establishes a false relationship between present and past, since it gives the past as representation. Accordingly, the image of what is past appears as an optical effect of the recollection-image, rather than signifying the event of memory that is expressed in the form of the recollection-image which cannot be said to resemble the past in any way (any more than the event designated by the statement 'I remember' can be adequately represented by a particular object of recollection). Here, Deleuze takes up the Bergsonian distinction to argue that the past can never resemble the recollection-image, but withdraws or diverges from its representation as its profound cause. Secondly, the recollection-image is inadequate because Deleuze himself comes to the striking conclusion 'that memory is no longer the faculty of having recollections'; but rather,

> it is the membrane which in the most varied ways (continuity, but also discontinuity and envelopment, etc.) makes the sheets of the past and the layers of reality correspond, the first emanating from an inside which is always already there, the second arriving from an outside which is always to come, the two gnawing at the present which is now only the point of their encounter. (TI 207)

If the past cannot be the object of representation, because it functions as its profound cause, then any attempt to construct a series of recollection-images in order to gain access to 'what happened' at Hiroshima, in short to 'Remember Hiroshima,' necessarily leads to an impasse – as Duras writes, 'Nothing is truly given at Hiroshima' (H 9) – and actually projects a false image or a sterile double of the past that is evacuated of all of its force (that is, the duration that connects it to the living body of the present), producing instead its corpse, or an empty and dead zone in time.

On the third level, the artificial and conventional sense of the recollection-image and of Hiroshima itself as a site of 'banal repetition' is further reinforced by the insertion of the documentary within the film and the appearance of Riva's character in the uniform of a nurse, thus providing us with a certain air of fantasy, that of the role (or mask) in the world-historical drama that Hiroshima has become for the rest of the world. In the synopsis of the script, Duras suggests that it is precisely an aspect of male fantasy, that of Riva's appearance in the white uniform, 'the official uniform of official virtue,' that initially attracts the Japanese. In this sense, it may be more or less accurate to compare the type of perception that appears in the recollection-image with the dream vision, since both dream and recollection-image lack a distinct 'point-of-view' in relation to which vision unfolds, emerging rather from that point where the subject who sees is already found to be elsewhere (for example, as what happens when someone wakes and recollects the perception-images that reappear from a vague and indeterminate region of the past). Duras herself refers to this sense of masquerade, as well as the air of fantasy that fills Hiroshima with a kind of dreamlike quality, as a 'baroque parade,' a festival procession of the world – dogs, cats, idlers, students protesting, children chanting – as if describing a canvas by Hieronymus Bosch. Thus, in her staging instructions, Duras places special emphasis on the fact that each time we are shown the 'peace square' at Hiroshima where the documentary is being filmed, we always witness the disassembling of the stage and the various props being removed. 'The cameramen are moving off (whenever we see them in the film they're moving off with equipment). The grandstands are being dismantled. The bunting is being removed' (H 11). This is clearly presented in Duras's synopsis that begins in Part Three of the script:

> It's four P.M. at Peace Square in Hiroshima. In the distance a group of film technicians is moving away carrying a camera, lights and reflectors. Japanese workers are dismantling the official grandstand that has been used in the last scene of the film.
>
> *An important note: we will always see the technicians in the distance and will never know what film they're shooting at Hiroshima. All we'll ever see is the scenery being taken down.* (H 39)

In the scene to which this last statement refers we come upon the French actress asleep under the bunting of a grandstand while the set of the film is being dismantled. The character of Riva is sleeping, which signals a duration that interrupts the point where she is acting. Thus, she is the actress asleep while she remains in her role as the character of the other film. As Deleuze writes, 'It is under these conditions of the time-image that the same transformation involves the cinema of fiction and the cinema of reality and blurs their differences' (TI 155). In the next scene, we are presented with a duplication of one of the earlier scenes of the documentary on International Peace, the students' protest march, this time with the stagehands taking the place of the actors who played the protesting students: 'Stagehands are carrying the posters in various languages – Japanese, German, French, etc. – NEVER ANOTHER HIROSHIMA' (H 39). There is a certain irony present in this moment since although we might believe in the intention of the film about Hiroshima as 'enlightening' (Duras), the form of this 'enlightenment' violates its message in the sense that it creates the possibility of Hiroshima happening again an infinite number of times. Thus, 'NEVER ANOTHER HIROSHIMA' in actuality means FOREVER ANOTHER HIROSHIMA.

Analogous to the role of Riva, the French actress who plays 'the eternal nurse of an eternal war' (H 10), Hiroshima itself is essentially 'played' rather than remembered; it is played again and again, and represents something like a broken chrono-tape of world-memory. In fact, we could argue that the past of Hiroshima is the past of 'pure representation,' the past of its montage, the moment just after it has been placed on film; the moment it ends, when it is disassembled and then assembled again, as Duras states, 'for all eternity.' Hiroshima is a moment eternally repeated. 'It will begin all over again. Two hundred thousand dead. Eighty thousand wounded. In nine seconds. These figures are official. It will begin all over again' (H 24). Thus, memory itself is reduced to its banal statistics, information, figures, images, duration. The event of Hiroshima would last nine seconds, or even an infinite number of nine-second loops. As a result, we might define it as a nine-second interval that is repeated eternally. Everything that happens, has happened and will happen at Hiroshima occurs as if in a past that has never been present, or rather, has been present countless times. Both alternatives amount to the same structure of time: pure past, or pure repetition. In other words, an eternal day of judgement: the origin of the world, the end of the world.

It is against this eternal return of the Same that Duras incorporates another kind of repetition that grasps Hiroshima from the point-of-view of Riva's past. Riva sees Hiroshima from the perspective of Nevers, almost in the sense that Hiroshima becomes the double of Nevers. It is from the perspective of her point-of-view that another Hiroshima unfolds; however, this double of the past functions in a different manner from the recollection-image since it forges a living connection with the present at Hiroshima (particularly from the perspective of the Japanese) and, moreover, bears a hypnotic trance-like vision, like the glowing eyes of the cat in the cellar of Nevers which Duras uses to figure the quality specific to Riva's perception.

More accurately, we might even say 'projected.' The past of Nevers is projected onto the present of Hiroshima, or even, it is through the lens of Nevers that Riva sees 'everything' at Hiroshima (which, in a sense, clarifies her statements at the beginning of the film). Resnais uses Riva's gaze as a hidden point of projection that rivals the 'objective' view-point of the camera and provides each scene with the 'feeling' of double exposure, as an effect of what Eisenstein called 'visual overtonal montage.'[2] This is first established in the montage sequence early in the film when Riva watches the Japanese man asleep, his arm outstretched behind him and his open hand visible, and suddenly falls into a trance over the confluence of this image with the hand of her dying German lover in the past of Nevers. ('While she is looking at it [the hand of the Japanese], there suddenly appears, in place of the Japanese, the body of a young man, lying in the same position, but in a posture of death, on the bank of the river, in full day-light' [H 29].) A small detail, but pivotal nonetheless – again, the word 'hypnotic' may even be a more accurate description – since it is from this point onward that the present at Hiroshima becomes haunted by the past at Nevers. Hence, the view-point of the camera falls under the spell cast by Riva's vision in such a manner that both perspectives are folded into contorted angles that confront each other violently, producing in the scenes a shock or disturbance in the coordination of the angle of projection with the characters' point-of-view. (I will return to further discuss the significance of this below.) It is by these 'two hands' that the past of Nevers and the present of Hiroshima are suddenly 'stitched together' in Riva's perception, in a manner that is strikingly similar to the function of what Lacan described as the *point de caption* ('the quilting point'). The apparent contradiction between Duras's description of 'hands' in the film-script and the film's presentation of only one hand is resolved when we understand that the hand of the Japanese is doubly exposed in Riva's vision. Moreover, this expresses the idea to the spectator that the Japanese himself is doubly exposed, being from this moment onward two men in one, his presence *at Hiroshima* completely possessed (or captured) by the presence of Riva's dead German lover *at Nevers*.

Finally, the mechanism of this over-tonal conflict that occurs in the visual layers of the image allows us to understand more clearly why the landscape of Hiroshima can be said to be 'haunted,' since it is illuminated from two angles and visibly 'glows' from the point where it is now seen from Nevers. It is from this 'glowing' that we might perceive the power of Riva's vision which bears two distinct senses: first, as we have already illustrated, a kind of hypnotic point of vision which illuminates (or irradiates) the present of Hiroshima; second, an eternity (a dead or empty form of time) which empties every perception of this present into a pure past that refuses to be, or rather, whose being itself is pure repetition (for example, the repetition of Nevers in Hiroshima). It is because of this second sense that we cannot say, any longer, that Nevers is a past in relation to the present of Hiroshima, any more than we can say that the place of Hiroshima can henceforth be distinguished from the place of Nevers.

On a more general level of interpretation, we might link these descriptions of the type of vision (or 'seeing') that appears from Riva's point-of-view to Deleuze's comments concerning the quality of perception and the 'new race of characters' that emerge in post-war cinema who belong to spaces that we no longer know how to describe: spaces that Deleuze calls 'any-space-whatever' (*espace quelconque*) and a mutant race of characters he describes as being reduced to pure functions of vision, as 'seers' (TI xi).[3] The novelty that Resnais introduced around the emergence of these new spatial and perceptual situations, according to Deleuze, is 'the disappearance of the center or fixed point.' Without a fixed and immutable point of reference to which it is related, 'the present begins to float, struck with uncertainty, dispersed in the character's comings and goings, or is immediately absorbed by the past' (TI 116). This can be immediately ascribed to the function of the present in Resnais's direction of *Hiroshima Mon Amour,* whether we are speaking here of the voice-over, the image, the use of flashback, or even the progression of scenes. As Deleuze writes, for Resnais

> [d]eath does not fix an actual present, so numerous are the dead who haunt the sheets of the past ('9 million dead haunt this landscape' [in reference to the landscape of Auschwitz], or '200,000 dead in 9 seconds' [in reference to Hiroshima]) ... In short, the confrontation of the sheets of the past takes place directly, each capable of being present in relation to the next: for the woman, Hiroshima will be the present of Nevers; for the man, Nevers will be the present of Hiroshima. (TI 117)

We might discern several things from the above statements. On the one hand, Resnais's characters do not occupy a present, or, rather, we can say that they exist outside the present defined chronologically, a fact that is supported by the nature of the affair, or 'one-night stand,' which temporarily interrupts chronological time, and installs in time a pause, or an 'in-between' of duration. This is further reinforced at the end of the film, when the characters return to the room in which, as Duras recounts, 'nothing happens.' 'Both are reduced to a terrifying, mutual impotence. The room, "The way of the world," remains around them, and they will disturb it no more' (H 13). This gives us a vivid illustration of the earlier statement that cinematic description stops presupposing a reality that precedes the filmed moment, because the world remains outside the duration they share together. It does not exist for them, or perhaps, it is because they – that is, who they were for the others – have become lost to the world that is populated by others. Therefore, who they are – or more accurately, who they are becoming – exists only within the duration that unfolds at Hiroshima, and only from the singular direction of each other's gaze. (In the last scene of the film, Duras writes: 'They look at each other without seeing each other. Forever' [H 83].) We must imagine that if they were to turn away and avert their glance, even for a second, they would be doubly lost: a first time to the world, a second time to each other.

On the other hand, we cannot infer from this that they are purely absent either, but rather that they occupy two points on the sheets of the past, pasts which are present to each other through the intersection of Hiroshima–Nevers. In this manner, for her, he becomes the present of Hiroshima; for him, she becomes the present of Nevers; as if all of the present has been encompassed by the present that exists at Hiroshima and all of the past by the past at Nevers, and the whole of time is stretched between these two points. This is why the Japanese must learn everything he can about her past in Nevers, since it is only because of 'what happened' at Nevers that she exists and becomes present to him at Hiroshima. Duras writes, 'she gives this Japanese – *at Hiroshima* – her most precious possession: herself as she now is, her *survival* after the death of her love *at Nevers*' (H 112). Thus, in response to Riva's question concerning why the Japanese wants to know about her past life at Nevers, Duras provides Resnais with three statements in the film's script, each of which designates Nevers as that point where time forks or bifurcates into different pasts. Rather than choosing just one, Resnais presents us with all three alternatives.

> HE: Because of Nevers. I can only begin to know you, and among the many thousand things in your life, I'm choosing Nevers.
> ...
> HE: It was there, I seem to have understood, that I almost ... lost you ... and that I risked never knowing you.
> ...
> HE: It was there, I seemed to have understood, that you must have begun to be what you are today. (H 51)

As we can see in these statements, it is not by accident then that Duras employs 'Hiroshima' as the catastrophic twin of 'Nevers,' since both signs, or place-names, designate the moment where time forks into incompatible worlds; therefore, the story that unfolds between Riva and the Japanese addresses in a striking way the same problem that was first taken up by Leibniz and then again by Borges (TI xii).

Recalling the earlier description of the time-image that concerns us in this example, 'forking-time' can be defined as the moment when time could have taken a different course. In *Difference and Repetition*, Deleuze first comments on the nature of forking time under the concept of the caesura (Hölderlin). This marks what later would appear as the succession of the 'movement-image' by the 'time-image,' in which the subordination of time to movement is overturned and time itself appears as an empty and pure form – i.e. time itself unfolds instead of things unfolding within it. This can be described as belonging to an order of time which no longer 'rhymes,' because it is distributed on both sides of an event that causes beginning and end, before and after, to no longer coincide. Thus, 'we may define the order of time as this purely formal distribution of the unequal in the function of the caesura . . . The caesura, along with the before and after that it ordains once and for all, constitutes the fracture in the I (the caesura is exactly the point at which the fracture appears)' (DR 89). Therefore, the caesura marks the appearance of an event which splits the whole of time into unequal parts, causing it to fall out of joint (or *cardo*), to appear different from itself, although this difference will continue to remain unequal, meaning that it will belong to an order of repetition rather than to representation. Since it causes the whole of time to be redistributed and to change sense, the symbol of its action must be understood to be adequate to time as a whole. 'Such a symbol adequate to the whole of time', Deleuze writes, 'may be expressed in many ways: to throw time out of joint, to cause the sun to explode, to throw oneself into a volcano, to kill God or the father' (DR 89).

Here, in the second of these possible symbols, 'to cause the sun to explode,' we can immediately recognize the classification of Hiroshima under the category of the caesura. In other words, we can see that Hiroshima functions as a pure order of time, that is, a time that 'orders' the series of before and after. There is the age of Hiroshima, which divides all of time into two parts: there is the world before Hiroshima; there is the world after Hiroshima; between them, there is a modification that remains unconscious and unknowable. 'What happened?' This is why the kind of repetition one finds there is characterized by 'banality,' a time in which nothing happens, without content. Time itself is no longer a form in which empirical events unfold, but rather a formlessness at the 'end of time,' a bare and empty repetition (repetition of the Same) which is both abstract and general and is thus equal to the whole of time. On the first level, therefore, we can see that it is by analogy to this pure formal repetition of an event that modifies and orders the series before and after that she finds at Hiroshima the conditions for the unfolding of Nevers. She repeats the empirical events of Nevers at Hiroshima, because from a formal perspective of time itself, the form of repetition and what is repeated are identical. Yet, there is also a repetition to be located on his side. She repeats Nevers at Hiroshima; he repeats Hiroshima at Nevers. What in the beginning was the 'absolutely subjective' becomes objectified in these two repetitions, making a mutual object of memory, what Deleuze calls a 'memory for two,' becoming finally 'ages of world memory.' Deleuze writes concerning Resnais's creation of 'ages of the world' as distinct cinematic characters:

> The idea of age tends to take on an autonomous political, historical, or archeological range ... There are constants: each age, each sheet, will be defined by a territory, lines of flight and blockages of these lines [signified, for example, by the statements 'I have seen everything,' 'You have seen nothing'] ... But the distribution varies from one age to another and from one character to another ... Throughout Resnais' work we plunge into a memory that overflows the conditions of psychology, memory for two, memory for several, world-memory, memory-ages of the world. (TI 118–119)

It is the passage of this purely subjective past that overflows the conditions of a limited psychological view-point, forming the condition of a shared memory, a memory for two, or a memory-age of world, that allowed us to take up the example of *Hiroshima Mon Amour*; specifically the intersection of Nevers/Hiroshima, the folding of Nevers upon Hiroshima as the superimposition of two sheets of the past that are stitched together through the present-point designated by each sign. What we are thus presented with is two incommensurable regions of the past, Hiroshima and Nevers, which are like two unconnected places in world-memory that undergo transformation by being placed in a direct relation to one another (a relation that is vividly represented by the final image: 'They look at each other without seeing each other. Forever.'). Here, memory is topologically understood which resolves, in a different sense from the solutions offered by Leibniz and then by Borges, the opening of the world to the existence of multiple pasts as well as different possible futures. Topological memory: the encounter of two different sheets of past that are designated by the signs Hiroshima–Nevers signals a transformation of the whole continuum of the past through its vital re-arrangement. Deleuze describes this transformation that takes place on two separate sheets of the past in terms of what mathematicians call a 'Baker transformation,' where in the smallest region of a square surface, two infinitely close points will be plied apart and separated, each allocated to one-half of a new square, 'with the result that the total surface is redistributed with each transformation' (TI 119).

A final problem that should concern us is the character of judgement that is attached to certain signs that might bear a global or world-character of memory. On the level of narration, the particular qualities that come to be attached to the names of Hiroshima and Nevers result from a system of judgement that differentiates them by assigning their referential function and distributing the actualization of each sign along a gradient that runs between the real and the fictional. In other words, 'Hiroshima' is a real name, evoking a real place, an historical event, a locus of world-memory; consequently, the point-of-view here is the most impersonal spectator – the world itself, the 'age of Hiroshima.' At first, it is from this perspective simulating a general subject of world-memory or an objective correlate of the real that Nevers might appear as a pure fabulation and an imaginary sign whose relation to the sign of Hiroshima is a form of improper signification, a construction of Riva's madness (*delire*); it either evokes a singular repetition of events, or designates the locus of another world that is encrypted within the world of 'Hiroshima.' Thus, it bears the topological attribute of a subjective region of the world that is singularized and unfolds within the interiors of one perspective; consequently, it is opposed to the 'objective' sign of the Hiroshima that unfolds within the interiors of a 'world' populated by others.

As we have discussed above, the camera occupies and mimics this 'objective' view-point in as much as it 'transcends' the purely subjective view-point and folds the two surfaces of vision into the movement-image (the sequence of shots): thus, the camera sometimes sees from the character's perspective through a series of highly stylized and artificial mechanisms that create the feeling of the purely subjective vision (soft memories, fuzzy and oblique angles, moving and contorted shots); at the same time, the camera 'sees' the character from the exterior and signals this 'objective' surface through an equally artificial means (clear and distinct resolution of the scene, high or direct angles which could not be occupied by the character such as the scene where she is walking along the river of Nevers). Then, a second perspective (or 'point-of-view') is introduced by the mechanism of the film within the film, of the documentary on peace within the film of their story, which reinforces the doubling that Hiroshima undergoes by being seen from the perspective of Nevers, or as the perspective of Nevers is 'projected' onto Hiroshima. In this manner, Resnais and Duras resolve this problem of equally falsifying perspective by making the camera itself appear within the frame of the film, as well as the apparatus of props, set constructions and, most importantly, the technicians and workers who are always shown carrying equipment in and out of the frame.

Otherwise, why would Duras place so much importance on the visibility of the machinery, of the identity of the 'technicians' and the 'Japanese workers,' of the system of exchange that motivates the production of modern film as an industrial art, if not to reveal the irony of the money system that conditions the production of what is essentially a fiction set at Hiroshima? The irony of an entire international economy (Franco-Japanese) funded to tell a personal story signals, perhaps, a more profound narrative of 'world-peace.' As Duras writes, 'the personal story always dominates the necessarily demonstrative Hiroshima story' (H 39).

> If this premise were not adhered to, this would be just one more made-to-order picture, of no more interest than any fictionalized documentary. If it is adhered to, we'll end up with a sort of false documentary that will probe the lesson of Hiroshima more deeply than any made-to-order documentary. (H 10)

Following this premise, the mechanism of the 'film within the film' is much more complex than a simple *mise-en-abîme* since the entire medium of the film itself becomes an aspect of the problem of memory and point-of-view. In other words, the film apparatus or camera itself is invested with a point-of-view that is sometimes confused between subjective (personal) and objective (real), revealing the 'analogy' between subjective personal memory and objective collective memory that the apparatus of film enacts. Because the apparatus of the camera is what first exteriorizes and distinguishes the cinematic image from simple mental image by placing the memory-image in relationship with external objectified space and providing it with an identifiable form (or genre), the indiscernibility of the actual point of projection results in an irresolvable confusion around which film is actually being shot at Hiroshima (particularly since Riva's 'point-of-view' occupies the same place as the production of the documentary on Hiroshima and uses the same equipment). Finally, it is this sense of confusion that illustrates the capture of Hiroshima by Nevers, that is, of the necessarily demonstrative documentary by the narrative plot of Riva's story. Does this mean that the 'personal' is simply laid over the 'desert' city of Hiroshima, the subjective captivates the objective, distorts or perverts its true reality? No. Rather, her past is projected onto the past of Hiroshima, causing it to undergo a metamorphosis, ultimately falsifying perhaps. Yet, all this reveals is that the locus of projection that constitutes the so-called 'true reality' is itself a supreme fiction, a convention that is made in order to avoid or 'to turn away' from the subjective condition of mutual past moments all of which converge around an artificially constructed present.

Once again this touches on the function of a species of 'banal repetition' that often characterizes the moral intention of the documentary. We might also invoke the images of concentration camps, the filmed sequences showing the piling of bodies in open trenches, in order to signal this dilemma as integral to the crisis of memory that concerns us here. What is the logic of their representation? How does the infinite 'representation' of Hiroshima – the 'description of horror by horror' – prevent the event from repeating itself, from happening again? That is, how does the content of this representation (information of 'what happened,' whether this 'information' arrives by purely visual or discursive means), prevent the future actualization of the event that such information cannot dispel or explain in a preventative manner? This is a central question that touches the kind of representation that has become naturalized by its moral purposiveness and supposedly prohibitive function, a question which we cannot take up here at length, but which might cause us to interrogate the physio-psychological presuppositions concerning its effect on the subject who becomes, in a very definite sense, its addressee. We might therefore expose the logic of this kind of representation to its inevitable contradiction; although it intends to prevent the event that it represents from being actualized, *it must nonetheless assert the 'nullity' (the horror) of this event by reducing it to information that can be endlessly repeated without touching the place where the past actually resides.* As Deleuze writes:

> All the documents could be shown, all the testimonies could be heard, but in vain: what makes information all-powerful ... is its very nullity, its radical ineffectiveness. Information plays on this ineffectiveness in order to establish its power, its very power to be ineffective, thereby [becoming] all the more dangerous. (TI 269)

We might understand the 'ineffectiveness' of this form of representation in simple psychoanalytic terms, in the sense that what is repeated is not remembered: Hiroshima is impossible to remember, which would entail that it also must be 'forgotten,' so that it must be repeated endlessly. What we have here is an abstract repetition of a 'past' without the possibility of memory, a past that does not pass into the past. In fact, what is repeated is the unconscious of the representation itself: that is, the powerlessness of the spectator to be involved, the distance and the impersonality of the type of recollection involved in the alibi, '[Y]ou know nothing, you have seen nothing.' As Duras suggests in the 'synopsis,' the infinite and impersonal representation of Hiroshima, the species of moral prohibition that produces a 'description of horror by horror,' may in fact represent a will to forget, to distance oneself from 'what happened' at Hiroshima. In order to follow Duras's own solution to this problem, I am emphasizing the problematic nature of this type of representation which is the dominant approach taken up in the post-war period and which Resnais himself utilizes in a contrapuntal montage at the beginning of the film. Yet, one might also understand the profound intention of this type of representation that Duras calls tautological representation, the 'description of horror by horror,' in a different sense. What if we were to understand its objective as installing itself completely 'on the sheet of the past,' to occupy precisely that moment 'when time could have taken a different course,' even if it only ends up memorializing this moment with an image of eternity? Perhaps the failure of this type of representation occurs precisely from its pedagogical and prohibitive function which it projects upon 'future actors' even though the image of the future it provides is vague and indeterminate, in fact, is only the negative or inverse side of the past it confronts passively. This passivity is both the source of its 'made-to-order' representations of the past as well as its 'ineffectiveness' concerning the future.

If we accept that the endless representation of Hiroshima may itself constitute a fundamental form of forgetting, why then is it that the powers of 'fiction' or 'imagination' are prohibited from the site of Hiroshima? That the type of memory that Duras allows to 'break in' to the zone of Hiroshima, to attach a personal perspective and point-of-view to the work of memory that takes place through her fable, and the consequent moral prohibitions this type of 'falsifying representation' of Hiroshima involves, only point to the moral-juridical quality of this other type of representation? It is odd, therefore, that the attachment of a 'personal perspective' would be condemned as a moral concupiscence, as deceit, betrayal or as a will-to-forget. The word 'sacrilegious' is used by Duras in the synopsis to evoke the aura of judgement that surrounds the film's story at Hiroshima. Why this word? 'Sacrilegious' denotes a transgression and offense of a sacred site whose ritual function involves both memory and repetition. For example, it is sacrilegious to lie with a corpse, to touch the dead, to profane a site of burial, a site consecrated in the memory of community and reserved as 'outside the boundaries' of certain forms of interest and sexual desire. There is an irony implicit in Duras's use of sexuality to open the question of the erotic relationship between memory: the desire to keep Hiroshima 'pure' and 'untouched' is itself presented in contrast to her desire to 'violate' Hiroshima in the most personal way. 'Everywhere but at Hiroshima guile is accepted convention. At Hiroshima it cannot exist, or else it will be denounced' (H 10). By setting up this extreme opposition, Duras highlights the moral-prohibitive determination of the kind of memory that Hiroshima represents: it is forbidden to touch the dead. It is sacrilegious to incorporate love with the crypt, to make love to the dead (necrophilia), to love the dead. Instead, Duras asks, is this not the ultimate sacrilege against 'Life'? Is not Hiroshima itself sacrilegious? In the opening scenes, is it offensive that they should be making love at Hiroshima, rather than being offensive that Hiroshima must always signify for us a place of death, a topical representation of horror? 'This is one of the principal goals of the film: to have done with the description of horror by horror, ... but to make this horror rise from its ashes by incorporating it in a love that will necessarily be special ...' (H 9). We might hear in Duras's phrase an echo of Artaud's famous dictum: 'To have Done Finally with the Judgement of God.'

Concerning Resnais's own relationship with 'the age of Auschwitz and Hiroshima,' Deleuze writes the following:

> René Prédal has shown the extent to which Auschwitz and Hiroshima retained the horizon of Resnais' work, how close the hero in all of Resnais is to the 'Lazarean' hero that Cayrol made the soul of the new novel, in a fundamental relation to the extermination camps. The character in Resnais cinema is 'Lazarean' precisely because he returns from death, from the land of the dead [the characteristic trait of 'philosophical identity']; he has passed through death and is born from death, whose sensory motor disturbances he retains. Even if he was not personally in Auschwitz, even if he was not personally in Hiroshima ... he passed through a clinical death, he was born from an apparent death, he returns from the dead. (TI 208)

By passing through all these stages represented by the journey that is enacted from Riva's point-of-view, Hiroshima is thus transformed from the name of death to the proper name of a love that survives the horror of its own past. Thus, the story is that of a survivor, one who survives the end of the world and who must live after Hiroshima. In telling her story, she offers a way out of Hiroshima by filling the place of Hiroshima with a love that is 'wonderful,' as Duras writes, 'one that will be more credible than if it had occurred anywhere else in the world, in a place that death had not preserved' (H 9).

> Between two people as dissimilar geographically, philosophically, historically, economically, racially, etc. as it is possible to be, Hiroshima will be the common ground (perhaps the only one in the world?) where the universal factors of eroticism, love, and unhappiness will appear in implacable light. (H 10)

Does this last statement imply that the only successful 'working-through' of the past is through its eroticization and disguise in the kind of repetition deployed by transference? In a certain sense, yes. Deleuze argues that what the selective game of transference discovers is nothing less than the positive principle of a form of repetition (the death instinct) which gives the past 'an immanent meaning in which terror is closely mingled with the movement of selection and freedom,' becoming at one time 'the source of our illness and our health, of our loss and our salvation' (DR 19). Concerning this necessary presence of transference (i.e. the eroticization of memory) within any 'living relation' to the past, Deleuze writes that

> it is necessary to seek out the memory where it was, to install oneself in the past in order to accomplish a living connection between the knowledge and the resistance, the representation and the blockage. We are not, therefore, healed by a simple anamnesis, any more than we are made ill by amnesia. Here as elsewhere, becoming conscious counts for little. The more theatrical and dramatic operation by which healing takes place – or does not take place – has the name of transference. Now transference is still repetition: above all it is repetition. If repetition makes us ill, it also heals us; if it enchains and destroys us, it also frees us, terrifying in both cases by its 'demonic' power. All cure is the voyage to the bottom of repetition. (DR 18–19)

By situating the absolute character of the past on the level of transference, signaling the character of an event that causes the past to become past, we see no more than a little 'demonic' trait in the type of repetition she introduces. She 'possesses' Hiroshima (meaning both the place and the Japanese, singular and plural nominative), in such a way that all of Nevers possesses all of Hiroshima.

She 'obsesses' him; in the end, he has no will of his own, nothing but what she has given him – to live on, to survive after Hiroshima. ('Impossible, not to come,' he declares as he returns to her room in the hotel the next morning.) Thus, what begins as a simple interruption ends by becoming an entire duration. What is 'demonic' but the emergence of a transference that authenticates the roles they play? 'In transference, repetition does not so much serve to identify events, persons and passions as to authenticate the roles and select the masks' (DR 19).

Set against the role she plays for the documentary on international peace is the more profound role that she is assigned through the repetition of Nevers, a role that causes him to finally abandon any pretension to know himself except through the role of Hiroshima that this eternal game of repetition provides. And might we not perceive the entire drama of *Hiroshima Mon Amour* as the theater where these two types of repetition of the past confront one another and threaten to destroy one another? The logic of the documentary, the archive, 'the description of horror by horror,' operates on the level of a simple anamnesis. Although it provides us with the visual and discursive layers of a past event, the fact of which, that is, its *quid facti*, or 'it happened,' is given as the content of its representation, as the informative side of the image; however, in truth, such information heals nothing, gives us no knowledge of what happened, is both representation and blockage of a relation to the pure past. Here, I recall the statement by Duras which becomes the axiomatic principle of the kind of representation she invokes: 'In truth, nothing is given at Hiroshima.' The representation of the past that belongs to banal repetition maintains the image of a past that is in-itself and projects it elsewhere – that is, outside or transcendent to a plane of immanence where the living dwell. Rather than constituting a 'living connection' with the past, its representation is always already a blocking and annihilation of such a connection, a 'dead-and-empty' connection which places a barrier or frontier between the living present and the dead past, a death zone that can never be crossed, understood or most importantly 'lived through,' gotten to the end of, which is why it launches an infinite repetition that becomes an age, a world.

If the objective of a 'world-peace' can only be achieved by a 'settling of accounts' with the past, or by an act of atonement for a past action, then perhaps we must recognize the impasse of the recollection-image and the documentary, the description of 'horror by horror,' which simply functions as another judgement of a God – the creation of an infinite debt to a past that cannot be atoned for or lived through. Contrary to this, we might see in her 'story,' as well as in his, a certain 'living connection' that is established with the past: the desire to seek out the memory of Hiroshima where it was – at Nevers – and to establish a living connection that is signaled by the transference of the past of Nevers onto the past of Hiroshima. Perhaps it is by means of their mutual story of 'what happened' at Hiroshima, which becomes a shared memory, a memory for two, that Duras is suggesting another narrative of world-peace. In other words, Duras shows us the truth of memory's global character in the sense that subjective memory, in a certain way and from a visible perspective, or distinct 'point-of-view,' is also a world-memory. Hiroshima is only an extreme example that Duras uses to make her case. Could we not say, then, that the structure of world-memory evolves and undergoes vicissitudes (divergences, abnormal and false movements, accidents) in a manner that can have a topological analogy to the subjective structure of time? What are Hiroshima and Auschwitz if not fatal events that cause a temporal series to diverge or bifurcate?

Yet, we must be careful at this point not to reduce ontological time to its psychological tropes, but rather to show how each is 'implicated' in the other, 'co-implicated,' and how the latter is 'deployed' in the first. We might understand, therefore, that the memory of the Japanese man and the memory of the French woman cannot be limited to a psychological view-point, but overflow this, and the nuptial (Duras says 'marriage'): the memory they create around the past at Hiroshima causes the entire volume of the past to undergo a rearrangement. This is why Deleuze raises the possibility that in their each forgetting his or her own memory and making a memory together, memory itself was detached from their persons and was now becoming world-memory. As Duras writes, 'it was as if all of Nevers was in love with all of Hiroshima' (H 9). This is also why their personal identities undergo a transformation as well, as if through the transformation of nothing in common to the common memory of Hiroshima–Nevers, the Japanese are present to the French, the East to the West. 'For in fact, in each other's eyes, they are non-one.' But since these people are no one it raises the chance of seeing film as the story-telling function of a new society, of a 'people to come,' the world-survivors of the age of Hiroshima and Auschwitz. They are names of places, names which are not names.

SHE: Hir-o-shim-a. Hir-o-shim-a. That's your name.
HE: That's my name. Yes. Your name is Nevers. Nev-ers-in-France. (H 83)

10

ARTAUD'S PROBLEM AND OURS

BELIEF IN THE WORLD *AS IT IS*

In *Cinema 2: The Time-Image*, Deleuze takes up Sergei Eisenstein's earlier argument that what is directly realized in cinema, the movement-image, was only indirectly present in the other arts. 'Because the cinematographic image itself "makes" movement, because it makes what other arts were restricted to demanding (or to saying) . . .' (TI 157). The weakness of the shock (the montage-effect) such as it occurs in theater, according to Eisenstein, precisely describes the architectural parameters of theatrical space itself which limits the possibilities proper to montage. The visual image and the aural image cannot accede to new arrangements; the visual image is limited to the confines of the stage, and the aural image to the speech of actors, or to the noise of props. Moreover, theatrical construction is limited by bodies, highly artificial conventions that have historically determined the possibilities of perception, for example, the 'role' of the actor in relationship to the audience as well as to the action itself. The 'outside' is reduced to a small opening in theatrical space by means of a referent (the world, reality) and the action-image appears as an oblique (or indirect) angle of reflection 'on everyday happenings,' as Brecht said. As a consequence of its indirect relationship with the whole, the 'shock' effect becomes overly didactic, since its power is mediated by a command structure that is often identified with the expression of political will. We should recall Benjamin's argument concerning the strategic and political effect of 'shock' upon the audience in Brecht's epic theater, although in this case 'alienation' (or *Verfremdungseffekt*) becomes the dominant affect of theatrical montage. Here, 'the truly important thing is to discover the conditions of life. (One might say just as well: to alienate [*verfremden*] them.) This discovery (alienation) of conditions takes place through the interruption of happenings.'[1]

A fundamental principle that one can find at work in both Brecht's epic theater and in Artaud's 'theater of cruelty' is therefore the destruction (or 'fissuring') of theatrical space itself (or at least its classical automatons), where the effect of 'alienation' entails the 'suppression of all protective barriers' and strikes against the mental automatons of artificial and exterior mimicry 'that cast the mind [not only of the spectators, but also the actors and creators as well] into an attitude distinct from force but addicted to exaltation.'[2] The 'goal' would be a spectacle acting as a force on rather than as a reflection of external happenings; for Artaud, as for Brecht, this would position the spectator in the center with the spectacle surrounding, the distance from the spectacle no longer abstracted from the totality of the sensory milieu. Yet, as in Brecht's 'gestic' theater, this cannot truly occur where thinking is presented (or rather, represented) by the demand for movement that is still virtual and not yet actualized in the image, since the image remains external to the movement, is still over there (representation), and has not yet touched the very cortex of the spectator. As Deleuze writes, 'it is only when movement becomes automatic that the artistic essence of the image is realized: producing a shock to thought, communicating vibrations to the cortex, touching the nervous and cerebral system directly' (TI 156). Here we find the dynamic principle of 'nooshock.' The cinematographic discovery of a higher faculty of 'emotion,' the figure of desire that is represented by the 'I feel' of the movement-image, is that which causes movement of the 'spiritual automaton' within the spectator; in other words, it causes the already constituted and partial subject to be surpassed in favor of another subject which is capable (or incapable as it were) of thinking, desiring or willing the Whole. This 'Whole,' Deleuze writes, is the 'subject' of modern cinema; '[t]he cinematographic image must have a shock effect on thought, and force thought to think itself in as much as it is thinking the Whole. This is the very definition of the sublime' (TI 158).[3]

But why does Deleuze compare here the effect of shock upon the nervous system of the spectator to the concept of the sublime? This is a very subtle comparison, but one which radically re-envisages the Kantian sublime from the modern perspective of the brain in its confrontation with chaos. Deleuze's interpretation of the Kantian sublime concerns the infamous violence experienced by the faculty of the imagination when confronted by a formless and/or deformed immense power and, as a result, is thrown back on itself as upon its own limit (or in an important phrase which echoes the original Kantian description, utilized prominently in *Anti-Oedipus* and elsewhere, '*se rabat sur*,' that is, 'falls back' or 'recoils upon itself'). This phrase represents the uniqueness of Deleuze's intuition around the function of the imagination in the Kantian analysis, which he reconfigures by resolving the impasse of the imagination no longer in terms of a principle of representation (as Kant did) but in terms of the Bergsonian definition of the brain as a pure interval (or 'gap'), opening onto a 'virtual whole' that is actualized according to divergent lines which 'do not form a whole on their own account and do not resemble what they actualize,' since the 'Whole is never "given"' (B 104–105). This comparison returns in the closing chapter of *What is Philosophy?* where the original Kantian faculties are reconfigured under the three sources of representation: science, art and philosophy. 'In short, chaos has three daughters, depending on the plane that cuts through it – art, science, and philosophy – as forms of thought or creation ... The brain is the junction – not the unity – of the three planes' (WP 208).[4] In the *Critique of Judgment*, however, it is reason which appears in the role of power and the figure of formlessness is itself the direct presentation of failure of the imagination 'to unite the immensity of the sensible world into *a Whole*'

(K 51). The figure of formlessness or deformation is, in fact, the sensible manifestation (let us say 'embodiment') of the relationship between reason and imagination which is experienced as contradiction (or conflict), as dissension, as pain. Yet, it is only within this very conflict that a relationship first emerges, and it is only on the basis of this feeling of pain that pleasure first becomes possible. 'When imagination is confronted by its limit with something which goes beyond it in all respects it goes beyond its own limit itself, admittedly in a negative fashion, by representing to itself the inaccessibility of the rational Idea [of the Whole] and by making this very inaccessibility something which is present in sensible nature' (K 51).

For Kant, the feeling of the sublime opens a 'gap' *(écart)* in experience through which the idea of 'subject as Whole' is engendered (literally given birth) as 'something which is present in sensible nature.' The faculty of desire is given an object, even though this object is immediately inaccessible, and a destination, even though this destination is 'suprasensible,' since 'the suprasensible destination of the faculties appears as *that to which a moral being is predestined*' (K 52, original emphasis). Therefore, as Deleuze writes,

> in the sublime there is a sensory-motor unity of nature and human, which means that nature must be named the *non-indifferent*, since it is apparently Nature itself that issues the demand for unification of the Whole within the interiority of a subject and it is by reacting to this demand that we discover that which is fundamental to our destiny. (K 52, my emphasis)

Art in the West – at least from the baroque period onward – can be said to be founded upon this demand in as much as through it the faculty of desire gives birth to the presentation of a 'higher finality' which is symbolized by the unity of the art-work. This underscores the significance of the Baroque for Deleuze and the importance it bears for establishing the direction and the problem of artistic and political representation in the modern period. The effect of 'alienation' (*Verfremdungseffekt*) and the different conceptions of 'shock' that we have been analyzing can therefore be understood as figures of the 'discordant-accord' (Deleuze) between finite, *a-posteriori* imagination and a spontaneous, *a-priori* power that belongs to the idea of the Whole. Thus, the feeling of 'alienation,' the aesthetic principle of modern political representation, can itself be understood to reproduce a central tension that belongs to the sublime in as much as the feeling of suffering that it immediately engenders in an audience of spectators also gives birth to the suprasensible idea of itself as another nature, that of a spontaneous collective subject, or 'a people.' Hemmed in and confined by the limit of theatrical space, however, a limit which fuses with and partially institutes the concrete and historical limits of the imagination itself, such a 'supra-sensible idea' must first appear as a negative or critical force which breaks open the frames of classical representation and spills over to link together thought and action, causing the base-brain or 'spiritual automaton' of a mass to undergo a change of quality.[5]

Whether this force takes the form, as in Brecht, of an 'interruption' of sympathetic identification (estrangement) or, as in Artaud, of 'cruelty' and even 'absolute sadism,' it marks the ferocity of desire for a higher finality that belongs to the nature of modern political theater, and of certain experimental traditions of modern art in general. To inflict a symbolic violence in perception, language, opinion, character, mood; to destroy common sense and wage a war against all forms of cliché internal and external; to bathe the prose of the world in the syntax of dreams; to wash the image in the grain of light or to evacuate it in favor of a pure 'blankness' that lies underneath – these are the hallmarks of modern art. We might understand these as figures of the 'negative apprehension' of an idea of the Whole that the art-work bears within itself like a seed, which marks both the temporal nature of its duration and the manic desire for total achievement which characterizes every finite attempt to express this nature in one formal unity. Within the contemporaneousness of the present that defines the current stage of its achievement, however, the idea of this nature is expressed as an internal dehiscence or bears the aspect of 'danger' (Artaud) like the violent frenzy of a wounded animal. Consequently, in the sensible appearance of this ferocious and violent nature, we might also see a *mise-en-scène* of the sublime itself. First, the perfection of the work of art represents the overpowering nature of a demand for the 'subject as Whole' and reproduces this demand within the inter-cerebral interval between stimulus and response, between image and reaction, or, as Kant defined this interval in classical terms, between apprehension and comprehension (that is, between the presentation of the art-work and the comprehension of the spectator). Second, in as much as the Whole of this interval extends beyond its own powers to actualize within a complete circuit that would run between image and brain (what Deleuze calls a 'sensory-motor unity'), a certain figure of 'formlessness' appears which comes to symbolize this unity in a negative manner and also to characterize the appearance of the art-work generally.

It is this moment of 'failure' that also characterizes a certain cyclical movement (the 'cyclone,' or spiral) through which modern art 'recoils' from manifesto to cliché, then from a state of inertia (or fossilization) to its renewal in the next movement, the next manifesto, the next style, each promising to discover the means of restoring the vital connection between nature and human. *In other words, the cerebral interval becomes a deep 'gap' or 'void' that it cannot fill, an immense distance or abyss that it cannot cross, emerging instead as the crack or fissure that creases its body and constitutes an 'outside' which cannot be expressed in language or present in the image: 'deeper than any interiority, further than any exteriority' (employing a formula that Deleuze adapts from Foucault), the outside describes that mute and formless region that appears at the center of the modern work of art and becomes the principal cause of its 'deformation' and even appears as its defect, its symptom or its neurosis.* This characteristic quality of 'deformation' or 'formlessness,' however, cannot be understood simply as an aspect of the style of the modern art-work, but rather belongs to the 'total physiological sensation' (or 'I FEEL') that defines the experience of modern experimental art, in particular, and is caused by the failure to attain the 'action-image' it posited as its higher finality. That is to say, the sensation or 'feeling of formlessness' gives us an indirect representation of the Whole that, although it can propose an image of it in a negative manner, remains outside the powers of art to realize.

The event of this repeated failure whereby art comes to a limit and recoils upon itself can be understood to lie behind two principal tensions that can be found in the movement of art. First, the sense of 'recoil' can be expressed as the *schism* between the 'culture' of the artist as creator and a mass or popular cultural subject, underlying the tendency of modern art to withdraw and to enclose itself in an aristocratic social form. This 'schism' characterizes the relationship between the 'spiritual automaton' of modern art and the major-brain or mass subject which is mediated by the forms of conflict, opposition and even disgust; at the same time, it expresses the quantitative degree of its failure in the sense that its power (or '*nooshock*') is capable of affecting only the minor-brain of an elite or aristocratic class comprised mostly of artists themselves. The second sense of the 'recoil' of modern art can be figured as its *obsession* over the idea of self-achievement and of conceiving the *work* of art as a total movement that passes historically through uneven stages of development in order to reach an absolute expression (e.g. Mallarmé's 'Absolute Poem') or to restore it to an immanent relationship with the movement of life itself (e.g. Artaud's 'theater of cruelty'). The duration occupied by each art-form must be conceived from the perspective of this idea of this Whole in such a way that each successive 'failure' also represents the possibility of teleological renewal in its progress toward achieving a final 'goal.' Eisenstein's dialectical theory of the art-work that finds its penultimate expression in the emergence of modern cinema participates in this teleological image of the modern art-work.

As Kant wrote nearly two centuries earlier concerning a kind of 'knowing' (thinking, apprehending) that is specific to the experience of art, one which breaks with the conditions of a knowledge that is immediately connected to a mental image of 'action' (as in the cases of science and handicraft): 'Only that which a human, even if he knows it completely, may not therefore have the skill to accomplish belongs to art' (K 146). But how does the emergence of cinema change this state of affairs? Let us recall that, for Eisenstein, the movement-image promises 'the subject as Whole' (that is, to represent the synthesis of image and thought in a sensory-motor unity). How is this subject different from that of art? As an industrial art-form, the cinematographic subject of knowledge is distinct from that of the fine arts (or from the kind of knowing that belongs to art as Kant defined it above) in that it comprises, at least potentially, a synthesis of science, handicraft (skill) and art. Therefore, in its confrontation and struggle with chaos (i.e. 'formlessness'), cinema behaves like a science when it knows how to slow down and place limits on this chaos by providing it with a reference, the 'Open,' by which it makes the Whole appear indirectly as the 'object' of the movement-image; at the same time, cinema behaves like an art when it allies itself with the force of chaos in order to forge new visions and new sensations which it uses in its struggles against the pre-established clichés and ready-made linkages of image and thought (including those clichés, as we have seen above, that belong to the field of art itself). Under this second aspect, what formerly appeared as chaos here becomes a 'fourth dimension' which cinema discovers through its knowledge of the process of montage as 'the inexhaustible storehouse, as it were, of laws for the construction of form, the study and analysis of which have immense importance in the task of mastering the "mysteries" of the technique of form' (to cite again a passage from Eisenstein's 1935 speech). As a synthesis of these two aspects of knowledge, therefore, Eisenstein's theory of cinema appears both, like science or handicraft, as a set of 'functives' (or axioms) that comprise a machinic assemblage for the construction of cinematographic form and, like art, as a 'monument' of sensation, or 'compound of percepts and affects.' Deleuze defines this distinction in the following manner: 'Art takes a bit of chaos in a frame in order to form a composed chaos [or "chaosmos"] that becomes sensory, or from which it extracts a chaoid sensation as variety; but science takes a bit of chaos in a system of coordinates and forms a referenced chaos that becomes Nature, and from which it extracts an aleatory function and chaoid variables' (WP 206). Recalling the Kantian statement above, contrary to the other arts, cinema both posits or thinks the Whole and, at the same time, is capable of – or at least posits for itself – the knowledge and technical skill of realizing it as well.

If the 'realization of the Whole' becomes the highest task of classical cinema, this is because in a certain sense it is already completely given. 'The material universe, *the plane of immanence*, is [itself only] a machinic assemblage of movement-images,' as Deleuze writes earlier in *Cinema 1: The Movement-Image* (MI 59, original emphasis). A question only remains concerning whether this realization will be accomplished by the primacy of montage or by the technical perfection of the movement-image itself. By situating this achievement within the region of the sublime, Deleuze is also suggesting the emergence of a new subject which categorizes space-time: a purely cinematic subject, or I THINK, which is interposed between the brain and the world, or between the brain of a supra-intelligence and the 'Open' through which the Whole itself undergoes a dialectical 'conflagration' (TI 159ff.). However, because this subject necessarily bears the character of an absolute knowledge, we might discern here the portrait of what Deleuze calls a 'cinematographic Hegel' in Eisenstein's theory of cinema as the dialectical automaton in the service of social realism. If according to Hegel, 'Spirit [or mind] is alienated' and must pass through the stages of the dialectic in order to become reunited with its own form of expression, then for Eisenstein this passage is accomplished by the cinematographic technique of montage, which breaks open the historically 'alienated' forms of perception, language and character in order to reconnect thought to its primordial immediacy and immanence for the subject. As Deleuze writes, '[a] circuit which simultaneously includes the author, the film, and the viewer is here elaborated':

> The complete circuit thus runs from the sensory shock which raises us from the images to conscious thought, then the thinking in figures which takes us back to the images and gives us an affective shock again. Making the two co-exist, joining the highest degree of consciousness to the deepest level of

> unconsciousness: this is the dialectical automaton. The Whole is constantly open [the spiral], but so that it can internalize the sequence of images [within the subject], as well as becoming externalized in this sequence [as total object, or world]. The Whole forms a knowledge, in the Hegelian fashion, which brings together the image and the concept as two movements each of which goes towards the other. (TI 161)

It is only by technically achieving this dual movement between the most unconscious region of the image and the most abstract region of thought that cinema will construct a knowledge of the Whole as the condition of montage and will gradually become equal to the task of realizing the true promise of the dialectic which Hegel had earlier defined for philosophy as 'Spirit thinking itself as Subject.' It does this by gradually mastering the dialectical progression between image and concept, or, using Eisenstein's terminology, between 'pre-logical, sensual thinking' and the highest forms of symbolic logic, thus surpassing both forms and uniting instinct and reason in an image of thought that at the same time discovers at the 'deepest level of the unconscious' the conditions of action for the historical subject (thereby becoming 'action-thought,' or what Eisenstein refers to elsewhere as the 'habit logic of the future').[6] This constitutes the highest goal of the culture of montage, according to Eisenstein, which is to present within the vivid immediacy of the movement-image the unity of the 'Subject as Whole,' that is, to individuate the perceptions of the masses so that the consciousness of the spectator no longer appears isolated, but rather as the collective subject of his or her own reaction, or even as an objective force of nature itself. Nature appears on the side of the subject of cinema (becoming 'the non-indifferent'); cinema appears on the side of the masses (becoming spirit or 'I feel' of a people to come). This is why Deleuze refers to Eisenstein's theory as essentially monist. 'Action thought simultaneously posits the unity of nature and human, of the individual and the mass: cinema as *the art of the masses*' (TI 162, my emphasis).

Cinema, art of the masses! If this slogan sounds a bit hollow, like a modern advertising jingle, it is because something has happened in the interval that has made us extremely skeptical of all such beliefs concerning art. It is around the nature of belief that Deleuze's teleology of modern cinema diverges significantly from that of Eisenstein, and he must resort to Artaud and to Blanchot in order to situate the relationship between thought and cinema in its modern period, after the belief in a pure or revolutionary cinema has remained unrealized; or, much worse, after the discovery of cinema's potential to attach itself to the cortex and to touch the cerebral system directly has been perverted and 'has degenerated into state propaganda and manipulation, into a kind of fascism which brought together Hitler and Hollywood, Hollywood and Hitler' (TI 164).

> Hence the idea that cinema as art of the masses, could be the supremely revolutionary or democratic art, which makes the masses a true subject. But a great many factors were to compromise this belief: the rise of Hitler,

> which gave cinema as its object not the masses become subject, but the masses subjected; Stalinism, which replaced the unanimity of peoples with the tyrannical unity of the party; the break-up of the American people, who could no longer believe themselves to be the melting-pot of peoples past nor the seed of a people to come. (TI 216)

This does not come about because cinema fails to accomplish everything that Eisenstein dreamed it would, but rather it is that the dynamic principle upon which it was founded, the movement-image, succeeds in the worst manner.

The optimism with which Eisenstein originally held the muscular syntax of inner-speech and the forms of 'sensual, pre-logical thinking' as primary sources for montage and of a 'habit logic of the future' also harbored the possibility of fascism, manipulation and the infinite alienation of the masses. Thus, rather than breaking through to achieve a form of thinking that would give birth to the idea of 'a people' as a collective and international subject, instead it revealed a dead and mummified 'sensualism' and an archaic and familial unconscious as its wellspring. (Like both Artaud and Bataille before him, Deleuze rejects the Surrealist and Modernist definitions of the unconscious and the dream as sources of liberation.) The dream, as it turns out, was a false source of profundity; and the unconscious, rather than constituting a true depth and wellspring for the creation of forms, was a basement filled with junk. Even worse, when these are attached to an apparatus of mass projection they give birth to a world filled with mummies, ghouls and vampires. Thus, the ideological force that finds its privilege in the cinema of the modern period can be seen as the 'return of these archaic norms and laws of conduct' (the murderous impulses that belong to racism, genocide and nationalism) which are provided with newer and more effective eidectic combinations through the cinematographic inventions that surround the development of the movement-image in the first and second waves of cinema. The state finds in the dominant principle of classical cinema (the action-image) the very means of breaking into the 'storehouse of primitive or sensual thinking' and new techniques for establishing these patterns of habitual thought or normative laws toward the achievement of its own desire for finality (totality, absolutism, immanence). Hitler becomes the 'spiritual automaton' who gives birth to the German people in the Nazi period, 'the subject as Whole.'

Eisenstein himself had also perceived this danger in what he called 'psychological retrogression' where cinema becomes subordinated to the automaton of 'sensual, pre-logical thinking' which can suddenly become a 'dominant' even in the most complex of social constructions, since the margins between the higher phases of intellectual order and the primitive and baser instincts are extremely mobile, are volatile, and often undergo sudden shifts at each stage of development.

> This continual sliding from level to level, backwards and forwards, now to the higher forms of an intellectual order, now to the earlier forms of sensual thinking, occurs at ... each phase in development ... The margin between the types is mobile and it suffices a not even extraordinarily sharp

> affective impulse to cause an extremely, it may be, logically deliberative person suddenly to react in obedience to the never dormant inner armory of sensual thinking and the norms of behavior deriving thence. (FF 143)

The common example he gives for the above is that of a girl who tears the photo of her beloved into fragments 'in anger,' thus destroying her 'wicked betrayer' by destroying his image in an act of magical thinking (based on the early identification of image and object) (FF 143). In other words, development does not proceed in a straight line, on the level either of the individual or of the whole social construction: e.g. 'the regress of spiritual super-structures under the heel of national-socialism' (FF 145). However, rather than recoiling in fear and thereby avoiding further research into these early forms which comprise the basis of any possible action-image (or 'habit-logic'), Eisenstein sees in the cinematic apparatus the potential of a dialectical progression that maintains the pursuit of highly complex intellectual forms and processes and, at the same time, the 'analysis' of the early forms of sensual thinking.[7]

This represents Eisenstein's wager: to invent not merely a rhetorical cinema, but an analytical cinema, a cinematographic science of thinking. Cinema must achieve by means of technical montage and the contrapuntal method what Engels had earlier defined as 'the third stage' in the construction of thinking through which humanity must pass: neither the primitive and diffuse complex of sensual thinking of the first stage, nor the formal-logical stage which negates the former (perhaps even 'forecloses' it in the psychoanalytic sense), but rather the 'dynamic perception of phenomena' which dialectically absorbs the first two 'in photographic detail' (i.e. social realism). It is for this reason that Eisenstein's theory of cinema is founded upon a dynamic principle of conflict with these two other automatons. It must avoid becoming too sensual, on the one hand, and too formal and abstract, on the other, always seeking as the principle of its development a certain balance (in a Whiteheadian sense). Here, the total process achieves the figure of a dialectical circle or a 'spiral,' as Deleuze calls it, following a 'dual-unity' in which the highest form of art has as its correlate the deepest form of subconscious.

> The effectiveness of a work of art is built upon the fact that there takes place within it a dual process: an impetuous progressive rise along the lines of the highest explicit steps of consciousness and a simultaneous penetration by means of the structure of the form into the layers of profoundest sensual thinking. The polar separation of these two lines of flow creates that remarkable tension of unity of form and content characteristic of true art-works. Apart from this there are no true art-works. (FF 145)

Of course, we do not need to demonstrate that Eisenstein lost his wager for a cinema which maintained a certain balance that could insure both a higher form of satisfaction (intellectual complexity) and, at the same time, a higher form of 'feeling' (passionate sensibility), the achievement of which repairs the broken accord between conscious perception and thoughtful action. The unfolding of history and the development of the cinematographic art in the modern period give us ample evidence to forgo a demonstration, and I have already underlined the major points of this evidence above. Such a balance could only describe an ideal cinema, that is, one that grew from the seeds that were planted in the soil of another world and would require for its actualization an entirely different nature than that of the masses, that is, a wholly 'other' brain. These, moreover, would have to be prerequisites or initial conditions of the cinema that Eisenstein describes, rather than its 'products' or even its 'revolutionary effects.'

Concerning the existence of such an ideal cinema, Artaud probably said it best: 'The imbecile world of images caught as if by glue in millions of retinas will never perfect the image that has been made of it. The poetry which can emerge from it all is only a possible poetry, the poetry of what might be, and it is not the cinema we should expect' (cited in TI 165). The primary reasons Deleuze gives for this failure are quantitative mediocrity of products and fascist principles of production; these are generalized as the shortcomings of author and audience. Again, 'Hollywood and Hitler.' 'Popular cinema' and 'Nationalist cinema.' In the former, we find a figurative cinema based upon the automaton of vulgar sensualism (clichés of sex and violence); in the latter we find a cinema based upon the automaton of the state (clichés of history and action). Here again, in Eisenstein's defense, we should recall the earlier discussion of the 'fourth dimension' of intellectual cinema and the contrapuntal method in the approach of the sound film, since both were conceived as preventative measures to avoid precisely the above state of affairs from determining the future of the cinematographic form. First, by linking the montage process to an 'outside' which could not be determined by simple visual or aural images, Eisenstein hoped to avoid the situation where the 'focus' of the visual image would be trapped on the surface of already composed and defined bodies (whether of objects, persons, already divided sexes, or even peoples). Second, by means of the contrapuntal method, he hoped to liberate the sound-image from a situation where its 'sense' would be determined mono-linguistically, or bound too closely to the literary and dramatic conventions that might define a single national character or cultural imagination. These aspirations underlie a truly international cinematographic vision (an aspect often overlooked, even willfully ignored, in Deleuze's reading of Eisenstein), although it is a vision, perhaps even an 'inner-monologue,' that is often hidden or obscured in the official rhetoric of the speeches and lectures that had to pass under the gaze of the Soviet censors and, in general, had to be concealed from the race of impudent masters Eisenstein's films were to serve. In fact, Eisenstein came under direct criticism of the Stalinists several times, particularly around the improperly dramatic treatment of the action-image in the heroic portrayal of Alexander Nevsky, which was judged as being too 'Hamletian' in proportion and not an adequate vehicle for collective sentiment of the Soviet people.[8]

But then, this underscores a third reason – the most obvious one, perhaps – which even conditions the first two in the sense that the art of industrial cinema depends for its existence less on genius than on the interest of modern institutions and their systems of majority, either in the form of the state or of a culture industry, and this distinguishes it from the other arts (with the exception of architecture) and even predisposes it to assume an overtly ideological shape in its classical period or, in the modern period, frequently causes it to confront the limit of its internal presupposition, that is, money. 'The film is movement,' Deleuze writes, 'but the film within the film is money, is time':

> Modern cinema thus receives the principle which is its foundation [what causes it to exist in the first place]: endlessly relaunching exchange which is dissymetrical, unequal and without equivalence, giving image for money, giving time for images, converting time, the transparent side, and money, the opaque side, like a spinning top on its end. And film will be finished when there is no more money left ... (TI 78)

In the current period especially, not encountered by Eisenstein, Capital assumes the force of the Whole, as that power which is equal to the 'Being' of the Whole; at the same time, it apportions the limit to this representation precisely at that moment where the money runs out, which is also where the forms of desire (or interest) and imagination encounter their own internal limits as well. This final reason marks the 'no-exit' of modern industrial cinema which can become pure and disinterested only at a price, which can be tangibly measured and even calculated in advance as a condition of its production; however, the only place where it is really free (that is, from the pressures of these institutions) is that place, or those places, where it doesn't exist. A cinema of pure possibility, or 'of pure poetry,' as Artaud said, but one we shouldn't expect – not an art of the impossible, but merely an impossible art.

Deleuze argues that two dominant responses to loss of the idea of a just world in the West have been the creation of two spiritual ideals. The first is the revolutionary (or critical) ideal which responds to the loss of the true world by an active engagement of science, politics and art in the destruction of the previous world and the 'fabrication' of a new world that will replace it. This amounts to the belief in a principle of creation (or negativity) that would be able to intervene between human and nature in order to set right, rectify or even radically to transform this relation. The other ideal Deleuze calls 'catholic' which amounts to spiritualizing the human in the hope of a transformation (through an act of conversion or mysticism) into another nature. (Here, we might perceive an implicit kinship between Catholicism and Buddhism.) The former can be illustrated by Eisenstein's image of revolutionary cinema to intervene into the very brain of the human and thereby to transform its nature, which is the nature of its perception-consciousness system (or the spiritual automaton within us). Although Deleuze underlines a deficiency in Eisenstein's 'monism,' as well as in his tendency to express the conflict between these two spiritual automatons in terms of opposition, in actual fact, there is less difference between their theories of cinema than one might expect. Their 'goal' is identical: that is, a total provocation of the human brain. Where is the point of divergence to be located? On the first level, it can be located in simple chronology. Eisenstein conceived of the possibilities of cinematic art in its earliest stages, and his experience belongs to the first and second periods of the 'old cinema.' On the other hand, Deleuze defines his earliest experiences with cinema in the period that runs immediately before and after the Second World War. As already outlined above, his experience occupies a moment of transition not encountered by Eisenstein, when something happens that robs cinema of this total provocation (or 'nooshock') as the dynamic principle of the achievement of cinematographic art as an art of the masses, something which causes the belief in the revolutionary nature of cinema now to appear as an overly naïve and even fantastic premise, worthy of a museum filled with the lost aspirations of the golden age of art in the West.

On the second level, intimately bound up with the first, the point of divergence can be located in the 'image of thought' that defines as its goal the total provocation of the brain (i.e. the principle of 'nooshock'). Simply put, the difference is between thought identified as a power that would be placed in a circuit with the automatic image to effect a change in the Whole, and thought that appears deprived of this power *a priori* and, in fact, reveals a subject that is haunted by the automatic character of movement that animates it as well as by the source of images it is given to think. A qualitatively new monster emerges in the world at about the same time as it becomes a frequent character of modern cinema (particularly science fiction): an alien who latches on to the human face, smothering its victim without letting it die, and at the same time who lays eggs inside the victim's mouth. These eggs are the physical, optical and auditory clichés – the 'little organs' of the reproductive imagination – to which the spiritual automaton of modern ideology gives birth.

> Nothing but clichés, clichés everywhere ... They are the floating images which circulate in the external world, but which also penetrate each one of us and constitute our internal world so that everyone possesses only psychic clichés by which he thinks and feels, is thought and is felt, being himself a cliché among others in a world which surrounds him. Physical, optical, and auditory clichés and psychic clichés mutually feed on each other. In order for people to be able to bear themselves and the world, misery has to reach the inside of consciousness and the inside has to be like an outside ... How can one not believe in a powerful concerted organization, which has found a way to make clichés circulate, from outside to inside, from inside to outside. (MI 207–208)

Here we can discern the figure of a crisis that interrupts the achievement of the movement-image and which is already foregrounded in the above passage from the conclusion of *Cinema 1*. Instead of opening to the birth of thought, the achievement of the movement-image in cinema not only hastens its own death, but opens the subject to the moment when the possibility of thought itself can be 'stolen away' by force and this only deepens the subject's passivity before this possibility that appears like a 'powerful concerted organization' installed at the deepest point of its interiority. Ultimately, this crisis will lead to an absolute break in which modern cinema recoils from its desire for higher finality, understood in terms of the 'action-image,' and even renounces its power to give birth to 'the subject as whole,' understood in terms of the movement-image. As Deleuze writes, 'this is the first aspect of the new cinema' that follows, which is 'the break in the sensory-motor link (action-image), and more profoundly in the link between human and the world (great organic composition)' (TI 173).

The above reflections on the inner mechanism of the movement-image offer us the occasion to understand more clearly the direct relationship between modern cinema and Ideology. If we find an implicit analogy here between the crisis of the movement-image and the crisis of the imagination in the encounter with the sublime, it is because Deleuze uses this analogy to figure the relationship between the 'failure' of classical cinema and the 'deformation' that the power of reason suffers in the advent of the modern notion of Ideology. Consequently, there has never been the possibility of a non-ideological cinema and it is not simply by chance that modern critiques of ideology have found in the appearance of film one of the principal culprits in the reproduction of political, class and racial ideologies. However, many of these critiques pursue a false distinction, believing that the subject of ideology is qualitatively distinct from the movement-image and appears 'behind it' or 'speaks through it' like a homunculus (reinforcing a classical mind–body dualism), rather than forming the material basis of the image and the laws of association peculiar to 'sensual thinking' as Eisenstein discovered. Likewise, such critiques must propose an 'inside' of conscious perception that is also qualitatively different from the 'inside' of the image as if there was first a subject whose perceptions were clear and distinct, and then where the transparent waters of consciousness were muddied over by false projections, illusions, lies and clichés. In other words, they must believe in a subject that is not already composed of a tissue of clichés ('the veil of Maya'); such a subject must appear as composed of another nature, whether as an original nature like that of God, or pure *cogito*, or as the final nature of a transformed human (whose apotheosis becomes the shared goal of science, art and politics in the West). On an historical level of the concept of knowledge, this situation addresses the problem faced by post-Enlightenment philosophies generally, in which the idea of Reason, rather than guaranteeing to the subject of knowledge the certainty of its link with the world, becomes deformed and reappears in the guise of opinion (*doxa*), even as transcendental opinion (or *Ur-doxa*). However, in the life of the conscious subject this feeling of disbelief points to what Deleuze calls a 'real psychic situation' that both ideology (as the modern concept of truth) and cinema (as the modern concept of art) share as a formal condition of representation; the suspension of any verifiable link with the 'true' world happens at the same time that human appears as the subject of purely optical and aural situations. As Deleuze writes, 'The Modern fact is that we no longer believe in this world. We do not even believe in the events which happen to us, love, death, as if they only half concerned us' (TI 171). And if the 'real' subject cannot believe in the world that is presented, it is because the world has become nothing but bad cinema, and the subject has become a pure voyeur who regards his own being as well as the being of others, like in an episode of *The Jerry Springer Show*, as 'stock characters' in a psychic drama which unfolds from the hidden perspective of a real that, although external to the subject, is somehow internal (or necessary) to the world as it is.

> The sensory-motor break makes the human a seer who finds himself struck by something intolerable in the world, and confronted by something unthinkable in thought. Between the two, thought undergoes a strange fossilization, which is as it were its powerlessness to function, to be, its dispossession of itself and the world. For it is not in the name of a better and truer world that thought captures the intolerable in the world, but, on the contrary, it is because the world is intolerable that it can no longer think a world or itself. (TI 171–172)

The figure of Artaud occupies the moment of this break where the 'image of thought' instead of becoming identified with the power of the Whole, that is, the power of a subject capable of externalizing itself in a series of images by which the Whole undergoes change, becomes fissured and more receptive to a fundamental powerlessness which testifies to 'the impossibility of thinking that is thought' (Artaud). 'It is indeed a matter, as it was for Eisenstein, "of bringing cinema together with the innermost reality of the brain," but this innermost reality is not the Whole, but on the contrary a fissure, or crack.'[9] Here, thought does not accede to a form that belongs to a model of knowledge, or fall to the conditions of an action; rather, thought exposes its own image to an 'outside' that hollows it out and returns it to an element of 'formlessness.' We might conceive of this event in terms of the notion of formlessness that we explicated above in relation to modern art or literature, or even in terms of Eisenstein's discovery of the 'fourth dimension' (although here, separated from its 'dialectical automaton'), except in this instance the relationship to the Whole is not even given a negative expression, but rather undergoes an absolute break, which in the subject takes the form of a permanent and irreparable state of disbelief. Thus, the problem of ideology receives its most authentic expression from Artaud when he cried: '*my body was stolen away from me before birth*'; '*my brain has been used by an Other who thinks in my place*.' Artaud experienced and gave expression to this problem in its most extreme form, as if suffering from the memory of a physical, mental and spiritual rape – that is, the cry of schizophrenic man. However, 'rape' is not being employed here as simple metaphor, but rather as the most direct translation of Artaud's complaint; it reveals the nature of 'the total physiological sensation' of the automaton that enters to violate the subject even before birth.[10] In response to this intolerable situation, our question must then become how it is possible to distinguish between all the images that comprise the subject's existence in order to choose the right one, or how to extract thought from all its various clichés in order to set it up against them. According to Deleuze, Artaud experienced this question as the problem of thinking, which can be summarized in the following manner: the impossibility of not thinking, the impossibility of thinking, the impossibility of thinking differently.[11] Commenting on the first part of this triad, 'the impossibility of not thinking,' in relation to the subject of cinema this concerns the automatic character of thought which it shares with the movement-image, since even my refusal to think only signals that place where another thinks in my place. Not thinking, consequently, appears to Artaud as impossible *a priori*. Likewise, the second and third concern thinking as a power or quality that belongs to the subject which are impossible *a priori*, the first in the sense that all thinking is composed of clichés, the second in the sense that thought itself (or 'What is called thinking?' represented either as a common notion, an opinion, or as a kind of dominant image) must ultimately be determined as transcendental cliché, or an *Ur-doxa*.

It was only because the automatic character of thought already found a resemblance with the automatic character of the movement-image that cinema discovered the dynamic principle by means of which it could appear as the force that causes the subject to think. The dominant image of thought appears in this resemblance as a power in accordance with the power of Nature, or with the order of techné by which knowledge intervenes to disturb, 'work over,' and to fundamentally transform the interval between Nature and Culture. According to this dynamic representation, thinking is a Power which has as its beginning a point of projection (a subject) and as its end a transformed nature or a fabricated object (a world); between these two points there is a certain directionality or orientation by which thought is translated spatially from subject to object, from culture to nature and back again; and temporally from idea of Whole to the Whole transfigured. It is because of this mere resemblance that the movement-image acquires a certain power to determine the Whole, and the appearance of this power is then consolidated as a specialized technical knowledge, that, finally, the whole problem of the resemblance between the movement-image in cinema and the ideological images deployed by the apparatus of the state ensues. And it is only on the basis of this resemblance that Virilio's thesis is correct, namely that there has been no diversion of the movement-image to ideological ends, but rather the 'movement-image was from the beginning linked to the organization of war, state propaganda, ordinary fascism, historically and essentially' (TI 165).[12] However, this resemblance in fact only implies that the problem of ideology was already implicit in the 'image of thought,' that is, it was already latent in the subject and was simply awaiting its final birth: the automatic character of thought as a power, as either an 'habitual' or a transformative force, one that could internalize the Whole within a subject, and externalize the subject as a Whole (a world, a state, a national conscience).

Should the failure of a classical cinema founded upon the movement-image, such as its goals and aspirations were formulated by Eisenstein, not be inferred from an image of thought that was still attached to this problematic resemblance? Did this resemblance not condition Eisenstein's belief that cinema will eventually achieve by perfecting its knowledge of movement-image the means to repair the broken interval that appears as the cause of the subject's collective fragmentation? To unify the subject by crossing in both directions the gap between instinct and intelligence, and between thinking and action – both would amount to absorbing the interval into the synthesis of the movement-image. Because this perfection was understood primarily in terms of the action-image, conceived as the solution to art's neurosis and to collective fragmentation suffered by 'a people who is missing' (both of which are conceived as figures of 'negative apprehension'), it is ironic to see that it was precisely this conception of the action-image itself which was the cause of this neurosis. All movement through space is constructed by clichés, and the 'action-image' was itself a cliché of a special type; to evoke the 'revolutionary' potential of the new cinema seems contradictory since it constitutes a cliché of the highest order, an *Ur-doxa*, which posits either the total transformation of the Whole or the 'subject as Whole.' It was, in fact, a false solution that only furthered the break between the human being and the world, even realizing this impasse as an absolute and giving it an objectified form of the purely optical and sound situations in which thought appears to be trapped.

As a result of these situations, as Deleuze writes, 'the spiritual automaton is in the psychic situation of a seer, a true visionary who sees better and further than he can react, that is, think' (TI 172). Deleuze's thesis is that this is precisely the 'no exit' that the new cinema founds itself upon. Nihilism, therefore, is not a spirit that is restricted to philosophy alone. At the same time, he suggests, there may still be hope and the example of Artaud's relationship to cinema offers a way of 'thinking through cinema by means of cinema.' Beginning from this situation and even affirming it as the fundamental condition of the modern subject, to make the interval appear directly is the solution that Artaud offers: not to attach thought to a motor image that would extinguish it in action, or absorb it in knowledge, but to attach it directly to the interval itself so that thought would find its cause no longer in the image, but rather in what within the image refuses to be thought. In other words, if the whole problem of thought was that it was attached to an image that represented it, then Artaud turns this problem around to reveal its true experience for the subject. What this experience reveals is precisely the automatic, habitual and instinctual character of the thought that thinks me, interpolates me and determines me as a subject. One might still define this experience as 'total provocation' or 'nooshock'; yet, the nature of this experience with the cause of thinking has undergone a radical change. Under its previous image, shock, the neuronal messenger, simply travels along the same path that was opened, according to Artaud's cry, by a more fundamental power, thus referring the shock-effect that appears as the basis of the projects of art and ideology to an event that occurs before my birth. But this implies that the cause of thinking remains unconscious in principle, since it can never really emerge as a motive of conscious understanding or to become the condition of deliberative action. Instead, thought leaps over the interval to become, in principle, the condition of an action that remains fundamentally unthought, like an involuntary reaction, habitual response or nerve impulse.

Under its new image, this dynamic representation of thinking as a force is no longer 'the goal,' and the problem is no longer in attaining an 'image of thought' that would be equal to the force of the Whole (i.e. the perfection of 'the action-image'), but rather, according to Artaud, it is this 'image' of thought as a force or a power that itself is suddenly revealed as the problem of thinking. It reveals precisely the shock that 'I am not yet thinking' or that 'what is called thinking' is a power that belongs to a subject who 'I am not.' The effect of this awareness bears a certain 'dissociative force' which pries thought from its image, at the same time as it cuts the image off from the world, and exposes it to what Deleuze calls its 'reverse proof,' *the fact that we are not yet thinking.*[13]

Both cinema and ideology are expressions of the same broken interval between the human and the world, an interval that has reduced the link to only what the subject hears or sees; moreover, both have participated in the transformation of the world into an object of belief – even if this belief should prove illusory. It is precisely because everything that I see and hear is capable of being false, the expressions of deceit or trickery, of false oaths and betrayal, that only my belief is capable of reconnecting me with what I see and hear. This situation that I have been outlining as the basis of both the cinematic mechanism and the mechanism of ideology amounts to an extreme Cartesianism, however, one without any recourse to the principle of God who provides the subject of the *cogito* with fundamental certainty of knowledge. This is because, under the axiom of I = the Other, the subject I feel myself to be in perceiving, willing, desiring, can always be an 'Other.' As Deleuze writes, 'It was already a great turning-point in philosophy, from Pascal to Nietzsche: to replace the model of knowledge with belief' (TI 172). Likewise, modern cinema by reducing the world to the image can only intervene into the fold that runs between the human and the world; it is by changing the signs and affects of perception and consciousness that it is alone capable of provoking a change in the nature of consciousness itself. After all, what is a human being but the totality of her conscious perceptions, her affective qualities and her memory signs. The loss of the direct relation to the body, such as Artaud experienced it, is only the ultimate expression of a universal predicament. Thought is full of clichés, memory is not to be trusted, and perception is made-to-order. It is ironic, then, that the only means we have of restoring a connection that has been broken or damaged is by the very means that has caused our separation, by means of perception-images, memory-images, sounds and statements. This is why modern cinema, in particular, will be concerned with rendering an experience or connection between the body and the world, of creating new visual and aural images that might 'give back' the body's relationship to the world which has been lost in a chaos of clichés. Therefore, as Deleuze argues, although cinema cannot intervene directly into the world, or cause this world to be transformed into another, it may be the one and only means we have of restoring our belief. A strange optimism, which can be formulated as follows: to continue to believe in cinema, despite everything, despite even the repeated 'failures' of cinema itself, is to believe in the actualization of the world *as it is.*

Now, Eisenstein's belief in the power of 'revolutionary cinema' is well known and we have underlined many of its principles above. In Artaud, however, we have the figure of a 'true believer' in the cinema, who had to suffer through the stages of renouncing a too-simple faith in cinema in order to discover a more profound reason to believe. 'The nature of the cinematographic illusion has often been considered,' Deleuze writes, '[and] restoring our belief in this world – this is the power of modern cinema (when it stops being bad). Whether we are Christians or atheists, in our universal schizophrenia, we need reasons to believe in this world' (TI 172). The situation we face today only expresses this fact to an extreme degree, which underlies the radical uncertainty when the appeal to earlier models of knowledge and reason is exposed to the accusations of 'bad faith.' Nevertheless, the affirmative principle expressed by Nietzsche (but also by Kierkegaard before him) can be understood as being the most sobering response to this predicament: to believe in the world as it is, neither in a transformed world nor in another world, and to provide an image of thought that thoroughly belongs to this world which is ruled by the powers of the false; moreover, to raise falsehood to a positive principle in the service of those who choose to live in this world and not in another. In either case, what we have been calling the 'modern subject,' for lack of a better name, is faced with a terrible choice: either to continue to live in such a way that he or she can no longer believe anything he or she sees or hears (resulting in the loss of any connection to the world), or actively to cultivate the reasons to believe in this world of which fools, confidence men and tricksters are a part. Restoring our connection to the world, but also assuming a constant vigilance over clichés and ready-made linkages – these are the tasks of the cinema that emerges today from this new situation of thought.

11

THE USES (AND ABUSES) OF LITERATURE FOR LIFE

In the introductory essay of his last work, *Critique et Clinique* (1993), the translation of which was published in 1997 under the title *Essays Critical and Clinical*, the plane of immanence upon which the question of literature is unfolded is defined simply as 'Life.' Deleuze defines literature as 'the passage of life within language that constitutes Ideas' (CC 5), somewhat in the same manner that Whitehead had earlier spoken of Ideas themselves as the 'passage of Nature' into the location of a place (Fold 73). Thus, it is only on the plane of immanence, that is 'Life' itself, where we can discover a point situated outside the critical representation of literature; and it is from this point or vista that we might begin again to pose the question(s) proper to literature itself. Keeping this in mind, that is, the strategic necessity of situating the question of the critical from a point 'outside' its historical representation (or representative discourse), I will turn to this introductory essay in order to interrogate the above passage, since it is from this point that Deleuze describes what happens when the questions of living are bound up with 'the problems of writing.' In this essay Deleuze outlines four criteria for defining the relationship of literature to life. Because these criteria may provide a good approximation of the 'uses of literature for life,' in the following passages I will illustrate each criterion.

FIRST CRITERION

> *Literature is a passage of life that traverses outside the lived and the liveable.* (CC 1).

This is what Deleuze means by the first sentence that begins the leading essay of *Essays Critical and Clinical*, 'Literature and life': 'To write is certainly not to impose a form of expression on the matter of lived experience' (CC 1). This statement recalls a question first proposed by Proust: 'If art was indeed but a prolongation of life, was it worthwhile to sacrifice anything to it? Was it not as unreal as life itself?' (C 339). Before Deleuze, Proust is probably the greatest apologist for the 'duty' of literature. 'How many have turned aside from its task,' he asked, 'lacking the instinct for it, which is nothing less than the instinct for life itself?' (TR 298). On the other hand:

> Real life, that is, life at last laid bare and illuminated – the only life in consequence to which can be said to be really lived – is literature, and life thus defined is in a sense all the time immanent in ordinary men no less than in the artist. (TR 298)

For Proust, therefore, literature is the most 'real' of all things, since the ideas formed by pure intelligence may be logical, but are not necessary; moreover, perception or knowledge which is common or general is likewise not necessary, because it has not been deciphered, developed, worked over, that is, created. (In a famous description, Proust writes that for most people memory is a dark-room containing too many negatives that have not been 'developed.')

Therefore, literature is life

> . . . remote from our daily preoccupations, [the life] we separate from ourselves by an ever greater gulf as the conventional knowledge we substitute for it grows thicker and more impermeable, that reality which it is very easy for us to die without ever having known and which is, quite simply, our life. (TR 298–299)

According to this principle, certain literary works often take the opposite path: to discern beneath the merely personal the power of the impersonal. Thus, literature sometimes concerns the question of living in the sense that the writer struggles with the problem of life in order to extract movements and becomings that are inseparable from the question of 'style.' 'Style,' however, does not reflect the individuated expression or personality of the artist or writer. As Proust argues:

> [A]rt, if it means awareness of our own life, means also the awareness of the lives of other people – style for the writer, no less than color for the painter, is not a question of technique but of vision: it is the revelation, which by direct and conscious methods would be impossible, of the qualitative difference, the uniqueness in which the world appears to each one of us, a difference which, were it not for art, would remain the secret of every individual. (TR 299)

In the passage that traverses both the lived and the livable, the identities of the terms do not remain the same, but enter into a process of mutual becoming; Deleuze calls this process a 'capture,' a kind of repetition that causes both to become unequal to their former definitions, and enter into a relation of becoming. Such a becoming, however, concerns the immanence of a life, and only in certain cases does it emerge to touch upon the immanence of a life that is lived and livable by others. We might ask then, what makes the life posed by literature exemplary; in other words, what causes its critical expression to pass over to the side of the clinical? It is upon this question that the value of the literary enterprise is posed, whether it receives justification and a 'use' or falls into a miserable state of its own univocity. This is where the question of 'passage' receives a definite qualification: literature concerns the passage of a life into language. It is only through this passage that Life itself can achieve the repetition of a higher power, and the personal can be raised to the condition of a language.

Deleuze often remarks that the plane of life surpasses both the lived and the livable; the writer's encounter often proceeds from an encounter when life, defined in terms of the lived and the livable, becomes impossible, or when this encounter concerns something that is 'too powerful, or too painful, too beautiful' (TI 51). Accordingly, the writer often returns from the land of the dead and is 'a stranger to life' (TP 208). In other words, the writer does not simply write from experience or memory, but also from something too painful for memory or too light for experience, perhaps even 'an unbearable lightness' as in Kundera. It is for this reason, second, that the act of writing and the figure of the writer always entertain a relationship with a fundamental stupidity (*bêtise*), which is not simply a lack of experience as the fictionalizing factor, as well as with a fundamental amnesia or 'forgetting,' which is not simply a weak memory as the factor of an overly active imagination. (The *récits* of Marguerite Duras are exemplary in this regard.) Both stupidity and forgetting are the forces that define the writer's strangeness and estrangement from 'the lived and the livable.' For example, is there not a stupidity proper to Kafka's relationship with women that initiated the desire of the bachelor (hence, his famous statement, 'Prometheus was a bachelor'), or a forgetting of language and speech that one finds in Artaud, Beckett and Joyce? As in the famous case of the *'jeune homme schizophrène'* (an earlier essay on which is included in *Essays Critical and Clinical*), the relationship to a maternal language has undergone a fundamental trauma and dispossession and must be either invented anew (as in the case of Joyce and Proust) or pushed to its extreme limit to the point where Language itself confronts its impossibility (*impouvoir*, using Blanchot's term) and comes into contact with its own outside. The latter can find its various strategies in Artaud (where the outside is the cry beyond words), or in Beckett, who pushed the language of the novel to an extreme repetition that unravels into tortured fragments at the same time that his characters devolve into partial objects (e.g. a mouth, a head, an eye, a torso, a stomach, an anus).

Perhaps we can illustrate the immanence of a life with the following statement taken from Primo Levi which implicitly points to the example of Kafka: 'The shame of being a man – is there any better reason to write?' (CC 1). Here, 'shame' defines the fundamental trait of a life that is not simply the life of Kafka, but of a 'situation' particular to his case. For Kafka, moreover, the problem of writing is posed within an immanent relation to the escape from a 'situation' of shame. Benjamin had earlier perceived this shame as the 'elemental purity of feeling,' which is fundamental to Kafka's writings and, consequently, 'Kafka's strongest gesture [*gestus*]' (Benjamin, *Illuminations*, 25). What is the 'shame of being human'? For Benjamin, shame is primarily a social feeling: it is something one feels in the presence of others, something one feels for others. Because of this origin, the individual is innocent and cannot be found to be its cause. Consequently, in Benjamin's reading, the situation of shame always returns to the character of the law and its officers (the judge, the father, the mother, even the son and the daughter, or the sister); the character of law is that of an incredible filth that covers everything and everyone – a defilement of being. The father in 'The judgement' wears a dirty nightshirt; in 'The metamorphosis,' the father's uniform is covered in filth; in *The Trial*, the Examining Magistrate pages through a dusty volume of the Law which, when K. discovers its contents, is filled with dirty pictures. One might think this is a characteristic particular to the fathers and the officials only; however, nothing could be further from the truth. In fact, the son has become the embodiment of filth; he is vermin. Neither does woman escape, since, as many have noticed, she is touched with the filth of the law that defiles her own sex, and appears as a slut, a court prostitute, or a hunchback among the assembly of harpies who assemble on the stairs outside the painter Titorelli's studio. Shame – i.e. the shame of being human – is nothing 'personal,' but rather belongs to an unknown 'family' which includes both humans and animals alike. And Kafka writes concerning his indefinite relationship to this family: 'He feels as though he were living and thinking under the constraint of a family ... Because of this family ... he cannot be released.'[1]

SECOND CRITERION

> *To write is not to recount one's memories and travels, one's loves and griefs, one's dreams and fantasies; neither do we write with our neuroses, which do not constitute 'passages,' but rather those states into which we fall when our desire is blocked or plugged-up – consequently, 'literature then appears as an enterprise of health.'* (CC 2–3)

We might ask why Deleuze seems to love children and writers so much? Or rather, why are writers so often described in the process of 'becoming-child'? Kafka's letters often demonstrate this directly, particularly those to Felice where he takes a child's point-of-view in talking about her 'teeth' or in day-dreaming over the idea of curling up in her dresser drawer next to her 'private articles,' or, finally, in the passages where he describes a thousand agitated hands fluttering and out of reach, which can be understood as prefiguring of Gregor Samsa's thousand tiny legs waving helplessly in front of him. In addition to Kafka, we might think of Beckett as well, particularly the trilogy, where the transformations of the characters – Molloy, Malone, Jacques, Mahood, the Unnameable – all undergoing incredible and hilarious journeys and transmigrations, are haunted by endoscopic perceptions. The answer, it seems, would be simple enough: because the child knows how to play (to experiment), and the writer in the process of 'becoming-child' does not imitate children but repeats a block of childhood and allows it to pass through language. However, to avoid allowing the notion of 'play' to remain too simplistic (since most will say they know what 'playing' is), we should turn back to Freud who entertained an original intuition of the child-at-play in his 'Creative writers and day-dreaming.'[2]

First, Freud noticed that the child, contrary to the adult, plays in the full light of day, plays openly, and even causes his or her creations to transform the external world of perception. By way of contrast, the adult can only play in secret and often actively hides his or her creative activities (perhaps even from himself or herself). Adults are, first and foremost, guilty; consequently, they have lost the innocence of play, have repressed it, meaning that they aggressively prohibit all 'public displays' of such an activity, transforming the nature of play itself into an unconscious source of pleasure. Freud used this distinction primarily to distinguish the play of the child from the fantasy life of the adult; to show that the origin of the phantasm itself has this sense of 'hiding,' a guilty source of satisfaction for the adult who can only play in secret (and alone). At the same time, even Freud noticed that the artist constitutes the exceptional case to this internalization and continues to play out in the open. What's more, Freud exclaims with a certain amount of surprise, society allows it! Even if the artist must usually pay the price in terms of a suffering that compensates for the artist's enjoyment and seems to satisfy the cruelty of society itself toward the artist for enjoying too much and in a manner that civilization first of all demands to be sacrificed, cut off. This economic arrangement of cruelty and pleasure, according to Freud, is the guarantee that the creative writer and artist have to exist.

Returning now to emphasize that the writer, like the child, plays openly and in the full light of day, this would seem to imply that the nature of the activity cannot find its source in the secret, internalized and guilty affects of the adult. As Deleuze writes, 'we do not write with our neuroses' (CC 3). Wouldn't this imply that we should look for the sense of the process on the surface of the writer's activity, for a process that seeks to hide nothing? It seems odd, then, that often the function of interpretation is to reveal or to expose a 'secret' behind the appearance of the literary effect, underneath the more overt and all-too-evident transformations: to locate the 'figure in the carpet' or the figure of ideology. Is there any difference? Couldn't this activity be seen as an extension of the earlier repression: to transform what is out in the open, on the surface, to what is hidden and secret? Wouldn't this transform the very intentionality of the writer, so that the figure itself would appear to have been ferreted away, and desire becomes the desire of the phantasm? This is why interpretations of ideology begin with a false premise: that the writer was hiding anything to begin with. Perhaps this is why Deleuze and Guattari choose to highlight the most problematic of writers from the perspective of an adult morality (Carroll and his love for little girls, Faulkner and Melville's racism, or that of Celine, the misogyny of Miller and Burroughs, Proust's 'closeted' homosexuality, Artaud's mania and crypto-fascism, Kafka's bachelor-desire, Woolf's frigidity, etc.), as if to say, 'Well now, there's nothing hidden here!' 'All perverts – every one of them!' Or perhaps, 'If we are to judge, if we must arrive at a judgement, then we must find a better evidence; but at least, we must find something more interesting to say.' But then 'perversion' may not be the right word. Again, this evokes the sense of symptomatology, since the writer 'plays' – openly, without shame, or guilt – with what the adult chooses to keep 'secret,' even though secrecy makes these symptoms no less determining of a life and perhaps even more so. How many times lately have we had to suffer the moralism of perverts, racists, misogynists and pederasts who choose to persecute others for their own most secretive desires? Thus, the publicity with which the writer plays with his or her desires is not perverse in the least; rather, the function of 'perversion' describes the position of a normative morality under the condition that enjoyment either remains 'a dirty little secret' of the individual, or undergoes a strange reversal into sadism and cruelty.

THIRD CRITERION

> *'Health as literature,' as writing, consists in fabulation, which Deleuze defines as 'the invention of a people who is missing'; thus, 'the ultimate aim of literature is to set free, in the delirium, in this creation of a health, in this invention of a people, the possibility of a life.'* (CC 5)

Under this criterion, we should recall the three characteristics that belong to the concept of 'minor literature': first, a certain situation occurs when a major language is affected with a high coefficient of deterritorialization; second, everything is political and the 'individual concern' or 'private interest' disappears or serves as a mere environment or background; third, everything takes on a collective value. From these three criteria, we can locate the specific conditions that give rise to what Deleuze calls 'fabulation.' The concept of 'fabulation' first appears in *Bergsonism* (1966) and then disappears almost entirely until it is highlighted in the later writings, particularly in *Cinema 2: The Time-Image* (1989) and again in the interviews conducted between 1972 and 1990 that appear in *Negotiations* (1990), where Deleuze makes the following pronouncement: 'Utopia is not a good concept, but rather a "fabulation" common to people and to art. We should return to the Bergsonian notion of fabulation to provide it with a political sense' (N 174). In light of our effort to understand this concept in view of a generalized literary clinic, we might understand the concept of fabulation as having two sides: creation and prognosis. Fabulation is the art of invention as well as a conceptual avatar of a 'problem-solving' instinct that remedies an unbearable situation – particularly with regard to the situation of 'the people who are missing' (CC 4). The goal of fabulation, understood as a process, is where the writer and the people go toward one another (TI 153ff.); in this sense they share a common function. Deleuze writes, 'To write for this people who are missing ... ("for" means less "in place of" than "for the benefit of")' (CC 4). That is, they share a process, a vision beyond words, a language beyond sounds. In this sense, fabulation could be said to resemble the function of dream work and, by extension, the moments of selective rearrangement that mark historical discontinuities. What is power unleashed in revolution but the ideal game deployed within what is essentially a fiction; that is, the power to select and reorder the objects, artefacts and meanings that belong to a previous world? Utopia, then, rather than designating a static representation of the ideal place, or *topos*, is rather the power of the 'ideal' itself, which can bifurcate, time and create possible worlds. This is why Deleuze calls 'fabulation' a better concept than 'utopia,' since it designates a power or a vital process rather than representing a static genre – an ideal form of repetition rather than the repetition of an ideal form.

Fabulation entails a 'becoming' that happens from both directions – it is both the becoming-popular of the creator or intellectual, and the becoming-creative of a people. In many ways, this movement echoes the description of the cultural process of nationalist or post-colonialist art first examined by Frantz Fanon in *The Wretched of the Earth* (1963), which can be used to illustrate the concept of fabulation. First, in Fanon's analysis, the function of fabulation that determines the writer's cultural presence in colonial culture and the forms of 'socialization' and identification that underlie the perspective of the modern 'creator' are both explicitly developed:

> At the very moment when the native intellectual is anxiously trying to create a cultural work he fails to realise that he is utilising techniques and languages which are borrowed from the stranger in his country. He contents himself with stamping these instruments with a hallmark he wishes to be national, but which is strangely reminiscent of exoticism. The native intellectual who comes back to his people [as Fanon previously qualifies, 'whatever they were or whatever they were or whatever they are'] by way of culture behaves in fact like the foreigner. Sometimes he shows no hesitation in using a dialect in order to show his will to be as near as possible to the people; but the ideas he expresses and the preoccupations he is taken up with have no common yardstick to measure the real situation which the men and women of his country know. (W 223)

This incommensurability, which underscores the initial appearance of the colonized intellectual, also belongs to a preliminary phase in the creation of national conscience of culture in Fanon's reading. It must be followed by other stages, which reconfigure the attributes (or 'property') of culture between its contingent and exterior genres and its interior collective expression of 'inner truth' (W 225). (Fanon articulates the latter as culture's muscularity, in relation to political action, and rhythm, in relation to ethnic and regional identities.) In a post-colonial culture's incipient phase, however, these attributes are uncoordinated and this non-coordination can be seen to inform the very appearance of hybridity in the image of the cultural producer and his or her creative work. From the perspective of the post-colonial 'people' – who, at this stage, 'are still missing' – comes the initial schizoid image of culture, one which is also manifested in the appearance of the colonized intellectual as the result of the mutilating psychological effects and dehumanization of the colonizing situation. This addresses the problem of becoming from the perspective of the native intellectual and writer, where 'going back to your own people means to become a dirty wog, to go native as much as possible, to become unrecognisable, and to cut off those wings that before you had allowed to grow' (W 221). Part native and part stranger, near and distant at the same time, the creator only 'appears' to manifest a characteristic of proximity by imitating native dialects and speech patterns; however, this creator's 'ideas' are at first both unfamiliar and strangely distant from a people's perception of their own image.

Fanon himself accounts for this hybridity by assigning it two causes. First, hybridity results from an appearance of 'culture' itself that is uncoordinated with political and national conscience (i.e. a direct consequence of the colonial process that 'alienated' and even 'negated' any relationship between these two sites of mentality). Second, this appearance of the indigenous cultural producer and the national conscience of culture precedes the actualization of political revolt. This peremptory and premature appearance gives the creator and the cultural work the characteristics of 'a-temporality' and 'affective remoteness' in the minds of the people themselves:

> The artist who has decided to illustrate the truths of the nation turns paradoxically toward the past and away from actual events. What he ultimately intends to embrace are in fact the cast-offs of thought, its shells and corpses, a knowledge which has been stabilised once and for all. But the native intellectual who wishes to create the authentic work of art must realise that the truths of a nation are in the first place its realities. He must go on until he has found the seething pot out of which the learning of the future will emerge. (W 225)

This diagnostic and therapeutic narrative structures the dialectical stages that the creator (and the 'people') must pass through in order to arrive at the synthesis of collective political and cultural expression. Fanon traces these stages from alienation of an internalized cultural identification with the colonizer; to the spark of an original memory (which Fanon compares with the return of infantile and maternal associations); to a period of malaise, nausea and convulsion (expressions of 'vomiting out' the poison of the earlier cultural identification); and at last to the final stage of combat in the martyrological expression of a true popular culture, where the writer becomes 'the mouth-piece of a new reality in action' (W 223). Thus there is a deep analogy between the ethnography of a 'people' and the story of the coming-to-conscience of the creator's voice, the manifestation of a culture's essential 'property' and authentic expression of its innermost nature. At the end of the dialectic of culture outlined by Fanon, the 'mental space of a people' that had been distorted by the instruments of colonization gradually draws close to itself in the image of the creator and remembers in the voice of the poet the sound of its own voice. The final image of proximity occurs when the creator and the people become one mentality in which culture thinks itself in – and as – the substance of its own ideational life. The 'organic coordination' between the poet's plastic expression and the people's inner thought achieves such a synthesis of muscularity and natural rhythm that those who before would never have thought to compose a literary work 'find themselves in exceptional circumstances ... [and] ... feel the need to speak to their nation, to compose a sentence which expresses the heart of the people, and to become the mouth-piece of a new reality in action' (W 223).

We could see here in Fanon's description of the process between the marginalized writer and 'a people who are missing,' an echo of a lesson from Kafka that Deleuze often emphasizes in the context of his discussion of fabulation:

> The author can be marginalised or separate from his more or less illiterate community as much as you like; this condition puts him all the more in a position to express potential forces and, in his very solitude, to be a true collective agent, a collective leaven, a catalyst. (ML 221–222)

This is the solitude that Kafka addressed in terms of impossibility, where the 'problem of writing' is fundamentally related to a collective impossibility: the situation of a people who either live in a language that is not their own, or who no longer even know their own and know poorly the major language they are forced to serve (ML 19). To use an expression that is invoked throughout Deleuze's work, and is primarily inspired from Blanchot's writings, the writer's solitude cannot be reduced to a normal situation of solitude in the world, to an experience of being-alone and apart from others. This is because the figures above do not experience their aloneness from the perspective of this world, or of this society, or from the presence of others who exist, but rather from the perspective of another possible world or another community that these figures anticipate even though the conditions for this community are still lacking. Often this desire or longing, which brings about the condition of solitude, is expressed in the discourse of love as in the case of Kierkegaard with Regina, or of Proust with Albertine. In the latter case, Marcel is haunted by the fact that no matter how close he comes to Albertine, or no matter how he draws her near him even to the point of holding her hostage, he is always haunted by the fact that behind the face of Albertine, there always lies another Albertine, a thousand other Albertines each breaking upon one another like waves of an infinite ocean. Thus, it is this experience of solitude that burns into his mind the impossible and delirious desire of capturing each one, of 'knowing' all the possible Albertines, as the highest goal of Love.

Returning to the case of Kafka, according to Deleuze, the solitude of the writer is related most profoundly to the situation of the people who are missing. This is why the solitude of certain writers is in no way a private affair for Deleuze, and why the concept of 'solitude' must be qualified to evoke the uncanny experience of inhabiting a strange language, a language that is not and may never be one's own, where the very act of speaking brings with it the feeling of self-betrayal, or of 'falsifying oneself,' and where the alternative of remaining silent bears the threat of extinction. It is in this sense that the position of the writer is virtual to that of the collective, and, therefore, the so-called 'private' is immediately collective as well, that is, 'less a concern of literary history than of a people.'[3]

Deleuze writes concerning this situation which was specific to Kafka's predicament, but which can describe the situation of other writers as well (such as Melville or Woolf), that 'the most individual enunciation is a particular case of the collective enunciation' (ML 84). Moreover, 'this is even a definition: a statement is literary when it is "taken up" by a bachelor who precedes the collective conditions of enunciation' (ML 84). This last definition appears to reclassify the entire sense of the literary as emerging from 'a bachelor-machine,' a concept that Deleuze draws from the figure of Kafka but that also can be found to refer to the figure of Proust; however, the condition of a 'bachelor' can be redefined, outside its gender determination, to describe or refer to a situation in which one prefers the state of being alone (i.e. exceptional, singular, anonymous) rather than 'taking on' the identity of a subject one is assigned by the majority. The situation of preferring to remain a bachelor can find affinities, for example, with the situation of a Jew in eighteenth-century Europe, with that of a woman in nineteenth- and twentieth-century societies, or with the situation of minorities in America today.[4]

FOURTH CRITERION

Finally, literature opens up a kind of foreign language within language. (CC 5)

This invention has three aspects: (1) through syntax, the destruction of the maternal language; (2) through delirium, the invention of a new language which carries the first outside its usual furrows (*habitus*), and which, in turn, entails a second destruction: the clichés of visibilities and statements which, although not completely reducible to language, are nevertheless inseparable from it, being the 'ideas' and 'habits' that determine the forms of seeing and saying; (3) in the third aspect, as a result of the destruction of the maternal language and of the clichéd statements and stock visibilities (which are like its ghosts), the literary process bears the former language to its limit, turning it toward its own 'outside,' which Deleuze describes as its inverse or reverse side made up of visions and auditions, which 'are not outside language, but the outside of language' (CC 5). The final aim of these three aspects, according to Deleuze, is the concept of literature defined as 'the passage of life within language that constitutes ideas' (CC 5).

Taking up the first aspect, through the destruction of the maternal language, literature functions as a war machine. 'The only way to defend language is to attack it' (Proust, quoted in CC 4). This could be the principle of much of modern literature and capture the sense of process that aims beyond the limit of language. As noted above, however, this limit beyond which the outside of language appears is not outside language, but appears in its points of rupture, in the gaps, or tears, in the interstices between words, or between one word and the next. The examples of writers who define their relationship to language under the heading of this principle are too numerous to recount, although I will provide a few significant examples for the purposes of illustration. First, we might point to the poet Paul Celan, for example, whose poetry is precisely defined as the systematic destruction of the language of Goethe and Rilke in the sense that the poem itself expresses a word that no German mouth can speak (the deterritorialization of language from the teeth and the lips). In Celan, the poem itself is nothing less than a materialization of the mother's corpse that is gradually interned within the German language and given a specific place of mourning; thus, the image of the mother is a shadow of the lost object by which Celan draws the entire German language into a process of mourning. This is Celan's process: the 'passage' of the Mother's death into the German language; the passage of the living German language into an encounter with his Mother's death and, by extension, with the murder of his maternal race. The use of color in Celan's poetry gives us a vivid illustration of the Deleuzian and Proustean notion of vision. The poet is a true colorist who causes colors to appear as nearly hallucinatory visions in the language of the poem; however, in Celan's poems, the descriptive and neutral function of color is poetically transformed into the attributes of his mother's body – her hair, or her skin, her eyes; the green of a decaying corpse. It is as if each enunciation of each color will henceforth bear a reference to his mother's body, that the German language is modified to incorporate this cryptic reference into its poetic and descriptive functions. Thus, the green is the color of summer grass, but it is also the color of my mother's decaying shadow; blue is the color of the sky, but it is also the color of the sky the day it wore my mother's hair; red is the color of the tulip, but it is also the color of the silent one who that day 'comes to behead the tulips'; finally, yellow is the hair of Marguerite, but it is also the color of my mother's star, the star that marked her for extinction.[5]

Kafka also approaches the German language with the statement of his swimming champion, 'I speak the same language as you, but don't understand a single word you're saying' (quoted in CC 5), and at the same time draws on the resources of the all-too vernacular and deterritorialized Czech-German and the all-too symbolic and allegorical Yiddish ('a language of the heart') in order to purify the German language and the syntax of Goethe from its own cultural signification. In other words, as Deleuze often recounts, Kafka 'creates a kind of foreign language within language' (CC 5) that, although it bears an uncanny and perfect resemblance to the major language, it no longer bears the significance for German culture and emerges as a kind of war machine within its majoritarian sense. As Deleuze and Guattari write, by a kind of schizo-politeness hidden beneath an almost too-perfect German syntax, 'he will make the German take flight on a line of escape ... he will tear out from the Prague German all the qualities of underdevelopment it has tried to hide; he will make it cry with an extremely sober and rigorous cry ... to bring language slowly and progressively to the desert ... to give syntax to the cry' (ML 26). This marks the importance of animals in Kafka's shorter works – the musical dogs that appear in 'Investigations of a dog,' the singing mouse-folk in 'Josephine, the mouse-singer,' the song of the Ape in 'Report to the academy,' the low-cry of the Jackals in 'The jackals and arabs' – but also the musical auditions of the other fabulous creatures that

Kafka creates, such as Odradek in 'Cares of a family man' whose laughter bears the airy sound of dried leaves, or the silence of the Sirens in the tale of the same name. In all these cases, we have examples of pure sonorous auditions that are introduced into the German language. It is through the deterritorialization of the human that the German language passes through a becoming-animal, that animals introduce the notes of a strange music that has never been heard before in German literature, that Kafka introduces new possibilities into the German tongue, 'a music made up of deterritorialized sounds' (ML 26). In themselves, as pure sonorous material, these sounds may have already been possible: the melody of a dog's howl, the shrill silence of a mouse, the low moan of the jackal. However, the form they take in Kafka's language – for example, the first song that the Ape learns from a drunken sailor, which becomes his primitive language lesson – becomes an 'idea' in its passage through language, an 'audition' of a cry of humiliation and oppression that Kafka first introduces as such into the German ear. It is in this manner that he both escapes the oppressive, classical harmonies of the German language and, at the same time, institutes a pedagogy of syntax in which he teaches the German language to cry.

Taking up the second aspect, the invention of 'a delirium, which forces it out of its usual furrows' (CC 5), we should recall that one of the principal axioms of *Anti-Oedipus* is that desire always invests or is immanent to the social field of production, in order to apply this axiom to 'the desire to write.' The desire to write, at one level, is a delirium that is immediately social. How could we otherwise explain the institution of criticism that has secreted around the work in the modern societies based upon writing if not as an effort to submit this delirium to the identifiable categories of a 'proper delirium' that functions as the basis of the group? At the same time, if we were to attempt to grasp 'the desire to write' from its immanent perspective within society, we would need to conceive of the function of writing in all its occasions: from the legal or juridical and the legislative, to its hermeneutic and confessional modes. Perhaps, then, the figure of the writer emerges to 'represent' this delirium and, thereby, to isolate the 'problem of writing' to rare and exceptional cases we call 'writers,' almost in the same manner that Derrida had illustrated around the function of the pharmakon. It is as if society, which itself is constructed by and from writing, must also produce a being who embodies in order to protect itself from the madness that belongs to its own order of possibility. Is there any wonder then why the writer has so often been defined by the attributes of illness or bad health? Again, this may explain Deleuze and Guattari's selection of the series of problematic writers to combat this definition. To close the work off by applying these symptoms to the ethical or psychological character of an author, and thereby to 'psychologize' or to 'impeach' the writer, is to alienate the critical function of these writers – that is, the 'lens' they offer to perceive what otherwise remains obscure and misapprehended by its individuated or psychological forms. Recalling again the second criterion, the principal distinction is the incredible 'openness' these symptoms receive in the writing, which must be set against the usual secret forms that determine the expression of unconscious fantasies, or individual symptoms.

Here, the Borgesian formula of 'Fang has a secret' often recounted by Deleuze can be used paradigmatically of this moment of turning, or decision, in which nothing is guaranteed. That is, 'Fang has a secret' and 'there is a stranger at the door.' In order to illustrate the paradigmatic value of this formula, we could substitute for the nameless identity of the stranger the forces signalled by the emergence of a life based on silicon, the formation of the capitalist in the final stages of planetary deployment, the deterritorialization and crisis of disciplinary regimes and their reterritorialization by mechanisms of the 'control society,' the emergence of racialized identities and new fascisms of the flesh. In turn, each of these 'strangers' marks turning points for the human form, as well as a fullness of time, a time pregnant with possibility, the moment of a 'dice-throw.' (These are the sombre precursors spoken of in *Difference and Repetition.*) That is, each arrangement presents us with diverse possibilities, with possible futures that bifurcate, tracing the curve of the present that goes toward the future announced by the new assemblage of Life that appears on the horizon. Borges, for example, discovered a possible means of escaping a colonizing relationship with the past through a comic procedure of overturning the European library and parodying the God of European history in its colonial situation. Kafka discovered through the fictional personage of 'K.' a manner to research the diabolical assemblage of law and the institution of the state-form. Burroughs diagnosed the secret filiation of the alien, the homosexual and the junkie as victims of the paranoia unleashed by the 'bio-power' of the modern state that defines its internal enemies in terms of a virus. And there are countless more examples of these 'sombre precursors' in Deleuze's work (Buchner's Lenz, Nietzsche's Zarathustra, Welles's Kane, Melville's Ahab or Benito Cereno, Duras and Resnais's Hiroshima).

In *Anti-Oedipus*, it is with the discovery of the production proper to the schizophrenic that Deleuze and Guattari find a degree-zero of the delirium that the schizophrenic shares with society: 'he hallucinates and raves universal history, and proliferates the races' (AO 85). Thus, the schizo refers to the function of a delirium as the principle of 'desiring-production' that society itself uses to 'distribute races, cultures, and gods' – in short, to 'make itself obeyed' – on the body without organs (i.e. the full body of the earth [AO 84]). In Deleuze and Guattari's use of the concept of delirium we might detect a certain cosmological theory of madness (i.e. the thesis of 'madness as work' or a style of '*grande politique*' which they share in some ways with Blanchot and Foucault), which was first presented by Freud in his famous commentary on Daniel Schreber, who created a universe with his delirium and then proceeded to populate it with gods and with demi-gods (or demons), as well as with new races and sexes. These were the personages of Schreber's fabulous delirium; however, the structure of this delirium also describes the origin of the prohibitive mechanisms that society itself produces. In other words, the language of madness simply locates in the 'storytelling function' of figures like Schreber the very same mechanisms that society itself uses to engender a world populated with gods, cultures, races and peoples. Given the conservative function of this 'myth-making' faculty, we might ask how, according to the major thesis of *Anti-Oedipus*, the delirium proper to schizophrenic production and social production can lead to the potential of fabulation as a relay to revolutionary force. This is the point around which many commentaries on Deleuze and Guattari's use of the schizo fall into error by taking the clinical entity of the schizophrenic as a kind of model creator, a turn to romanticism. However, the equation of the fabulation of the clinical schizophrenic with social fabulation has the subtle effect of rendering social production the truth of the clinical equation, since the clinical personage of the schizophrenic constitutes that point where desiring-production is blocked, falls into an impasse, becomes reactive or sick. If the clinical entity of the schizophrenic is identical with society, then we find the true subject of schizoanalysis, which is social production. Within the literary process therefore, delirium undergoes a positive 'transvaluation' (Nietzsche) which differentiates it from its repressive or conservative functions in madness and society. That is, if the world itself 'is the set of symptoms whose illness merges with man,' it is by means of this process that 'literature is a health' (CC iv).

Finally, concerning the third aspect of these criteria, Deleuze writes: 'the final aim of literature ... *is the passage of life within language that constitutes ideas*' (CC 5 – my emphasis). In *Foucault* (1988), Deleuze situates this aspect that belongs to modern literature in what is essentially a psychology of the fold, whereby language is disarticulated from the 'grand unities of discourse' (*Foucault*) which structure the possibilities of enunciation. In *Essays Critical and Clinical,* Deleuze recalls the above formulation when he describes the event of literature as, 'in effect, when another language is created within language, it is a language in its entirety that tends toward an "a-syntactic," "a-grammatical" limit, or that communicates with its own outside' (CC iv). Deleuze locates this aspect of modern literary practices in an analysis that owes much to Foucault's stubborn persistence to privilege the question of literature in a time when it was being subordinated to the forces of the negative (work, communication, information, identity), particularly to privilege the possibilities of resistance that are potential in the recent and overt tendency of modern writers to uncover a strange language within language. Accordingly, modern literature creates within language a non-linguistic stammering that inclines toward 'a-typical expression' and 'a-grammatical effects' (e.g. Berryman, Celan, Queneau, Cummings, Mallarmé).

As a result of and from this process, ideas emerge as what Deleuze calls visions and auditions – these are the forms of seeing and hearing that are specific to the literary process in its passage within Language. As Deleuze further describes, however, these ideas appear only when the literary process achieves its aim and breaks through the limit of language, a limit that is not outside language, but rather the outside of language which language alone makes possible. 'These visions are not fantasies, but veritable Ideas that the writer sees or hears in the interstices of language, in its intervals' (CC 5). Although they bear a certain hallucinatory quality specific to the literary effect (e.g. Proust's 'madeleine,' Gombrowicz's 'hanged-sparrow,' Melville's 'white whale,' Silko's 'spider-web'), they cannot be reduced to the psychological fantasies of the author nor to 'ideologemes' of a collective unconscious, since they take place, as Kafka said, 'in the full light of day' and not 'down below in the cellar of structure.'[6] Consequently, it is often through words or between words that is the implicit aim of the literary process; this desire on the part of the writer is accompanied by a certain destruction of the stock forms of visibilities and statements, of linguistic and syntactical habits, clichés of the quotidian and common utterances, stock and made-to-order descriptions and categorical prescriptions that all too often imprison what is seen and heard in a fog of nothingness.

> This labor of the artist, this struggle to discern beneath matter, beneath experience, beneath words, something that is different from them, is a process exactly the reverse of that which, in our everyday lives in which we live avoiding our own gaze, is at every moment satisfied by vanity and passion, intellect and habit, extinguishing our true impressions that are entirely concealed from us, buried underneath a junk heap of verbal concepts and practical goals that we falsely call 'life.' (TR 299–300)

In a certain sense, then, we might say that modern literature creates the conditions for 'good habits' of language use. 'What are we but habits of saying "I"?' Deleuze first proposes this question in his study of Hume (*Empiricism and Subjectivity* x). The question of language that both philosophy and literature expound upon in different manners, therefore, is one of developing and promoting 'good habits' of language usage and diagnosing 'bad or destructive' habits. Philosophy has always concerned itself with the 'uses and abuses' of language for the purpose of living (and dying) well; however, this image of good sense is not an object of logic, but of ethics or even etiquette. Nietzsche understood this as the essence of logic, as well as an image of philosophy as 'the transvaluation of values' which, first of all, include linguistic values, or 'signs,' whose proper sense can only be the object of a genealogical study, such as Foucault later described in his essay 'Nietzsche, genealogy, history.' Consequently, we find in Foucault's work an original relationship of language to the 'body' (the materiality of the self), a relationship which is given an historical and diagnostic expression. Habits (*habitus*), understood as the modern form of repetition, stand for those institutions of the statements that interpolate us and which define us by determining the possible attributes that can belong to the 'I.' As a certain species of repetition, moreover, habits achieve a degree-zero of memory (where the particular equals the universal), producing the condition in which 'what we do not remember, we repeat' (DR 19). Thus, certain uses of language can be defined as the cause of our illness, since they lead to a botched form of life, self, individuality, power, etc. We must recognize the effects of these 'habits' upon the process of thinking as well, particularly in the sense that the 'interiority of thought' (the grand circuit of associations, signs, concepts, memory and feeling) is 'limited' (contracted or disciplined) by the external forms of discourse and language. It is not a question of thought that is without language, but rather of thinking which appears in its most extended circuit, which enters into combinations with the elements of seeing and speaking that are 'exterior' to a language defined by formed statements and the visibility of objects. Consequently, we can define this problematic as a part of the Deleuzian critique of representation, since the particular form of repetition that belongs to this order and determines the habits of language-use also determines the unconscious of our representations.

On the other hand, certain modern literary practices, rather than being founded by their representational function, can be understood as a profound experimentation that reveals the positivity and the limits of our language-habits (our addiction to saying 'I'). In the statement 'I love you,' for example, why is the 'I' meaningless, as well as 'love'? Perhaps one might attempt to explain the first by the power of the shifter and the second by the privilege of the performative statement. On the other hand, we can understand this as a particular species of repetition, which has become abstract and too general, in the case of the first, and meaningless and too particular in the case of the second. What Deleuze refers to as 'the curve of the sentence' can be understood as a profound experimentation that reveals the limits of certain expressions, negates their abstractness for a 'new' positivity of language. Deleuze writes as early as *Difference and Repetition* that the event of positivity occurs necessarily in the advent of the 'new' that introduces variables into a previous repetition. Statements such as Kafka's 'I am a bug' or Fitzgerald's 'I am a giraffe' lead to the discovery of the nonsense that belongs to the statement 'I am a man' (TP 377). Consequently, the first two statements repeat the last one and at the same time introduce a new predicate, causing the statement 'I am a man' to be lacking definition and, in a certain sense, in need of rectification. In other words, the statement 'I am a man' leads to nothing and can be criticized as a bad use of definition. It defines no one and, thus, makes the 'abstract' predicate of man possible as a real relationship. Rather than representing, Kafka's proposition 'selects' and corrects the imperfections of the former definition. It reveals the limits of the statement as well as the visibility of the language-predicate; it introduces new variables into old habits of being, clearer and more definite articulations, new possibilities for the passage of a life into language.

In conclusion, we should return to situate the question of literature as one of the principal themes of the two volumes of *Capitalism and Schizophrenia*. In order to do so, it would be necessary to pay more specific attention to the status of the literary that occurs in the work of Deleuze and Guattari. When and in what manner is it evoked? For example, in the cries of poor A.A., the stroll of Lenz, the sucking-stones of Molloy, Kleist's Marionettes or Michael Köhlhaas on his horse. In each case, literary expression is allied to a 'war machine,' which means it draws its force directly from 'the outside.' Deleuze and Guattari constantly pit this condition of literary enunciation against any representation that subjugates it to a form of interiority (whether that of the subject-author, the private individual, a culture, or even a race). It is not by accident that the lines from Rimbaud are always recited like the lyrics of a favorite song: 'I am a bastard, a beast, a Negro.' The relationship of the concept of literature to a war machine is essential, and we should note that many of the examples of the war machine are drawn from writers (Artaud, Buchner, Kafka and Kleist), as well as philosopher-artists such as Nietzsche and Kierkegaard. In *A Thousand Plateaus*, the conflict between the literary war machine and the critic as 'man of the state' is first attested to by the confrontation between Artaud and Jacques Rivière (although not a man of the state, he was, according to Deleuze, not the first or last critic to mistake himself for 'a prince in the republic of letters'), who found Artaud incomprehensible and poorly organized, and he made no hesitation in giving his advice to 'pauvre A.A.' – 'Work! Work! If you revise, then soon you will arrive at a method (*Cogitatio Universalis*) to express your thoughts more directly!' (TP 377). Next, the literary war machine is attested to by Kleist's conflict with Goethe ('truly a man of the State among all literary figures'). In the case of the figures like Nietzsche and Kierkegaard, there is the conflict between the 'public professor' and the 'private thinker,' although Deleuze qualifies the latter notion in order to argue that, in fact, the 'private thinker' may not be a good term, since it too closely follows the reductive notion of the 'private individual,' and is too simple of a form of interiority where the so-called spontaneity of thought is said to occur. Instead, Deleuze argues that the 'solitude' one approaches in the writings of Nietzsche, or in Kafka, is a solitude that is extremely 'populated' (TP 467).

The concept of literature we have been discussing above fundamentally invokes a situation of language where the collective subject of enunciation (different from the official enunciation of a 'people,' or of a 'national consciousness') exists only in a latent or virtual state that cannot be located in the civil and juridical language of statutes and laws, the 'paper language' of bureaucracy, the technocratic and vehicular language of administrators, entrepreneurs and capitalists. It would not be an exaggeration to assert that most technical and administrative language, even in the first world, bears an historical relationship to the early techniques invented by colonial administrations – a language composed purely of 'order-words' (*les mots d'ordre*), a language of command in which the law finds its purest expression, just as Sade discovered the essence of Enlightenment reason, not by accident, in the categorical imperatives of pornographic speech: 'Do this!', 'Submit!', 'Obey!' Concerning the status of this language, as Fanon asserts, we have every reason to believe the colonizer when he says, 'the colonized, I know them!' since he [the colonizer] has created the categories that were installed at the deepest point of their interiority by the colonizing process, categories that continue to legislate their own knowledge of themselves as 'a subjected people.' Moreover, Fanon writes, 'colonialism is not satisfied merely with holding a people in its grip and emptying the native's brain of all form and content. By a kind of perverted logic, it turns out to be the past of the oppressed people, and distorts, disfigures, and destroys it' (W 210). Deleuze refers to this as the condition by which a 'people as Subject' falls to the condition of a 'people-subjected' (ML 164ff.). As we have witnessed many times, the question of 'identity' is always a dizzying and even treacherous problem from the position of the colonized, leading often to the very 'impasse' from which this category was created, underscoring an 'intolerable situation,' since the identity they assume in speaking, in saying 'I (the colonized)' has been essentially fabulated and only serves to subject them further. This intolerable condition of enunciation is a condition that is specific to the concept of 'minor literature.' At the same time, we must take inventory of the fact that the history of literature in the West is full of examples of this impossible situation; for example: Hippolytus and Phaedra, Antigone; in Kafka's 'metamorphosis,' there is Gregor who cannot speak, but rather emits a shrill note that can barely be discerned; but also in Melville, we have the character of Babo in 'Benito Cereno' who refuses to speak 'as the accused' and chooses to remain silent (therefore, in full possession of his speech), but also in the figure of Bartleby with his intractable formula, '*I would prefer not to* . . .'

Why does this situation appear as a fundamental problematic, if not to signal something genetic to the literary enunciation: the problem and the power of 'falsehood,' of the fictional status of the enunciation that essentially haunts the situation of writing? Taking up the notion of the 'public sphere,' such a concept already refers to the particularly 'striated openness' (*Oeffentlichkeit*) which is established when the dominant institutions of language and culture reflect the pre-conscious interests of the nation-state or class. In such a condition, the literary machine itself has already been 'reterritorialized' and now functions to reflect the genius of the national character or the spirit of *Kultur*. Thus, we might refer to this moment, one that has prepared the way for the strictly ideological representation of literature in the academy today, which is reduced to a sub-compartment of the 'political unconscious' or to the poetics of the State-form. This representation of literature is necessarily one-dimensional, and must sacrifice the variable relationships that originally belonged to the production of the art-work, and above all, must repress the whole question of art often by reducing it to the category of aesthetics which can, in turn, be prosecuted for its falsifying production. Here we might refer to the process of this reterritorialization, again using the analysis of the relationship between the 'war machine' and the 'State-form' outlined earlier. When a literary machine is captured by the State-form and provided with an end, what is that end except a war directed against 'the people' in the form of national memory and an official story-telling function? However, the very taxonomy and organization of literature soon repeat the rank-and-file order of major and minor tastes, as well as the striated organization of the story-telling function into a form of a canon. On the contrary, the writer does not often seek to represent the truth since, as Deleuze remarks, the 'truth' is often the category invented by the colonizer and the oppressor. Rather, citing another anecdotal phrase that Deleuze often employs, the writer seeks to raise the false to a higher power, that is, beyond the moral-juridical opposition of true–false that is maintained by the model of truth. To raise the false to a higher power is to discover the principle of fabulation that governs even truthful representation, to turn this principle into a critical force which addresses the intolerable situation of 'a people who is missing.' Accordingly, literature bears within its fragmented body – scattered, torn to pieces, or 'dispersed on the four winds' – the seeds of a people to come. These seeds are the germs of a 'collective assemblage of enunciation,' which, as Deleuze often declares, are real without necessarily being actual and ideal without necessarily being abstract.

Today, Deleuze and Guattari situate the conditions for the emergence of minor literature in a world where the forms of collective enunciation and national consciousness are breaking down on several fronts, as a result of the immigration patterns and displacement of national labor forces, and the decline of the 'State-form' itself.

> How many people today live in a language that is not their own? Or no longer, not yet, even know their own and know poorly the major language that they are forced to serve? This is a problem of immigrants, and especially of their children, the problem of minorities, the problem of minor literature, but also a problem for all of us: how to tear a minor literature away from its own language, allowing it to challenge the language and making it follow a sober revolutionary path? How to become a nomad and an immigrant and a gypsy in relation to one's own language? (ML 19)

In understanding the above passage, in order to determine the status of the 'literary,' the primary emphasis must fall upon the absence of a particular collective enunciation from official and public institutions of language and national culture. In the absence of a distinct majoritarian formation of the 'public sphere,' which gives enunciation weight and reference – which 'orders reality,' in so many words – a body of literature assumes the shadowy and non-essential region of a collective enunciation, a 'minor public' whose existence is always haunted by the 'imaginary' (or fabulous) nature of its agora (its open space). But, as Deleuze and Guattari write,

> The literary machine thus becomes the relay for a revolutionary machine-to-come, not at all for ideological reasons but because the literary machine alone is determined to fill the conditions of collective enunciation that are lacking elsewhere in the milieu: literature is the people's concern. (ML 17–18)

In order to strip this last statement of any romanticism in association with the nationalist or ethnic entity of a people invented during the nineteenth century, I should stress that without specific attention to the position of enunciation that is evoked here, we lose both the status of what Deleuze and Guattari call the 'literary machine' and the specific relationship that is being drawn up between a collective enunciation and the concept of minor literature. Here, the status of a minor literature is the problem of its multiple forms and locations, since it does not have an institution that organizes and disciplines its forms. This does not mean that it is formless, but rather that it has its organization of collective enunciation, which is dispersed across several registers of the major language it inhabits (legends, private letters, songs, heated conversations, stories, fables, etc.)

and has the character of dream-language in the various operations it performs upon the form of visibilities and on the organization of statements. Only when these criteria of minor literature are fulfilled can we begin to understand the statement that 'literature is a concern of the people' – a concern that may demand a new definition of the uses of literature for life.

CONCLUSION
ON THE ART OF CREATING CONCEPTS

Earlier, I proposed that the current relationship between philosophy and non-philosophy can be premised on the observation that, to a certain degree that has not yet reached a level of generality, the philosopher's conceptual activity is no longer founded on a notion of 'common sense.' The statement 'everyone knows' does not provide the commencement of a philosophical dialectic which then mediates between error and correct reasoning. Of course, this statement is not true of a certain tradition of analytic philosophy that continues to proceed by posing the nature of problems and questions first in the realm of common sense, which are then taken up and 'worked over' by logic. However, from as early as *Difference and Repetition*, particularly in the chapter on 'the image of thought,' Deleuze's understanding of the role of philosophy, and with the 'beginning' of the philosopher's procedure of 'questions and problems,' can in some ways be posed in a direct confrontation with this tradition.

My second thesis has concerned the encounter between philosophy and 'non-philosophy' among several modern thinkers, particularly where this encounter is situated in the domain of the arts (formerly subsumed under the category of 'aesthetics'). This definition must be qualified to understand the exact nature of the creation involved and, primarily, to take account of the fact that it is only in its encounters with non-philosophy that, following Deleuze's assertion, the task of concept creation can be proposed anew. It would not be difficult to propose that many modern philosophers extract their concepts from other semiotic regions (and from literature, the plastic arts and cinema, in particular), Deleuze being exemplary of this new approach. A precedent for this approach can also be found in the philosophy of Foucault who, in *The Order of Things*, systematically demonstrates that the contemporary philosophy no longer grounds its operation on the priority of resemblance, but rather on a profound dissemblance between the order of words and that of things (*les mots et les choses*). This dissemblance points to a certain baroque legacy highlighted in Part Two, 'On the (baroque) line,' and to a moment when the world of things threatened to become unreal and to topple over into a dream, that is, where representation no longer found a prior relationship with reality and where its categories (including that of the 'Subject') were exposed to a certain loss of the power to discern the relationship between the order of words and the order of things.

It has been my argument that Deleuze is one of the first to have observed this as a constitutive moment within the genre of contemporary philosophy, and his turn to 'certain other arts' was devised as a strategy or tactic that was employed to repair the broken interval with the world *as it is*. Again, I cite the passage from the preface of *Difference and Repetition* where this 'program' is clearly announced: 'The search for a new means of philosophical expression was begun by Nietzsche and must be pursued today in relation to the renewal of certain other arts, such as theater and cinema' (DR xxi). Perhaps this modulation in the genre of philosophy is, in part, due to the problem of expression that philosophy shares with the field of modern art and literature, which has to do with breaking through a chaos of clichés, common perceptions and ready-made representations in order to restore a broken connection with immanence, to institute its image of thought on another plane. This other plane that contemporary philosophy is in search of would not, for that reason, be more ideal or more transcendent, but rather more 'intensive' and it is precisely the role of art to produce the conditions for experience becoming more intensive. As Deleuze claims, 'Empiricism truly becomes transcendental, and aesthetics an apodictic discipline, only when we apprehend directly in the sensible that which can only be sensed, the very being of the sensible: difference, potential difference and difference in intensity as the reason behind qualitative diversity' (DR 57). The formula (or *ritornello*) that Deleuze cites many times to describe the conditions of experience that art reveals is drawn from Proust: 'Ideal without being abstract, real without being actual.'

And yet, if it was simply a matter of creating new expression, new visibilities and new statements, or new *percepts* and affects, then the role of the philosopher would be interchangeable with that of the artist, the writer or the director. This could be said to be the greatest temptation for contemporary philosophy, the temptation for the philosopher to become an artist or a writer, a poet or a dramatist. We have several examples of this temptation, beginning with Nietzsche's *Zarathustra* or Heidegger's pedantic poetry, the results of which could be judged to have been mixed. In the case of Nietzsche's *Zarathustra,* or his 'Hymn to friendship,' we might wonder if these moments represent the creation of a philosopher, a theologian, or a prophet (albeit of the 'Death of God'). In the case of Heidegger's *Denker als Dichter*, perhaps the less said about it the better. If both occasions are exemplary, they could be said to abdicate the duty of philosophy, or the problem of expression that is specific to philosophy defined as the *creating* of concepts. As Deleuze wrote many times, particularly in the later works, the only proper domain for philosophical creation is the domain of concepts. Thus, 'the question of philosophy is the singular point where the concept and creation are related to each other' (WP 11). Surveying Deleuze's entire corpus we have a vivid illustration of the philosopher's frenetic creative activity, from the opus of *A Thousand Plateaus* (with Guattari) to the sheer number of concepts introduced by the cinema studies alone. It seems that everything that the philosopher sees or touches is destined either to become a concept, or to comprise a support or partial plane that is combined with other concepts in a general co-creation. What is called a concept then becomes the signature and the most remarkable trait of this philosopher's vision.

In the last book written with Guattari, *What is Philosophy?*, Deleuze defines the philosopher as the true friend of the concept. 'The philosopher is the concept's friend; he is the potentiality of the concept ... Because the concept must be created, it refers back to the philosopher as the one who has it potentially, or who has its power and its competence' (WP 5). However, such a definition immediately raises a question concerning what is 'a true friend,' and calls for a method to distinguish between true and false friends (*faux amis*). This returns us again to perhaps Deleuze's most seminal text on the idea of philosophy, 'Plato and the simulacra,' where Deleuze describes the earlier *agon* (struggle, conflict) between different 'pretenders,' all of which lay claim to being the true friend ... of the truth, of virtue, of love or of 'the Good' (*ta Agathon*). Deleuze makes an even stronger claim: that the concept belongs to philosophy by right. 'The concept belongs to philosophy and only to philosophy' (WP 34). Here we can perceive a bit of an organizer in Deleuze, a trait which can be linked to Kant despite his own protests to the contrary, and here we recall that Kant had earlier defined the role of philosophy in comparison to other activities within a veritable division of labor, by relegating to the different faculties their own proper duty and precinct. This is nowhere more apparent than in *The Conflict of Faculties* where Kant determines this division of labor within the historical faculties themselves in order to intervene into the conflict between the higher and lower faculties. Accordingly, in *What is Philosophy?* Deleuze partitions the new faculties in terms of art, science and philosophy: to art belongs the extraction of *percepts* and *affects*; to science, the invention of *functions*; but to philosophy 'and only philosophy' belongs the creation of concepts.

At the same time, like the Kantian conflict, we might understand Deleuze's claim as essentially a defensive one; it is usually the weaker party in a conflict that lays claim to ownership *de jure*, if only because such ownership is not *de facto*. Therefore, according to this possibility, we might ask who lays claim to the concept today? Two pretenders whom Deleuze identifies as the greatest rivals of the philosopher today are the modern journalist and the market advertiser modeled after the conceptual artist (e.g. Andy Warhol as the new avatar of the 'concept-man'), each of whom claims to be the best friend of the concept, or the 'true creator.'

> In successive challenges, philosophy confronted increasingly insolent and calamitous rivals that Plato himself would never have imagined even in his most comic moments. Finally, the most shameful moment came when computer science, marketing, design, and advertising, all the disciplines of communication, seized hold of the word *concept* itself and said: 'This is our concern, we are the creative ones, the *ideas men*!' We are the friends of the concept, we put it in our computers! (WP 10)

Although this seems to be a somewhat frivolous antagonism – certainly there are more serious and threatening rivals? – what is implicit in this identification of these other pretenders is Deleuze's warning that philosophy itself is in danger of abdicating its only proper role, the creation of concepts, by becoming a kind of mass marketing, on the one hand, and performance art, on the other. Deleuze expressed his antagonism against the former very clearly in an interview he once delivered against '*les nouveaux philosophes*':

> Journalism, in its alliance with radio and television, has to be learned to a greater and greater degree of its own powers to create an event. And while they still must refer to external events, which they themselves have created for the most part, this need is often ameliorated by referring any external analysis to journalists themselves, or to characters like 'the intellectual,' or 'the writer': *journalism has discovered within itself an autonomous and self-sufficient image of thought* ... This is a new kind of thought: the thought-interview, the thought-conversation, the thought-minute.[1]

It is not that modern journalism and advertising care or even know that much about their conflict with philosophers, but rather that the desire that conditions the fields of interests and commodities in late-capitalist societies is effecting a change in the philosopher's own expression, and the concept is beginning to look more and more like a product made to satisfy a particular demand.

> Marketing has its own particular principles: First, it is necessary to talk about a book, rather than having the book itself offering anything on its own behalf. Ultimately, there must be a multitude of articles, interviews, colloquies, radio and television spots to replace the book, which could very well not have existed at all ... Second, for marketing purposes, the same book or project must have many different versions, in order to include everyone: a pious version, an atheistic one, a Heideggerian, a leftist, a centrist, even a Chiracian or neo-fascist, or even a version for the 'union of the Left,' etc.[2]

As Deleuze warns in *Negotiations*, this is not creation proper, which in fact should stimulate a desire for something we didn't know we desired beforehand. Moreover, these modern pretenders to the art of the concept cannot be understood simply as definite individuals who belong to different regions *outside* philosophy, but rather as a combination of forces that are emerging within the genre of philosophy itself and are beginning to cause its expression to become modified in order to meet particular ends. Whether these ends flow back to the individual or to a corporation of interests, they amount to the same form. As Deleuze writes,

> Philosophy has not remained unaffected by the movement that replaced Critique with sales promotion. The simulacrum, the simulation of a packet

> of noodles, has become the true concept; and the one who packages the product, commodity, or work of art, has become the philosopher, conceptual persona, or artist. (WP 10)

In contrast to this new conceptual persona of the philosopher, therefore, we might return to an earlier text where Deleuze outlines another image of the philosopher which can be offered in direct contradistinction to this image, *Spinoza: A Practical Philosophy*. It is there that Deleuze defines the three virtues of the philosopher: *poverty*, *chastity* and *humility*. Although these virtues may now seem a bit outdated, they underline the importance of a stoic understanding of pragmatism as a wisdom for *Life*; the goal of the philosopher's exercise has always been the question how to live (and to die) well. Thus, as Deleuze comments, these virtues 'are not moral ends, or a religious means to another life, but rather the "effects" of philosophy itself. *For there is absolutely no other life for the philosopher*' (S 3). This defines the possibilities of *a life* no longer based on needs, but rather 'in terms of means and ends, but according to a production, a productivity, a potency, in terms of causes and effects' (S 3). Here again, the nature of creativity is emphasized as a fundamental *ethos* of the philosopher.

How is this *ethos* different from the philosopher who creates in terms of means and ends, or on the basis of needs? But then we might turn the question around and ask whether 'to create on the basis of needs' is really creation proper? Does it really 'make' anything? As Deleuze writes, 'To create concepts is, at the very least, to make something' (WP 7). On the other hand, to create out of need is to conform to already established notions of 'the subject' (whether individual or corporate), of 'desire'; one does not create anything in this sense, but merely replenishes an already existent need with an object whose outline was already known beforehand. The object is like an answer posed at the level of too general a question of the type 'What do the people want?' or 'What does woman want?' In each case, because the question was badly posed, the concepts that are offered as solutions like morsels of food could not satisfy the reality of the questions themselves. This is very different from the concept of creation that Deleuze has in mind, in which the answer is not presupposed in advance, and causes the subject to enter into a movement of 'becoming equal to' the task of creating both questions and answers that are singular or specific to the passage of a life: immanence.

I argued above that Deleuze's *cry* can be understood as a cry for multiplicity, but the condition of every multiplicity is singularity. 'Every creation is singular, and the concept as a philosophical creation is always a singularity. The first principle of philosophy is that Universals explain nothing but must themselves be explained' (WP 7). From the above statement, we might discern the outline of his incessant cry against Universals, whether we are speaking here about his cry against the concept of DESIRE framed by psychoanalysis, or the concept of CONSENSUS that determines the possibilities of communication. Today, what Deleuze seems to be horrified most by is the incredible monotony of creation (or the lack thereof), by the machines for producing Universals, by the apparatus of consensus, which he defines as the current inter-subjective idealism that determines the Universals of communication that 'provide rules for the imaginary mastery of markets and media' (WP 6–7). *Consensus, consensus*, everywhere, but not a singularity to be found.

Where there is no singularity, Deleuze argues, then the conditions of philosophical creation are found to be lacking as well, since the periods known for a thriving philosophical activity are primarily recognized for the sheer number of concepts that were created, which continue to exist well after the societies themselves have vanished. This marks the importance of Greece for Deleuze in his last book with Guattari, in the sense that it populated the earth with concepts, concepts which continue to spread out, problematically perhaps, a plane of immanence that defines the internal history of 'the West' that somehow reaches its penultimate point in the globalized markets that have replaced the territories of nation-states. This is our problem today, as much as it was for the Greeks. As Deleuze and Guattari write, '*Only the West extends and propagates its centers of immanence*' (WP 101). Imperialism, colonialism, capitalism, all express the same problem at different moments, in as much as these moments are themselves the different expressions of the problem of immanence specific to 'the West.'

To conclude, let us return once more to the concept of the 'Other Person,' which I argued above is perhaps Deleuze's first concept of philosophy. If every concept refers to or encompasses a singularity, then there can be no concept of the 'other person in general,' understood either as a category of the subject ('I'), even as a universal subject ('Thou'); or as a peculiar object that emerges within the perceptual field of the subject, but assumes the same form. Every other person encompasses a singular expression of universe, contains a singular point-of-view, which is why there must be as many concepts of the Other Person as there are others. This is Deleuze's profound Leibnizianism, but also is inspired by his apprenticeship with Proust who taught him that the name Albertine can in no way be understood as referring to an individual, or to another person somehow different but related to Marcel, but to the expression of a finite number of singularities (a look, a certain moment, the figure of someone sleeping, a walk on the beach, at Guermantes, or *not* at Guermantes) the problem of which is how to compose all these singularities into a concept that expresses the secret face of Albertine, the face that expresses the possibility of Albertine's love. Therefore, before this hidden face of Albertine, the face of God pales in comparison.

It seems appropriate, then, to end my commentary by citing a long passage from Deleuze's study of Proust on the concept of creation that runs between philosophy and non-philosophy:

> The world has become crumbs and chaos. Precisely because reminiscence proceeds from subjective associations to an originating view-point, objectivity can no longer exist except in the work of art; it no longer exists in significant content as states of the world, nor in ideal signification as stable essence, but only in the signifying formal structure of the work, in

its style. It is no longer a matter of saying: to create is to remember – but rather, to remember is to create, is *to reach that point where the associative chain breaks, leaps over the constituted individual, is transferred to the birth of the individuating world.* And it is no longer a matter of saying: to create is to think – but rather, to think is to create and primarily to create the act of thinking within thought. To think, then, is to create food for thought. To remember is to create, not to create memory, but to create the spiritual equivalent of the still too material memory, or to create the view-point valid for all associations, the style valid for all images. It is style that substitutes for experience in the manner in which we speak about and the formula that expresses it, which substitutes for the individual in the world the view-point toward a world, and which transforms reminiscence [or the fulcrum of representation] into a realized creation. (P 111)

NOTES

In these notes, full bibliographical entries are given for works that do not appear in the Bibliography, but a short form (author's surname + abbreviated title + date) is used if a full entry appears in the Bibliography.

PREFACE

1 For example, there has been a tendency in the French reception of Deleuze's work, to present a clean and shaven portrait of the philosopher which has amounted to extracting a purely philosophical Deleuze from its admixture with the presence of Guattari. This can be detected in the work of Alain Badiou, *Deleuze: The Clamour of Being*, which even goes so far as to relegate the more iconoclastic image of Deleuze, the thinker of 'fluxes and multiplicities,' to the status of a *misinterpretation* which has too often been promulgated by Deleuze himself. Badiou writes, 'This "purified automaton" is certainly much closer to the Deleuzian norm than were the bearded militants of 1968 [including, I might add, Badiou himself] bearing the standard of their gross desire.' Alain Badiou, *Deleuze: The Clamour of Being*, trans. Louise Burchill (Minneapolis: University of Minnesota Press, 2000), p. 11.

2 Jacques Derrida, *Positions*, trans. Alan Bass (Chicago: University of Chicago Press, 1981), p. 12.

3 James, 'The figure in the carpet,' in *The Figure in the Carpet and Other Stories* (1986), pp. 355–400.

4 The question of commentary is already doubled in the case of the works by Deleuze and Guattari where each already functions as the double of the other. As Deleuze remarks in *Negotiations* (1990): 'When I work with Guattari, each of us falsify the other, which is to say that each of us understands in his own way notions put forward by the other' (N 126). Thus, to comment on these works is already to enter into a series of falsifications.

5 On the concept of *ritournelles*, see Charles J. Stivale's excellent discussion in *The Two-fold thought of Gilles Deleuze* (New York: Guilford Press, 1998), pp. 174ff.

1 PHILOSOPHY AND 'NON-PHILOSOPHY'

1 For Deleuze's critique of common and good sense, see especially Chapter 3 of his *Difference and Repetition* (1994), pp. 129–167.

2 Gilles Deleuze, 'Plato and the simulacrum,' Appendix One of *The Logic of Sense* (1990), pp. 53–266.

3 For a description of these new idiots and their relation to the modern question of literature in Deleuze's thought, see my 'The subject of literature between Derrida and Deleuze: law or life?', *ANGELAKI*, 5, 2(2001), 56–72.

4 See Deleuze, 'Postscript on control societies,' in *Negotiations* (1990), pp. 177–182.

5 Michel Foucault, *Madness and Civilization: A History of Insanity in the Age of Reason* (New York: Pantheon, 1965); Derrida, 'Cogito and the history of madness,' in *Writing*

and Difference (1978). On the dreams of Descartes, see Gregor Sebba and Richard A. Watson, *The Dream of Descartes* (Urbana: Southern Illinois University Press, 1987).

6 Klee, *Théorie de l'art moderne* ([1920]1964), p. 107.

7 After all, what is the concept of the fold in Deleuze's thought but a vertical line (transcendence) which has been declined horizontally to follow a plane of immanence that is implicated by others? At the same time, perhaps this represents not as much an 'over-turning of Platonism,' which still retains a dimension of verticality even by its famous inversion as in Heidegger, as the conditions of what Deleuze calls its 'reversal.' This reversal can also be found at the basis of the systems of other modern philosophers such as Derrida and Levinas, each of whom replaces transcendence with the problem of immanence introduced by the 'Other.' Around this point, it could be said that Deleuze, Derrida and Levinas share the same problematic, or image of thought, although each begins to treat this problem by means of different concepts (Derrida's *differance,* Levinas's *visage*), and these concepts, in turn, are led back to other concepts and thus produce a different history of the concept of the Other Person, or what Deleuze calls a different 'combination' (*chiffre*). See 'What is a concept?' in *What is Philosophy?* (1996), pp. 15–16.

2 HOW TIME PLACES TRUTH IN CRISIS

1 Serres, 'Lucretius: science & religion,' in *Hermes* (1982), p. 121.

2 In *Difference and Repetition* (1994), Deleuze describes this event by employing Hölderlin's figure of the *caesura*, where the expression 'out of joint' can be understood as the moment where time is itself divided between two unequal distributions which no longer 'rhyme' *before* and *after* the event that marks its declension. Thus, 'Hölderlin said it no longer "rhymed" because it was distributed unequally on both sides of the caesura, as a result of which beginning and end no longer coincided. We may define the order of time as this purely formal distribution of the unequal in the function of the caesura' (DR 89).

3 Emanuel Levinas, 'Philosophie comme transcendance,' in *Noms Propres* (Paris: Galilée, 1987).

4 For example, in *Bergsonism* ([1966]1988) this fundamental duality, or 'difference *in kind*' (Bergson), motivates Deleuze's inquiry into the Bergsonian division between matter and memory; thus, the importance he places upon the difference in memory which is not equal to the difference in perception.

5 As Deleuze writes, 'contrary to the form of the true which is unifying and tends to identification of a character (his discovery or simply his coherence), the power of the false cannot be separated from a positive multiplicity. "I is another" ["*Je est un autre*"] has replaced Ego = Ego' (*Cinema 2: The Time-Image* [1989], p. 133). Therefore, 'it is not an other which is an other I, but the I which is an other, a fractured I' (*Difference and Repetition* (1994), p. 261.

3 THE PROBLEM OF JUDGEMENT

1 Although it is not entirely accurate, I have sometimes resorted to the word 'actor' for the original term *personnage conceptuel*, and at other times employ 'character' (Massumi) or 'persona' (Tomlinson, Burchell), in order to highlight the problematic aspect of the 'double' which is characteristic of dramatic presentation, and to underline the ambiguity that occurs when we identify the figure of the philosopher – or, by extension, the image of thought itself – with its quasi-fictional character in the narrative of philosophy. This ambiguity can be illustrated when we refer to Aristotle, Descartes or Hegel not in the

sense of their persons, or even their works, but rather in the sense that their names signify a certain event or quality that seems to characterize a distinct image of thought or to mark an episodic moment in the history of philosophy. Thus, the term can be understood to have a relationship with Foucault's definition of the 'Author-function.' See Foucault, 'What is an author?', in *Language, Counter-Memory, Practice* (1977), pp. 117–138.

2 See Deleuze, *The Logic of Sense* (1990), pp. 318–320.

3 Gilles Deleuze, 'Seminar on Leibniz' (15 April 1980): www.imagenet.fr/pinhaus.html

4 See Deleuze, *The Fold* (1993), pp. 76–82. See also Bruno Paradis, 'Leibniz: un monde unique et relatif,' *Magazine littéraire*, 257 (September 1988), 26–29.

5 See Christiane Fremont's remarkable analysis of necessity and ideal causality in relation to the problem of evil: 'Complication et singularité,' *Revue de Métaphysique et de Morale*, 1 (1991), pp. 105–120. However, it appears that Fremont concedes to Leibniz's God his necessity (which corresponds to the justification or, better, rationalization of a necessary evil of sacrifice in the *Theodicy)*, since the labyrinths offered by Gombrowicz and Borges would ultimately lead nowhere and prevent the possibility of any new series from extending into the real. Consequently, Fremont retains the language of a jurist (essentially descriptive and economic) which leaves the event within the domain of the law to unfold (or not), or to express clearly and understand completely.

4 THE PARADOX OF CONCEPTS

1 Deleuze suggests that atypical statements may reveal the inherent problems of other common utterances such as 'John will arrive at 5:00 pm,' or 'Tomorrow there will be a naval battle,' or 'This evening there will be a concert'; all of which are contingent upon the series that actualizes them and reveal a moment when time can place truth in crisis just as effectively as, for example, in the statement from Beckett's *The Unnamable*: 'It is raining. It is not raining.' See Chapter 6, 'What is an event?', in *The Fold* (1993), pp. 76–82.

2 For a discussion of 'the crystalline surface of narration' (i.e. 'the time-image') see 'The powers of the false,' in *Cinema 2* (1989), pp. 126–155.

3 Heidegger, *Kant and the Problem of Metaphysics* ([1965]1990), p. 123.

4 *ibid.*

5 *ibid.*

6 Gilles Deleuze, 'Seminar on Leibniz' (15 April 1980): www.imagenet.fr/pinhaus.html

5 'THE MIND–BODY PROBLEM' AND THE ART OF 'CRYPTOGRAPHY'

1 According to the French sociologist, Gabriel Tarde, opposition should not to be conceived as a maximum of difference; rather, it is a very singular species of repetition in which two doubles enter into the destruction of each other by virtue of their very resemblance. See Tarde, *Les Lois Sociales* (1921), pp. 70f. Deleuze evokes Tarde, from as early on as *Différence et Répétition* (1968), as 'next to Leibniz, one of the last great philosophers of Nature.' In fact, it is Deleuze's early reading of Tarde's 'Microsociology' that prepares for the evaluation of Foucault's later works. With regard to the question of opposition above, I cite a footnote on Tarde from *Difference and Repetition*: 'Opposition, far from autonomous, far from being a maximum of difference, is a repetition *minima* in relation to difference itself' (DR 264*n*).

2 See Kant's statement in the 'Transcendental doctrine of method,' in *The Critique of Pure Reason*, ed. Werner S. Pluhar (London: Hackett, 1996), Chapter 1, Section 1. Also see

Heidegger's explication in 'Leibniz's doctrine of judgment,' in *The Metaphysical Foundations of Logic*, trans. Michael Heim (Bloomington: University of Indiana Press, 1984), pp. 78f.

3 This diversity forms a constant preoccupation through all of Deleuze's work and can be traced to his early description of the role of ideas within phenomena in *Difference and Repetition* (figured under the notation of 'an object = x' which is drawn from several diverse fields: biology, economy, literature), as well as to *Foucault*, which takes as its central project a cartography of the different historical (or epochal) formations of the couple *savior/pouvoir.*

4 G. W. von Leibniz, *Philosophical Papers and Letters*, Vol. 2 (Boston: Reidel Publishing Co., 1969), p. 433.

5 This is the metaphor of light that Derrida postulates both in 'The white mythology' and in 'The double session' where the act of reading in philosophy constitutes itself by a catachresis in order to establish itself as a higher order of perception. This allows for a usurpation of the eye by the 'point of light' placed at the level of the idea in Platonic philosophy, which causes the series formed by perception, echoing the position of a 'common sense,' to *defer* to a latent series traced by the conceptual path of the philosopher who represents an *anamnesis* of the Idea. Hence, Derrida shows that the movement of logo-centrism is inseparable from the establishment of a 'vulgar series' in the social field, which entails the production of clichés as well as the social and conceptual personages to embody them. See Jacques Derrida, 'The white mythology,' in *Margins of Philosophy*, trans. Alan Bass (Chicago: University of Chicago Press, 1982), pp. 207–273; 'The double session,' in *Disseminations*, trans. Barbara Johnson (Chicago: University of Chicago Press, 1981), pp. 173–227.

6 Sarah Koffman, 'L'Usage de la *chambre obscure* à Gravesande,' in *Camera Obscura* (Paris: Galilée, 1973), pp. 79–97.

7 Serres, *Hermes* (1982), pp. 93–94.

8 Inclination, from the Greek *clinamen*, is used throughout the *Theodicy* to denote the determinateness of the will within a free act and is set against a condition that Leibniz refers to as 'mere possibility.' See Leibniz, *Theodicy* (1985), §324–327.

9 Emile Benveniste, *Problèmes de linguistique générale*, Vol. 1 (Paris: Gallimard, 1966), pp. 258–266. I cannot pursue this further here than to indicate the striking resemblance between some formations of the secret and those of indirect discourse. Both indicate a transcendental status of human speech by introducing the possibility of a reference to a third term which is both inter-subjective and temporal.

10 It may be important to clarify terms, specifically around the resemblance of the secret to the problematic first introduced by the psychoanalytic perspective. Here, the secret could correspond to what Guy Rosolato has called the 'object of perspective' which emerges in the Freudian theories of infantile sexuality in the constitution of the Phallus: the capability of the infant to compose an unreal object in place of a void, and equally the capability to negate this object in favor of its substitutes which will have a central function in the imaginary as the objects corresponding to the partial drives. See Guy Rosolato, 'L'Objet de perspective dans ses assises visuelles,' *Le Champ Visuel, Nouvelle Revue de Psychanalyse*, 35 (Spring 1987), pp. 143–164.

6 THE RIDDLE OF THE FLESH AND THE '*FUSCUM SUBNIGRUM*'

1 Nowhere is the articulation of this relationship between 'having a body' and the form of the command more clear than in Kant who, in the first formulation of the 'categorical imperative,' must immediately articulate the distinction between the 'property' of the I of 'elective or arbitrary will' (*Willkühr = arbitrium*) from the body as 'property,' the

'man in my person.' Thus, in the hypothetical contemplation of 'suicide' (in the 'wish,' *Wunsch*, to dispose of my life by striking against the man in my person), Kant provides a guard-rail in the prohibition, 'I cannot dispose of *man in my person* by maiming, spoiling, or killing.' The body then, for Kant, is not a static thing, but represents the 'other in me as other than me,' or in Kant's metaphysical system, as 'the humanity in the form of my person' which maintains an interest in determination of the body as its 'property,' as a representation of an *end-in-itself*. See Immanuel Kant, *Groundwork for a Metaphysics of Morals*, trans. H. J. Paton (New York: Harper, 1948), pp. 97ff.

2 Leibniz, *Philosophical Papers and Lettres*, p. 530 (see Chap. 5*n*4).

3 See Deleuze and Guattari's famous criticism of the Freudian concept of the Unconscious, that is, their accusation that Freud botched the concept by insisting on the representation of parental figures and infantile associations, in 'One or several wolves?' (*A Thousand Plateaus* [1987], pp. 26–38).

4 This could give us a more precise illustration of the crypt as the body without organs. On the question of perception as hallucination, see *Le Pli* (1988), Chapter 7, '*La perception dans les plis*,' pp. 113–132.

5 Martin Heidegger, *The Metaphysical Foundations of Logic*, trans. Michael Heim (Bloomington: University of Indiana Press, 1984), p. 78.

6 In her *Gilles Deleuze and the Ruin of Representation*, Dorothea Olkowski also struggles with phenemenology over the question of 'orientation,' the logic of sense, which can be understood outside the question of sense that is already established by an order of signification, or language. This goes hand in hand with the objective of gaining access to a principle of creative individuation that is not already made or composed by fixed social and psychological schemes, hexagonal solids, hard bodies, static or 'cold' identities. Here, the question of perspective, or rather point-of-view, is as crucial to Olkowski as it was for Deleuze in *The Fold*. The question is 'How do we look?' What is the form of vision and feeling that is not already reduced to the 'subjective,' to the 'in there,' which is opposed or appears over-against (*Gegenstand*) the world 'out there'? This question is doubly important as well divided when it comes to representing the experience of women as different, yet already within the frame or scheme which reduces this difference to identity, that is, to the category of representation itself. It is around this question of orientation that Olkowski follows Deleuze's criticism of phenomenology for maintaining the last vestige of the scientific *cogito*, and thus perhaps for not being philosophical enough, for not achieving the purity of the concept of visibility without already reducing the visible to the infinite murmuring of LANGUAGE. See Olkowski, *Gilles Deleuze and the Ruin of Representation* (1999).

7 Klee, *Théorie de l'art moderne* ([1920]1964), p. 56.

8 *ibid.*

7 ON GOD, OR THE '*PLACE VIDE*'

1 Gottlob Frege, *Ecrits logique et philosophique* (Paris: Editions du Seuil, 1971), p. 92.

2 This is essentially Deleuze's argument against Badiou, who he says begins with a 'neutralized base' or 'any multiplicity whatsoever.' See Badiou, *Deleuze: The Clamour of Being*, pp. 23–28; also Deleuze and Guattari, *What is Philosophy?* (1996), pp. 151–153.

3 Lyotard, 'Time today,' in *The Inhuman: Reflections on Time*, trans. Geoffrey Bennington and Rachel Bowlby (Palo Alto, CA: Stanford University Press, 1988), pp. 58–77.

4 Frege, *Ecrits* p. 82*n* (see above, *n*1).

5 On the relation of the Baroque to other areas of modern sensibility, see Tom Conley's very suggestive discussion in the translator's foreword to *The Fold* (1993), pp. ix–xx.

6 Klee, *Pedagogical Sketchbook* (1968[1953]), pp. 54, 11.

7 Germain Bazin, 'La Gloire,' in *Figures du Baroque* (Paris: Presses Universitaire de France, 1983), p. 55.

8 Concerning its economic significance, Deleuze often reminds the reader of *Le Pli* about the frequent association of the Baroque to the structures of late capitalism along the axis of 'inclusion'; hence, the complete inclusion of the world within the monad finds its analogy in the entire circuit of exchange comprehended within each instance of *capital*.

8 THE BAROQUE DETECTIVE: BORGES AS PRECURSOR

1 In Deleuze's *Proust and Signs*, Plato and the contemporary status of the '*Agathon*' is read by none other than Proust; therefore, one might invoke Proust's Platonism in the sense that for Proust *to learn is still to remember*. However important its role, memory intervenes only as a means of apprenticeship that transcends recollection both by its goals and by its principles. The search is oriented toward the future, and not to the past. *Proust and Signs* (1972), p. 3.
2 De Saussure, *Course in General Linguistics* (1959), p. 69.
3 *ibid.*, p. 71.
4 The information is provided by Emil Rodriguez Monegal and Alastair Reid in their notes to 'The total library,' in *Borges: A Reader* (1981), pp. 346ff.

9 HOW THE TRUE WORLD FINALLY BECAME A FABLE

1 On the concept of 'crystalline narration,' see also Rodowick's very comprehensive reading of the cinema books in *Gilles Deleuze's Time Machine* (1997).
2 Eisenstein, *Film Form* (1949), p. 70.
3 See also the chapter on 'Any-space-whatevers' (*espace quelconque*) in Deleuze, *Cinema 1: The Movement-Image* (1986), pp. 111–122.

10 ARTAUD'S PROBLEM AND OURS: BELIEF IN THE WORLD *AS IT IS*

1 Walter Benjamin, 'What is epic theater?', in *Illuminations*, trans. Harry Zohn (New York: Schocken Books, 1968), p. 150.
2 Artaud, *The Theater and its Double* (1958), p. 10. Cf. also Derrida's exposition of this principle in 'The theater of cruelty,' in *Writing and Difference* (1978), pp. 232–250.
3 It is interesting to note that the argument that Deleuze makes for the cinematographic image, here, is exactly the same argument for the function of the drug in the section 'Becoming molecular' from *A Thousand Plateaus*; consequently, there is an implicit connection between a dynamic representation of the sublime (i.e., the principle of *nooshock*), the experience of the drug, and what happens within the brain (and body) of the cinematic spectator. Eisenstein himself had first commented in 'Film form: new problems' on this relationship, which he identifies with the forms of pre-logical, sensual thinking. 'That is, that art is nothing but an artificial retrogression in the field of psychology toward the earlier thought-processes, i.e. a phenomenon identical with any given form of drug, alcohol, shamanism, religion, etc.' (FF 144).
4 In fact, the manner in which chaos is figured will depend upon how it is 'cut up' by the three planes (a process resembling montage): each plane engages chaos from its own distinct procedures and problems and this causes chaos to appear differently within each. See *What is Philosophy?* (1996), Part Two, 'Philosophy, science, logic, and art,' pp. 117–218.

5 As I will return to discuss below, however, the direct realization of this force between the unification movement and the action-image, or between politics and art, also addresses a problematic relationship that Benjamin discovers at the basis of fascism. See especially 'The work of art in the mechanical age of reproduction,' in *Illuminations*, pp. 217–251 (see above, *n*1).

6 Eisenstein writes: 'The point is that the forms of sensual, pre-logical thinking, which are preserved in the shape of inner speech among the peoples who have reached an adequate level of social and cultural development, at the same time also represent in mankind at the dawn of cultural development the norm as of conduct in general, i.e. laws according to which flow the processes of sensual thought are equivalent for them to a "habit logic" of the future' (FF 131).

7 However, contrary to Deleuze's assertion, Eisenstein's 'goal' appears less Hegelian and more Whiteheadian in his aspiration to draw up more primitive states of satisfaction and emotion into higher orders of intellectual satisfaction and complexity; the aesthetic or artistic dimension of the cinematographic process figured in this process as the achievement of 'balance' between the two forms. See Whitehead, *Process and Reality* (1978), especially 'The higher phases of experience,' pp. 256–280.

8 This criticism is the sub-text of his 1935 speech 'Film form: new problems' (FF 122–149).

9 Deleuze, *Cinema 2* (1989), p. 167. On the nature of this 'crack' or caesura in thought, see Peter Canning's important discussion of this Deleuzian topic in 'The crack in time,' which appeared in *Gilles Deleuze and the Theater of Philosophy,* ed. Constantin Boundas and Dorothea E. Olkowski (New York: Columbia University Press, 1993), pp. 73–98.

10 I could apply this event to two different discursive regions of modern knowledge in order to validate the statement that Artaud's expression of spiritual rape is integral to the problem of ideology. The first region is that of psychoanalysis where, in the Freudian concept of the primal scene, this event, although not explicitly attached to the notion of ideological automaton, takes on the character of something that occurs outside or before consciousness life. It becomes the temporal form of a 'trace' (like the shadow of an earlier force) that returns to disturb and even to *deform* perception and thought. The second region would be contemporary forms of ideology critique where the figure of rape, this time as 'metaphor,' is frequently used – particularly by feminism (e.g. Pratt, Mohantry, Suleri) and post-colonial theory (e.g. Fanon) – to represent the nature of psychic violence that is suffered by the subject, and to signal the affective disturbances of memory and thought (feelings of disconnection, splitting or 'dual-consciousness' [Fanon], parodistic or hybrid forms of socializing this crack or splitting of the subject, even as prescriptions for resistance [Bhabba]). My argument (which represents a reading of Deleuze around this point) is that Artaud's expression clarifies the affective image of powerlessness which appears as the problem of thought in the modern critiques of ideology, even perhaps addressing a 'universal' condition of the modern subject – that, indeed, Artaud's problem is also ours. On this last point, it is interesting to note that most of criticism around the subject of Artaud ('*pauvre A.A.*') has concerned precisely, if not exclusively, whether his experience represents either an 'exemplary,' or merely an 'exceptional,' case. On this point, see particularly Derrida's 'La parole soufflé,' in *Writing and Difference* (1978), pp. 169–195.

11 This is a formula I have adapted from Kafka and it represents a problem that modern literature has discovered as well, which can be proposed in terms of movement. As both Kafka and Beckett can testify, any movement is infinitely treacherous and is filled with hallucinations of motor-coordination and the false hopes of arriving somewhere. As Beckett asked, 'Where now, who now?' – that is, 'Where would I go if I could go, who would I be if I get there?' On the one hand, as Kafka proposed with the character of Gregor Samsa, it is better not to move at all, 'to lie on my back with a thousand tiny hands waving desperately in front of me'; however, Gregor discovered that this solution was too unbearable, if not already impossible, since he was already moving in his nature and this 'metamorphosis' was a movement that he could neither remember willing nor

was it something he could control. On the other hand, this is Beckett's proposal in the characters of Molly, Malone and the Unnameable: he could achieve another means of movement; thus, if he could not walk, he could crawl, if not that, he might roll, if not that, then what? Likewise, this solution became impossible, even when he found himself without arms or legs, just a floating head in a barrel, he was tortured by the organs of thought that moved within him.

12 Paul Virilio, *Speed and Politics*, trans. Mark Polizzotti (New York: Semiotext[e], 1986).

13 Deleuze borrows this formulation from Heidegger's famous statement which occurs in *What is Called Thinking?*: 'the most thought provoking thing that we are given today to think is the fact that we are not yet thinking.' See Martin Heidegger, *What is Called Thinking?* (New York: Harper & Row, 1952).

11 THE USES (AND ABUSES) OF LITERATURE FOR LIFE

1 Benjamin, *Illuminations*, p. 25 (see above, Chap. 10*n*1).

2 Freud, 'Creative writers and day-dreaming,' in *The Standard Edition* (1963), pp. 143–153.

3 Kafka, *Diaries* (1948), p. 149.

4 It is here, I would suggest, that we might seek to understand the affiliation or nuptial, which has recently occurred between feminism and the work of Deleuze and Guattari. In other words, the significance of their work for many feminists including Elizabeth Grosz, Rosi Braidotti, Moira Gattens and Dorothea Olkowski I would argue has less to do with the so-called authority or representative value of their philosophy for feminism (an explanation that only repeats, in the most traditional sense, the history of philosophy as masculine); rather it has to do with a certain alliance that can be said to occur from the fact that more than any other so-called modern philosophy the work of Deleuze and Guattari is founded upon one of the most powerful historical critiques of both psychoanalysis and phenomenology. In other words, we might begin to understand this difficult association or this often 'unholy alliance' by the historical convergence of two very different 'problematics' around a common or shared antagonism with 'the history of philosophy' (including phenomenology), on the one side, and with 'the institution of psychoanalysis', on the other – and by the fact that each of these critical discourses shares the same philosophical urgency concerning what, in her book, Olkowski defines as 'the ruin of representation.' At the same time, to converge around the same problematic is not the same thing as to incorporate one representational system of concepts into another, or to invoke the authority of one philosophical system to secure the objectives of a second, and this is where the true sense of the 'problematic' that the work of Deleuze and Guattari shares with feminism today usually gets lost; it gets lost precisely by treating this phenomenon in representational terms. Situating these observations in the context of Olkowski's argument, if phenomenology does not confront the difference of 'point-of-view' but rather baptizes a generalized and objective point-of-view that is impervious to the question of sexual difference, would sexual difference then be the name of this force of exteriority, of the 'Outside' that Deleuze has thought this region of our experience? Would the thinking of 'sexual difference' (the thought of the effects of sexual difference upon the organization of statements and visibilities, the thinking of feminist philosophy) not in fact have the greatest chance of entering in to break open the phenomenological subject, to reopen this ancient *polemos,* which had been resolved or pacified too precipitously? And already, has not a feminist 'point-of-view' been most responsible for bringing this second figure of Being, this power-Being, most clearly into view? 'From epistemology to strategy' – would this not already be the slogan for much of feminist philosophy today? See Olkowski, *Gilles Deleuze and the Ruin of Representation* (1999).

5 Paul Celan, *Poems* (1972), p. 53.
6 Kafka, *Diaries* (1948), p. 148.

CONCLUSION: ON THE ART OF CREATING CONCEPTS

1 Gilles Deleuze, 'A propos des nouveaux philosophes et d'un problème plus général,' *Faut-il brûler les nouveaux philosophes? Le dossier du 'procès,'* established by Sylvie Bouscasse and Denis Bourgeois (Paris: Nouvelles Editions Oswald, 1978), p. 190.
2 *ibid.*, pp. 188–189.

BIBLIOGRAPHY

Artaud, Antonin (1958) *The Theater and its Double*, Mary Caroline Richards (trans.), New York: Grove Press.

Benjamin, Walter (1968) *Illuminations*, Harry Zohn (trans.), New York: Schocken Books.

Borges, Jorge Luis (1962) *Labyrinths*, New York: New Directions.

—— (1981) *Borges: A Reader*, Emil Rodriguez Monegal and Alastair Reid (ed.), New York: E. P. Dutton.

Celan, Paul (1972) *Poems of Paul Celan*, Michael Hamburger (trans.), New York: Persea Books.

Deleuze, Gilles ([1966]1988) *Bergsonism*, Hugh Tomlinson and Barbara Habberjam (trans.), New York: Zone Books.

—— (1967) *Présentation de Sacher-Masoch: le froid et le cruel*, Paris: Minuit.

—— (1968) *Différence et Répétition*, Paris: Presses Universitaires de France. (For English-language edn, see 1994.)

—— ([1970]1988) *Spinoza: A Practical Philosophy,* San Francisco: City Lights Books.

—— (1972) *Proust and Signs*, Richard Howard (trans.), New York: George Braziller. UK edn, London: Athlone Press.

—— (1984) *Kant's Critical Philosophy*, Hugh Tomlinson and Barbara Habberjam (trans.), Minneapolis: University of Minnesota Press.

—— (1986) *Cinema 1: The Movement-Image*, Hugh Tomlinson and Barbara Habberjam (trans.), Minneapolis: University of Minnesota Press.

—— (1988) *Foucault*, Sean Hand (trans.), Minneapolis: University of Minnesota Press.

—— (1988) *Le Pli: Leibniz et le baroque*, Paris: Galilée. (For English-language edn, see 1993.)

—— (1989) *Cinema 2: The Time-Image*, Hugh Tomlinson and Robert Galeta (trans.), Minneapolis: University of Minnesota Press.

—— (1989) *Masochism: Coldness and Cruelty*, New York: Zone Books.

—— (1990) *The Logic of Sense*, Constantin V. Boundas *et al.* (trans.), New York: Columbia University Press.

—— (1990) *Negotiations,* Martin Joughin (trans.), New York: Columbia University Press.

—— (1991) *Empiricism and Subjectivity: An Essay on Hume's Theory of Human Nature*, Constantin V. Boundas (trans.), New York: Columbia University Press.

—— (1993) *The Fold: Leibniz and the Baroque*, Tom Conley (trans.), Minneapolis: University of Minnesota Press.

—— (1994) *Difference and Repetition*, Paul Patton (trans.), New York: Columbia University Press.

—— (1995) 'Postscript on control societies,' in *Negotiations*, Martin Joughlin (trans.), New York: Columbia University Press, pp. 177–182.

—— (1997) *Essays Critical and Clinical*, Daniel W. Smith and Michael Greco (trans.), Minneapolis: University of Minnesota Press.

—— and Guattari, Félix ([1977]1983) *Anti-Oedipus: Capitalism and Schizophrenia*, Robert Hurley, Mark Seem and Helen R. Lane (trans.), Minneapolis: University of Minnesota Press.

—— (1986) *Kafka: Toward a Minor Literature*, Dana Polan (trans.), Minneapolis: University of Minnesota Press.
—— (1987) *A Thousand Plateaus: Capitalism and Schizophrenia*, Brian Masumi (trans.), Minneapolis: University of Minnesota Press.
—— (1991) *Qu'est-ce que la philosophie?*, Paris: Minuit.
—— (1996) *What Is Philosophy?*, Hugh Tomlinson and Graham Burchell (trans.), New York: Columbia University Press.
Derrida, Jacques (1978) *Writing and Difference*, Alan Bass (trans.), Chicago: University of Chicago Press.
Descartes, René (1986) *Meditations on First Philosophy*, John Cottingham (trans.), Cambridge: Cambridge University Press.
Duras, Marguerite and Resnais, Alain (1963) *Hiroshima Mon Amour*, Barbara Bray (trans.), 1st edn, New York: Grove Press.
Eisenstein, Sergei (1949) *Film Form: Essays in Film Theory*, Jay Leyda (trans.), New York: Harcourt Brace Jovanovich.
Fanon, Frantz (1963) *The Wretched of the Earth*, Constance Farrington (trans.), New York: Grove Press.
Foucault, Michel (1977) 'What is an author?', in *Language, Counter-Memory, Practice: Selected Essays and Interviews*, Donald Bouchard and Sherry Simon (trans.), Ithaca: Cornell University Press, pp. 117–138.
Fremont, Christiane (1991) 'Complication et singularité,' *Revue de Métaphysique et de Morale*, 1, 105–120.
Freud, Sigmund (1963) 'Creative writers and day-dreaming,' in *The Standard Edition*, Vol. 9, Ernst Jones (ed.), New York: Grove Press, pp. 143–153.
Heidegger, Martin ([1965]1990) *Kant and the Problem of Metaphysics*, 5th edn, Richard Taft (trans.), Bloomington: Indiana University Press.
James, Henry (1986) *The Figure in the Carpet and Other Stories*, Harmondsworth: Penguin Books.
Kafka, Franz (1948) *Diaries*, Max Brod (ed.), New York: Schocken Books.
Kant, Immanuel (1951) *The Critique of Judgment*, J. H. Bernard (trans.), New York: Hafner Press.
Klee, Paul (1964[1920]) *Théorie de l'art moderne*, Geneva: Editions Gonthier.
—— (1968[1953]) *Pedagogical Sketchbook*, London: Faber & Faber.
Lambert, Gregg (1997) 'The Deleuzean critique of pure fiction,' *Sub-Stance*, 26:3, 128–152.
Leibniz, Gottfried Wilhelm von (1902) *Discourse on Metaphysics, with Letters to Arnauld and Monadology*, La Salle: Open Court Press.
—— (1965) *Monadology and Other Philosophical Essays*, Paul Schrecker and Ann Martin Schrecker (trans.), Indianapolis: Bobbs-Merrill.
—— (1985) *Theodicy: Essays on the Goodness of God, the Freedom of Man, and the Origin of Evil*, E. M. Huggard (trans.), La Salle: Open Court Press.
Nietzsche, Friedrich (1997) 'On the advantages and disadvantages of history for life,' in *Untimely Meditations*, R. J. Hollingdale (trans.), Cambridge: Cambridge University Press, pp. 57–124.
Olkowski, Dorothea (1999) *Gilles Deleuze and the Ruin of Representation*, Berkeley: University of California Press.
Proust, Marcel (1993) *In Search of Lost Time*, Vol. 5, *The Captive and the Fugitive*, C. K. Scott-Moncrieff and Terence Kilmartin (trans.), revised by D. J. Enright, New York: Modern Library.
—— (1993) *In Search of Lost Time*, Vol. 6, *Time Regained*, Andreas Mayor and Terence Kilmartin (trans.), New York: Modern Library.
Rodowick, D. N. (1997) *Gilles Deleuze's Time Machine*, Durham, NC: Duke University Press.
Saussure, Ferdinand de (1959) *Course in General Linguistics*, Charles Bally and Albert Sechehayle (ed.), Wade Baskin (trans.), New York: Philosophical Library.

Serres, Michel (1982) *Hermes: Literature, Science, Philosophy*, Josué V. Harrari and David Bell (ed.), Baltimore: Johns Hopkins University Press.

Tarde, Gabriel (1921[1898]), *Les Lois Sociales: Esquisse d'une sociologie*, 8th edn, Paris: Libraire Felix Alcan.

Whitehead, Alfred North (1978) *Process and Reality*, David Ray Griffin and Donald W. Sherburne (ed.), New York: Free Press.

INDEX

Note: Where more than one sequence of notes appears on a single page, notes with the same number are differentiated by the addition of letters a, b or c.